A Guide to Charlie Chan Films

Recent Titles in
Bibliographies and Indexes in the Performing Arts

A Guide to Charlie Chan Films

Charles P. Mitchell

Bibliographies and Indexes in the Performing Arts,
Number 23

GREENWOOD PRESS
Westport, Connecticut • London

Library of Congress Cataloging-in-Publication Data

Mitchell, Charles P., 1949–
    A guide to Charlie Chan films / Charles P. Mitchell.
        p.   cm.—(Bibliographies and indexes in the performing arts,
    ISSN 0742–6933 ; no. 23)
    Includes bibliographical references and index.
    ISBN 0–313–30985–X (alk. paper)
    1. Charlie Chan films Catalogs. I. Title. II. Series.
PN1995.9.C37M58   1999
791.43′651—dc21   99–12472

British Library Cataloguing in Publication Data is available.

Library of Congress Catalog Card Number: 99–12472
ISBN: 0–313–30985–X
ISSN: 0742–6933

First published in 1999

Greenwood Press, 88 Post Road West, Westport, CT 06881
An imprint of Greenwood Publishing Group, Inc.
www.greenwood.com

Printed in the United States of America

The paper used in this book complies with the
Permanent Paper Standard issued by the National
Information Standards Organization (Z39.48–1984).

10 9 8 7 6 5 4 3 2 1

Copyright Acknowledgments

The author and publisher gratefully acknowledge the following:

Title page illustration by Roberta D. Mitchell.

Photos courtesy of Robert Brosch Archival Photography.

Additional poster art from the Paul Parla Collection.

This volume is dedicated to friends:

Lynn R. Bayley
William Chadwick
Bob King, Editor of *Classic Images*
Dewayn & Jean Marzagalli
Ted Okuda
Paul & Donna Parla
William S. Reder
James & Janet Smyth
Paul Sclafani

and to my dearest friend of all, my wife Roberta

Contents

An unnumbered photo essay begins after page 126

Preface

Good morning, Mr. Chan. Charlie Mitchell sent
me to you. He said you might be able to help me.
-- Simon LaFontanne in *DOCKS OF
NEW ORLEANS* (1948)

As a child, I was absolutely astonished to hear my name quoted as an unseen, benevolent character who advises the protagonist in *DOCKS OF NEW ORLEANS* to seek out Charlie Chan. Thus began my lifelong devotion to one of the most unforgettable of all cinema characters. Charlie Chan is one of the most beloved screen detectives, the only serious rival to the legendary Sherlock Holmes. In fact, there are more American-made feature films with Charlie Chan than any other detective, including Holmes. There are a total of fifty Chan feature films, as well as three additional Spanish language efforts. Several unauthorized Chinese language films are also reported to exist. These films have an offbeat charm, and seem universally regarded with affection by film lovers. The purpose of this book is to provide a thorough and useful guide to this unique and memorable series and to detail both the plots and the overall formula that made the films so memorable to generations of film lovers.

A GUIDE TO CHARLIE CHAN FILMS is divided into three parts. The introduction and overview discusses the literary origins of the character of Charlie Chan, the development of Chan into a film series, the personnel of the various series, the origin and different types of Chan sayings, Asian-American criticism of the series, particularly by some Chinese groups, and the influence and appeal of the films.

The main body of the volume is an in-depth study of the forty-four extant Chan motion pictures, arranged in short chapters in alphabetical order. After the title, each film is given a subjective rating by the author, which should be interpreted in the following manner:

*	Poor to Fair
* *	Fair to Good
***	Good to Very Good
****	Very Good to Excellent
*****	Top of the Line Chan

No half stars are used in these ratings, although in one case alone a bonus star in brackets is awarded for the entertainment value of a wild and silly plot. These ratings are developed to rate the films as Charlie Chan films, not to be compared with other general ratings of films.

Each rating is followed by standardized production information: studio, screenwriters, cinematographers, editors, musical directors, producers and directors. This section concludes with the running length of the film, rounded off to the nearest full minute.

The next feature is somewhat unique: an annotated cast list. The name of the actor or actress appears on the left, and the character he or she plays appears on the right, including a notation describing the part. The cast list is often arranged to make these notations more fluid and logical and to show the relationships between the various characters. Chan is always listed first, followed by any of his offspring involved in the story. Care has been taken to have the names of the actors appear in a consistent manner. Victor Sen Yung, for example, received different billings during his career as Sen Yung, Victor Sen Young and Victor Sen Yung. In all cases, the most common version is used in the casts lists. Numerous actors also had name changes, so Rita Hayworth and Jon Hall appear in their well known appellations instead of Rita Cansino and Charles Locher. Some minor performers, such as Jean Wong and Barbara Jean Wong, have often been confused, but they are indeed two distinct actresses.

An analysis and plot synopsis is the central portion of each chapter, with a detailed study of the plot line. The identity of the guilty party is not included here, however, but is provided in the first appendix. The next section is a performance critique, and each chapter concludes with a collection of Chan sayings presented in the film. The number of Chan sayings can vary widely from picture to picture. I have tried to make these collections as complete as possible, including every comment and observation that appeared to stand independently of the plot. An adage is omitted if it is too closely related to a passing event in the story. For example, when Charlie falls off a donkey in *CHARLIE CHAN IN EGYPT*, he remarks, "Please remove offspring of Satan to some distant place!" Chan's usual dialogue is always interesting, but this comment and many others simply cannot stand on their own and are therefore not included. Sayings by other characters are included if they are quoting Chan, as his son Lee does at times.

The final section of the book is a series of appendices. Appendix A is a "Rogue's Gallery," where the guilty party from each film is revealed by both character name and actor. Occasionally other details are included, such as the meaning of the chess piece clue in *THE CHINESE CAT*. Quite often the killer is in disguise during the plot, and these hidden identities are also uncovered in the "Rogue's Gallery." Appendix B is a guide to Chan offspring as portrayed in the pictures. One of Chan's favorite remarks is "Contradiction, please!" This section details the numerous contradictions in the film series regarding the children of the great detective. Appendix C contains a review of the six lost Chan films. There are no ratings for these films, nor are the guilty parties included in the "Rogue's Gallery." Appendix D contains a study of a Warner Oland vignette where, as Charlie Chan, he urges voters to overturn Pennsylvania's blue law against Sunday public exhibition of films in a 1935 referendum. Appendix E concentrates on *EL MONSTRUO EN LA SOMBRA*, the 1955 Mexican Chan film. Appendix F covers the two television series that featured Chan, one live action and the other animation. Appendix G is a guide to the sixteen actors who played Charlie Chan on stage, screen, radio and television. An index to the main body of the book and the appendices completes the book.

Here is the entire Charlie Chan filmography of fifty-three films, arranged in chronological order:

1926	*HOUSE WITHOUT A KEY* (Lost)	Appendix C
1927	*THE CHINESE PARROT* (Lost)	Appendix C
1929	*BEHIND THAT CURTAIN*	
1931	*CHARLIE CHAN CARRIES ON* (Lost)	Appendix C
	ERAN TRECE (Spanish language film)	
	THE BLACK CAMEL	
1932	*CHARLIE CHAN'S CHANCE* (Lost)	Appendix C
1933	*CHARLIE CHAN'S GREATEST CASE* (Lost)	Appendix C
1934	*CHARLIE CHAN'S COURAGE* (Lost)	Appendix C
	CHARLIE CHAN IN LONDON	
1935	*CHARLIE CHAN IN PARIS*	
	CHARLIE CHAN IN EGYPT	
	CHARLIE CHAN IN SHANGHAI	
1936	*CHARLIE CHAN'S SECRET*	
	CHARLIE CHAN AT THE CIRCUS	
	CHARLIE CHAN AT THE RACE TRACK	
	CHARLIE CHAN AT THE OPERA	
1937	*CHARLIE CHAN AT THE OLYMPICS*	
	CHARLIE CHAN ON BROADWAY	
	CHARLIE CHAN AT MONTE CARLO	
	LA SERPIENTE ROJA (Cuban film)	Appendix E

1938   *MR. MOTO'S GAMBLE*
       (Revised from *CHARLIE CHAN AT THE RINGSIDE)*
       CHARLIE CHAN IN HONOLULU
1939   *CHARLIE CHAN IN RENO*
       CHARLIE CHAN AT TREASURE ISLAND
       CHARLIE CHAN IN CITY OF DARKNESS
1940   *CHARLIE CHAN IN PANAMA*
       CHARLIE CHAN'S MURDER CRUISE
       CHARLIE CHAN AT THE WAX MUSEUM
       MURDER OVER NEW YORK
1941   *DEAD MEN TELL*
       CHARLIE CHAN IN RIO
1942   *CASTLE IN THE DESERT*
1944   *CHARLIE CHAN IN THE SECRET SERVICE*
       THE CHINESE CAT
       BLACK MAGIC
1945   *THE JADE MASK*
       THE SCARLET CLUE
       THE SHANGHAI COBRA
       THE RED DRAGON
1946   *DARK ALIBI*
       SHADOWS OVER CHINATOWN
       DANGEROUS MONEY
1947   *THE TRAP*
       THE CHINESE RING
1948   *DOCKS OF NEW ORLEANS*
       SHANGHAI CHEST
       THE GOLDEN EYE
       THE FEATHERED SERPENT
1949   *THE SKY DRAGON*
1955   *EL MONSTRUO EN LA SOMBRA* (Mexican film) Appendix E
1970   *THE RETURN OF CHARLIE CHAN*
1981   *CHARLIE CHAN AND THE CURSE OF THE DRAGON
       QUEEN*

In addition to the dedicatees, the author wishes to thank the following individuals and organizations for their assistance in the preparation of this book: Hector Argente, Bangor Public Library, Ben Chapman, Jim Ciccolilli, Alex Gordon, Jack Hill, Fredy Paralta, Dr. Ron Schwartz, Pamela St. Clair, Bill Tredinnick of Video Specialists International and the University of Maine's Fogler Library. This book would never have been completed without the total involvement of my wife, Roberta Mitchell, who read every word of the text and helped to resolve questions of clarity and to avoid cases of twisted syntax. I am also grateful to the many individuals who shared their interest in Chan films with me. I was continually and pleasantly surprised to discover the degree of affection and enthusiasm which people have for the films of this era and the films of Charlie Chan in particular.

Introduction and Overview

THE CHAN NOVELS OF EARL DERR BIGGERS

The saga of Charlie Chan begins with his literary origins. His character was created by Earl Derr Biggers (1884-1933), a noted Ohio-born journalist and author. Biggers was educated at Harvard University, and shortly after his graduation in 1907, he became a staff member of the *Boston Traveler*. Before long, he began to make a reputation as a popular columnist. He married Eleanor Ladd in 1912, and he published his first novel the following year. It was called *SEVEN KEYS TO BALDPATE,* a comic thriller about an author who attempts to write a novel in twenty-four hours upon taking up residence in the deserted Baldpate Inn. He doesn't get much time to write, as he encounters a series of grotesque characters who turn up at the house. This novel was developed into a popular stage play by George M. Cohan. It proved to be a tremendous success, and in 1915, the production became a motion picture. It was remade in 1917, 1925, 1929, 1935 and 1947. The last film version, *HOUSE OF THE LONG SHADOWS* (1983), was distinguished by the unique teaming of four memorable giants of horror films, Vincent Price, Peter Cushing, John Carradine and Christopher Lee.

Biggers followed up his success with three popular mystery-romances: *LOVE INSURANCE* (1914), *INSIDE THE LINES* (1915) and *THE AGONY COLUMN* (1916). Biggers started to concentrate on play writing, developing a stage version of *INSIDE THE LINES* and following it with three additional plays. While on vacation in Hawaii in 1919, Biggers read an article in the newspaper about Chang Apana, a resourceful Chinese police detective in Honolulu. Years later Biggers recalled Apana when he was developing a novel to be serialized in *The Saturday Evening Post*. It was called *THE HOUSE WITHOUT A KEY*, and Biggers created a Chinese detective, Charlie Chan, "the best detective on the force" in Honolulu. The author intended

Chan to stand in stark contrast to the villainous Oriental stereotype that was then in vogue, best represented by Dr. Fu Manchu. Ironically, years later some came to also regard his creation as a stereotype. Biggers completed six novels featuring Chan, all of which originally appeared in serial form in the *Saturday Evening Post*. All but the last title were made into films.

The Chan of the novels differs in numerous ways from his portrayal in films. The real popularity of the books came after Biggers' death on April 5, 1933 when he was just under the age of fifty. It was at this time that the movie series began to gain wide popularity. In the novels, Chan is described as "very fat indeed" and his sayings are often more caustic in tone. There is no father/son byplay either. His assistant in several novels is a young Japanese man named Kashimo, who is far more disruptive and thick-headed than any of the offspring in the films. Very little of Chan's background is ever revealed in the books. One major exception is the revelation that in his youth Charlie served as a houseboy to the Phillimore family at their mansion in Honolulu. Charlie was treated well by the family, and he developed a lifelong friendship with some members of the clan.

Charlie's language skills in the novels are more awkward than in the films, the most irritating element being his substitution of the word "are" for "is." This is apparent from the very first words spoken by Chan in the book: "No knife are present in neighborhood of crime." Other than this flaw, Charlie is described as "dragging his words painfully from the poets." Several paragraphs later, Chan uses his first unattributed quote from Confucius.

Here is a brief summary of each novel:

1. *THE HOUSE WITHOUT A KEY* (1925)

Wealthy socialite Dan Winterslip is murdered in Honolulu. Detective-Sergeant Chan is assigned to the case, and he becomes friends with John Quincy Winterslip, with whom he shares many of his observations and discoveries. Together they trap the killer. At the climax, Charlie allows the killer to seize his unloaded pistol. This trick, as in many later films, eliminates the need for further evidence since it produces a confession. Adams' aunt, Minerva Winterslip from Boston high society, is very condescending to Chan at first. Charlie confronts this directly, urging her, "Friendly cooperation are essential between us." By the novel's end, they reach a strong mutual understanding. Charlie's farewell to her is most poetic: " The snowy, chilly days of winter and the scorching windless days of summer--may they all be springtime for you."

2. *THE CHINESE PARROT* (1926)

As a favor to his old friend Sally Phillimore Jordan, Chan delivers a valuable pearl necklace from Honolulu to the California desert mansion of millionaire P. J. Madden. Here, he encounters a curious murder which he solves with the help of a multi-lingual parrot named Tony. In an unusual turn of events, Charlie assumes an undercover disguise as a cook named Ah Kim. In the culmination of the plot, Chan exposes a criminal masquerade and conspiracy. Charlie also encourages the romance of Bob Eden and Paula Wendell, the hero and heroine. He paints a wonderful portrait of connubial love for the young couple. "The ramble hand in hand with wife on evening streets, the stroll by moonly seaside. I recollect the happy spring of my own marriage with unlimited yearning." This also later became a tradition in the film series.

3. *BEHIND THAT CURTAIN* (1928)

Perhaps the best of the novels, the plot is set in San Francisco, where Chan helps solve the murder of his friend Sir Frederic Bruce from Scotland Yard. In this book, the Chan of the novels seems very close to Chan as he appeared on screen. The plot is intriguing, with roots dating back to an old murder in London. An important clue is a pair of Chinese slippers found on both corpses. The motive of a long-delayed revenge also becomes a key element in the films. Another highlight of the book is Charlie's reflections on his large family back in Honolulu. He speaks of them frequently with his friend Barry Kirk, and when he receives news of his newborn son back home, Charlie names him "Barry."

4. *THE BLACK CAMEL* (1929)

Chan, now promoted to Inspector, solves the murder of famous film actress Shelah Fane. The motive again involves revenge. He is helped by the mentalist Tarneverro, one of the most colorful figures created by Biggers. Of course, Tarneverro has his own agenda that he keeps secret from Chan, so for much of the story they are working at cross-purposes. In the conclusion, Tarneverro apologizes to Chan, regretting he did not confide in him sooner. Charlie responds graciously, "The man who looks back sees his mistakes piled up behind."

5. *CHARLIE CHAN CARRIES ON* (1930)

Inspector Duff from Scotland Yard is attacked in Charlie's Honolulu office. As a matter of honor, Charlie takes Duff's place on the last leg of a world tour to catch the killer his friend was tracking. Chan only appears in the last half of this novel, which is intricately plotted. Biggers creates a number of entertaining individuals as the suspects in this novel, and it is interesting to compare the different styles of Chan and Duff, both excellent detectives, in cracking this complex case. The synopsis for *ERAN TRECE* provides the full details of this plot.

6. *KEEPER OF THE KEYS* (1932)

Opera diva Ellen Lindini is murdered, and her four ex-husbands are all suspects. Chan solves the crime while on vacation in Nevada. Instead of a motion picture, this novel was the basis for a play called *INSPECTOR CHARLIE CHAN* by Valentine Davies, whose short story was the inspiration for *MIRACLE ON 34TH STREET*. The last Chan quotation penned by Biggers appears in the novel's last lines. Charlie says, "Three things the wise man does not do. He does not plow the sky. He does not paint pictures on the water. And he does not argue with a woman."

THE FOX FILM SERIES

The first few Chan films were not considered to be part of a series but merely dramatizations of the latest Earl Derr Biggers' novels. The first three Chans on film were actually played by Orientals, but Charlie's role was minimalized in each production. In *BEHIND THAT CURTAIN* (1929), Chan is virtually eliminated, with less than three minutes of screen time. Most of Chan's actions are transferred to another character, Sir Frederic Bruce, who is murdered early in the novel.

The first bona fide Chan film is Fox's *CHARLIE CHAN CARRIES ON* (1931) for which Warner Oland assumed the part. The picture was a huge success with both critics and audiences, and it was soon followed by *THE BLACK CAMEL*. By this time, the Chan films were finally regarded as a full-fledged series, which continued (except for one brief hiatus) for the next eighteen years.

The two principal actors who played the role of Charlie Chan during the heyday of the series were Warner Oland and Sidney Toler. Both were exceptional actors who brought a special magnetism to the role. Oland has come to be regarded as the definitive Chan. He assumed the role in 1931 and performed the part sixteen times. Warner Oland was born Jonah Werner Ohlund on October 3, 1880 in Umea, Sweden, and his family emigrated to America while he was still a child. He grew up on a farm in Connecticut. Young Oland became interested in theater, and toured with Sarah Bernhardt's company. He also learned set design and became a specialist in the plays of Ibsen and Strindberg, a number of which he translated into English. In 1908, he married actress and artist Edith Shearn (1870-1968). Shortly thereafter, he launched his screen career, appearing with Theda Bara in *THE JEWELS OF THE MADONNA* (1909). In 1912, he played two parts, including the title role of John Bunyan in *PILGRIM'S PROGRESS*. He played the first of many Oriental roles in *PATRIA* (1917), an elaborate serial. He frequently played Asian characters after this chapterplay, and they were almost always villainous roles. Oland claimed to have inherited his Oriental features naturally, as a result of the Mongol invasion of Sweden centuries ago.

Oland's most memorable film appearance in the Twenties was as Al Jolson's father in *THE JAZZ SINGER* (1927), but his voice was heard with one dramatic word: "Stop!" He shouts this as he enters the room where Jolson is singing a popular song at the piano. Oland played Dr. Fu Manchu in three Paramount feature films as well as one spoof short entitled *PARAMOUNT ON PARADE,* in which Philo Vance (William Powell) and Sherlock Holmes (Clive Brook) encounter Fu Manchu. Oland played Chan with very little makeup, primarily a goatee on his chin. His Chan is endlessly fascinating, and he usually stresses the poetic side of the character. He seems the living embodiment of virtue as expressed in the philosophy of Confucius. Beneath his gentleness, however, is a fierce determination, as is shown in many films. Oland's Chan is also a study of respect for others. It is Charlie's basic humanity that is his most appealing trait. He is willing to bend the law whenever circumstances show that this path would achieve the greater good.

It is no secret that Oland had an alcohol problem while making the Chan films, but according to all reports this actually improved his performance until his last two pictures. Oland developed bronchial pneumonia while on vacation in Sweden, his ancestral home, and he died in Stockholm on August 6, 1938 at the age of fifty-seven.

Sidney Toler was born in Warrensburg, Missouri on April 24, 1874. He became a notable stage performer, and made his film debut in an early sound film version of *MADAME X* (1929). In 1938, he was cast as the new Charlie Chan after an extensive casting effort by Twentieth Century Fox. Toler, unlike some of the other candidates, did not offer an imitation of Oland, but instead provided his own characterization. Although he was of Scottish descent, Toler had slightly Oriental features, but unlike Oland, Toler needed to use additional make-up to slant his eyebrows. Toler had only minor screen parts before he took on the role of Chan. He appeared with Warner Oland and Marlene Dietrich in *BLONDE VENUS* (1932) and with Clark Gable and Loretta Young in *CALL OF THE WILD* (1935), but his most memorable role was as an irate ship captain in *OUR RELATIONS* (1936) with Laurel and Hardy. His comic timing was superb in his scenes with the great comedy duo. Toler's appearance as Daniel Webster in *GORGEOUS HUSSY* (1936) was also memorable. Toler developed into a credible Chan who was somewhat more brittle and emotional than Oland. In the later films he became very easily exasperated. In some ways he was closer to the Chan of the novels. Toler played Chan in a total of twenty-two films, eleven for Fox and eleven for Monogram studios.

Another performer critical to the success of the early Fox Chan series was Keye Luke. His parents owned an art store in San Francisco. Keye was born on June 18, 1904 while his parents were on vacation in Canton, China. After the death of his father, the Luke family moved to Seattle, and Keye attended the University of Washington where he studied architecture and design. Luke became an artist, and he worked at both RKO and Fox as an art publicity director. He did the artwork for posters for the early Chan pictures, never dreaming he would become an intrinsic part of the series. Luke was very popular with studio personnel, and later when he became an actor, his writer friends always tried to write a "fat" part for him in their scripts whenever possible. Luke never received degrading Asian parts, and his roles always had dignity.

Luke's feature film debut was as a doctor in *THE PAINTED VEIL* (1934) with Greta Garbo and Warner Oland. Another of Luke's earliest roles was as a surgeon in *MAD LOVE* (1935), a classic horror film with Peter Lorre based on Maurice Renard's famous novel *THE HANDS OF ORLAC*. He was cast in a featured role in *THE GOOD EARTH* (1937), and the cast also included Walter Connolly, who frequently played Charlie Chan on radio. Later, Luke became one of the first Asian actors to star in a Hollywood film when he replaced Boris Karloff as Mr. Wong in *PHANTOM OF CHINATOWN*

(1941). Unfortunately, it was the last film in the Wong detective series, but Luke's performance was refreshing, and infused new life into the character of the detective James Lee Wong. No doubt Luke was awarded the opportunity due to his magnificent work in the Chan films, where he brought enthusiasm and likability to the part of Lee Chan, "Number one" son. He provided the definitive characterization as the perfect Chan offspring, always keeping the character credible. His debut in the role occurred in *CHARLIE CHAN IN PARIS* in 1935. He continued with the part until Oland's death in 1938. Although he never performed in a Chan film with Sidney Toler, the two actors became friends and appeared together in the serial *THE ADVENTURES OF SMILIN' JACK* (1943). Keye's brother, Edwin Luke, later played Chan's studious "Number five" son Edward, appearing with Toler in *THE JADE MASK*. During the late Forties, Keye Luke himself returned to the Chan series to be featured in the last two Monogram films. Many years later, he assumed the role Charlie Chan, lending his vocal talents to a cartoon series about the great detective. He remained active in films and television, appearing during his later years in such films as *GREMLINS* (1984) and *ALICE* (1990). Towards the end of his life, he was honored with a star on the Hollywood Walk of Fame. Luke died after a stroke on January 12, 1991.

In 1938, after *MR. MOTO'S GAMBLE*, Keye Luke's contract with Fox expired, and he became involved in many other projects, so Fox needed to cast a new son to continue the generational theme in the Toler/Chan films. Victor Sen Yung (1915-1980) was then selected to portray "Number two" son Jimmy, ignoring the fact that Charlie, Jr. was the "Number two" son in *CHARLIE CHAN AT THE OLYMPICS*. The conception of Jimmy Chan was as more inexperienced, almost a bungler compared to Lee. Overall, Lee was a genuine help to his father, but Jimmy and the other offspring were often obstacles, and Charlie sometimes lost patience with them. Jimmy did have a knowledge of chemistry, however, that benefited his father at key moments. Sen Yung had a great degree of charm, so he never alienated the audience with his antics, although he sometimes came very close. The relationship between Charlie and Jimmy was more volatile, but still with a sincere measure of affection. Sen Yung was billed in his Fox features as "Sen Yung" but this was Americanized in the Monogram pictures as "Victor Sen Young." After his stint in the Chan films, Sen Yung maintained an active career, appearing with Humphrey Bogart in *THE LEFT HAND OF GOD* (1955) and *FLOWER DRUM SONG* (1961). The actor also was successful on television, and he became a regular on *BONANZA* as Hop Sing, the Cartwright's cook on the Ponderosa. He died in his home in North Hollywood in 1980, apparently the victim of a gas leak.

The overall cast for the series was outstanding, and many brilliant character actors gave credibility and color to the films. The two major stars who lent their talents were the terror film icons Bela Lugosi and Boris Karloff. Lugosi's one and only Chan appearance was immediately after his sensational performance as *DRACULA* (1931). Karloff was in two films, a bit part in *BEHIND THAT*

CURTAIN and the co-lead of *CHARLIE CHAN AT THE OPERA*. Among the most memorable supporting performers were C. Henry Gordon, Murray Kinnell, Drue Layton, Douglass Dumbrille, Francis Ford (elder brother of director John Ford), Kay Linaker, Ethel Griffies, Lionel Atwill and many others. Additional players on their way to stardom, including Ray Milland, Rita Hayworth, Lon Chaney, Jr. and Robert Young received good training in the series. The contribution of young Layne Tom, Jr. was also unique, since he played three separate members of the Chan family in three different films.

The Fox series owed much of the quality of the work to the contributions of the screenwriters. After Biggers' death in 1933, there was some trepidation about writing original Chan stories for the screen. British thriller author Philip Mac-Donald contributed the first effort, *CHARLIE CHAN IN LONDON* in 1934. Edward T. Lowe, Robert Ellis, Helen Logan, Charles S. Belden and Jerry Cady were among the fruitful writers who crafted some of the finest Chan stories. After Toler assumed the role in 1938, the principal writers became John Larkin and Lester Ziffren, and their work sustained a good overall standard.

The directors were also essential for the high level of excellence. Hamilton MacFadden (1901-) was responsible for the initial success of the series. The brilliance in these films was not reflected in his later pictures, such as *THE THREE LEGIONNAIRES* (1937) or *SEA RACKETEERS* (1939), which were fairly routine films. MacFadden also appeared as an actor in some of the Toler Chan pictures, such as *CHARLIE CHAN IN RIO*.

The finest directorial contributor to the series may be H. Bruce Humberstone (1903-1984), often called "Lucky," who helmed four of the most memorable pictures. Among Humberstone's later endeavors were *WONDER MAN* (1945) with Danny Kaye, *FURY AT FURNACE CREEK* (1948), with Victor Mature, and *THE DESERT SONG* (1953). Eugene Forde (1898-1986) and Harry Lachman (1886-1975) both directed five films. Some actors found Lachman rather abrasive, but it is hard to deny the merit of his work. Norman Foster (1900-1976) helmed *CHARLIE CHAN AT TREASURE ISLAND* and two other excellent entries. Foster, the mainstay of the Mr. Moto series with Peter Lorre, is also remembered for his work with Orson Welles in *JOURNEY INTO FEAR* (1942) and Walt Disney in *DAVY CROCKETT* (1955). Other impressive Chan pictures were led by James Tinling, Gordon Wiles and Lynn Shores. Most of these individuals shared the ability to make the "B" Chan pictures appear to be "A" products.

Music is another important element, and although Fox usually provided adequate and even interesting scores, the studio never actually developed a touchstone motif or musical theme for Charlie Chan that might have added a greater sense of unity to the series. Each film has an individual theme, occasionally with an Oriental flavor. It wasn't until midway though the Monogram series that genuine theme music for Chan was employed. A few of the Monogram scores were excellent, with music that sounded quite similar to the film music of Shostakovich.

THE MONOGRAM SERIES

After Twentieth Century Fox discontinued the Chan series in 1942, Sidney Toler acquired the rights to the character from Earl Derr Biggers' widow. He was hoping to arrange financing for his own series to be distributed by Fox, but he was unable to complete any arrangements. Two years later, Monogram producers Philip N. Krasne and James S. Burkett decided to revive the Chan series for the low-budget studio. A deal was struck with Toler to continue in the leading role.

There were numerous changes in the old formula to tailor it to Monogram's budget. Chan was no longer working for the Honolulu police department. Instead, he became an official agent of the federal government working with the Secret Service, as noted by the first title in the Monogram series. Therefore, the writers did not have to explain his frequent absences from Hawaii. The plots also began to fall into a more predictable pattern, as each film began to focus on a gimmick such as the forging of fingerprints, a process enabling dead bodies to walk, or elaborate deadly booby traps. The production values, of course, were far lower at Monogram, with each film budgeted at about $75,000, about one third the budget at Fox. Action was often limited to one or two claustrophobic sets.

Another significant change was the addition of popular black comic Mantan Moreland in the continuing character of Birmingham Brown. Moreland was born on September 3, 1901 in Monroe, Louisiana. He ran off as a teenager to join a traveling show, and over the years became an expert performer in nightclubs and vaudeville. In 1928, he made his Broadway debut in the *BLACKBIRDS OF '28.* He and Ben Carter became partners, and their clever routines and classic wordplay humor rivaled Abbott and Costello. Moreland appeared in over a hundred films in his career. He always had a sparkle in his delivery, and the many subtle comments he added to each scene were comparable to the wry observations of W. C. Fields. Later in his career, Moreland was upset and angry at the civil rights movement, because his brand of humor was being denigrated making it difficult for him to get work. Director Jack Hill hired Moreland for *SPIDER BABY* (1964) and reported that his comic timing and performing ability were still excellent, but Mantan was bewildered that some members of the black community regarded him as an embarrassment. After this, Moreland only had bits in several television shows and films such as *ENTER LAUGHING* (1967) and *THE YOUNG NURSES* (1973). When Moreland died from a heart attack on September 28, 1973, he was largely forgotten. In the Forties, however, Moreland was a huge star with black audiences, and his participation insured a strong run for a film in primarily black areas. Financially, Monogram guaranteed success by adding him to the series. Moreland was an excellent comic with broad appeal, but his presence altered the Chan formula, providing an even stronger dose of comic relief. This weakened the films to some degree as the storylines became split between Chan's investigations and the humorous antics of Birmingham.

A new member of Charlie's family, "Number three" son Tommy, was also included in the Monogram series, and actor Benson Fong was hired for the part.

Fong was born on October 10, 1916, the son of a wealthy merchant in Sacramento, California. He had no actual desire to pursue an acting career even though he worked as an extra in several pictures during the Thirties. In 1943, however, a talent scout approached Fong in a Sacramento restaurant. This led to his role in the film *CHINA* (1943) with Alan Ladd, Loretta Young and Victor Sen Yung. Fong got on-the-job training in many films, including *THIRTY SECONDS OVER TOKYO* (1944) and *KEYS OF THE KINGDOM* (1944). He became friends with Gregory Peck, who suggested they open a restaurant together. In 1946, Fong opened "Ah Fong's," which specialized in Chinese cuisine. Over the years he opened four additional branches. Fong did not neglect film work, however, and he later appeared in many productions, including *FLOWER DRUM SONG* (1961), *OUR MAN FLINT* (1966) and *MOONLIGHT* (1982). His performance as Fong died on August 1, 1987. Tommy was noted for his unassuming animation and drive. He played particularly well in routines with Mantan Moreland.

Other performers, including Frances Chan and Marianne Quon, also made appearances in the series as members of Charlie's large family. It was always a refreshing change of pace to watch Charlie deal with his daughters instead of his sons. It brought out a more gentle and indulgent side of his personality. They know how to get their own way when dealing with their father.

A company of stalwart performers also graced the Monogram series, and they included many veterans such as Tim Ryan (a semi-regular as Lt. Ruark), Emmett Vogan, Milton Parsons (also a Fox veteran), Bruce D. Kellogg, Tristram Coffin, Carol Forman, Janet Shaw, Joan Woodbury and others.

George Callahan was the featured writer for the Monogram pictures, and the film's quality declined markedly after his departure. Phil Karlson (1908-1985) directed two of the better efforts in the series. Karlson's career finally clicked during the Fifties, and he directed a large number of excellent mysteries. Phil Rosen (1888-1951) began his career as a cameraman working for Thomas Edison. His work was reliable and steady, and he directed a total of six pictures, making him the most prolific of all Chan directors. The weaker films in the series were by Terry Morse and Howard Bretherton.

Overall, Sidney Toler made less of an impact as Chan at Monogram. As he was in his seventies, Toler had slowed down considerably. Despite the numerous handicaps, Monogram still managed to produce a few worthy, entertaining films, particularly *DARK ALIBI* and *THE SHANGHAI COBRA*. Toler's final three films, however, were of basement quality, and with his death in his home in Beverly Hills on February 12, 1947, it would seem to be the end of the Chan series. But the films were still moneymakers for Monogram, so they decided to find a replacement for Sidney Toler.

Roland Winters (1904-1989) was chosen to carry on as Charlie Chan. Years later on *THE DICK CAVETT SHOW*, Winters expressed his own surprise at his selection. He was enthusiastic about the prospect, but he considered it to be a huge stretch for him to portray a Chinese-American effectively. A number of critics have dismissed the Winters/Chan series outright, mainly because Roland lacked the charm of Oland and Toler. On his own terms, Winters' portrayal has more depth than is immediately apparent. Roland was a Boston-born performer who had done most of his earlier work on radio and the stage. He also played Chan with very little make-up, squinting to give his face an Oriental appearance. His nose seemed inappropriate for the part, but overall he made a decent Chan visually. His delivery of lines was sometimes stilted, but he was able to imbue them with warmth and flavor. Winters' Chan reverted to the same syntax problem as the Chan of the novels, substituting "are" for "is" in sentences ("What are your good news?"). On the plus side, the writers returned to the original Biggers' novels for sayings and situations utilized in the Winters' films. There was a conscious effort by Winters himself to make his rendition as close as possible to the Chan of the novels. Winters obviously enjoyed playing the role. While it is clear he was easily and thoroughly outmatched by Oland and Toler, Winters had a measure of success as Chan, particularly in contrast with the performance of J. Carrol Naish in the role a few years later. Naish was unwatchable in the role, and one can appreciate the success of Winters' rendition in comparison. In later years, Roland was a busy actor, appearing in numerous films and television. Actor Richard Herd described Winters as a warm and engaging individual who was a delightful raconteur and a perfect host. Roland Winters died of a stroke in 1989.

The Winters series can be very entertaining on its own terms. There were a number of changes to the basic Chan formula as Winters assumed the role. All mention of Charlie's wife and home in Honolulu vanished. Instead, Chan acquired a house in San Francisco as his home base. He was no longer attached to the Secret Service, but had become a semi-retired private investigator. Another inexplicable alteration was that "Number two" son Jimmy had changed his name to Tommy. This is indeed confusing, and some fans have formulated reasons to explain this occurrence. The most popular theory is that "Number three" son Tommy died while serving in the war effort, and his brother assumed the name in his honor.

Screenwriter W. Scott Darling was a genuine Chan enthusiast, and it is his affection for Charlie and the Biggers' novels that provides the most interesting moments in these films. The main director for these films, however, was William "One-Shot" Beaudine (1892-1970), whose only interest at this time was to shoot each scene quickly and move on to the next one. Earlier in his career, Beaudine's work showed genius, with such films as *SPARROWS* (1926) and *THE OLD-FASHIONED WAY* (1934) with W. C. Fields. The last half of his career is typified by such dismal films such as *BILLY THE KID VS. DRACULA* (1966).

In 1949 after *THE SKY DRAGON*, Monogram planned to do a series of Chan pictures in England with Roland Winters and Keye Luke, but without Mantan Moreland. The studio was planning to revive the idea of a traveling Chan touring Europe. *CHARLIE CHAN IN LONDON* was the working title for the first film. Due to British financial rules, Monogram had accumulated significant funds in English banks which were limited for use within Great Britain. The studio planned to use these funds to finance the additional Chan films. Unexpectedly, however, the British Finance Minister devalued the English currency, and Monogram was forced to cancel the series, since their funding was undercut. In fact, Winters and Luke were notified of the cancellation while they were preparing to leave for England. So by a twist of fate, the Charlie Chan film series ended due to the unanticipated shift in monetary policy by the British government, and not the encroaching impact of television.

THE CHAN SAYINGS

Charlie Chan's sayings have become his trademark, and remain a memorable element of each film. Whether they are called aphorisms, homilies, proverbs, nuggets of folk wisdom, adages, quotes, maxims, precepts or fortune cookie comments, these sayings express the heart of his character. They have their basis directly in the Biggers' novels, and among the first words out of Chan's mouth was a statement reflecting the thoughts of Confucius. These sayings basically fall into six categories:

A. Direct Quotes: "Confucius has said, a wise man question himself, a fool others." (*CHARLIE CHAN IN CITY IN DARKNESS*)

Confucius is the only individual directly cited by Chan, but he also prefaces many of his remarks by declaring "Ancient Chinese philosopher say" or "Chinese proverb say." Confucius (551-479 B.C.) or K'ung Fu-tse was a influential teacher and moral philosopher. An important compilation of some of his thought is contained in *THE ANALECTS*, and the core of his philosophy is basically an exhortation for individuals to follow the course of virtue. His sayings are endlessly witty, practical, and relevant, even today. There are thousands of memorable quotes, such as "I have never yet seen people who are attracted to virtuous scholars as they are by beautiful women" or "What you do not like when done to yourself, do not do to others." Besides Confucius, many of Chan's sayings have their origin in Lao-Tzu (604-531 B.C.) the founder of Taoist thought, the scholar Mencius (372-289 B.C.), the elegant poet Li Po (701-762) and others. It is intriguing but sometimes difficult to trace many of these quotes. In *CHARLIE CHAN IN SHANGHAI,* Charlie says, "Long journey always start with one short step," which can be traced to Lao-Tzu's statement, "A journey of a thousand miles begins with a single step." This same thought later inspired President John F. Kennedy, who quoted it in his speeches.

B. Paraphrases: "Ship with too many pilots sometimes have difficulty in reaching port." (*DOCKS OF NEW ORLEANS*)

A good number of Chan's sayings are paraphrases of common sayings, such as this variant of "Too many cooks spoil the broth." These sayings are sometimes quite amusing, because the listener can easily identify an old chestnut decked out in elaborate new garb by Chan. Another amusing sample is "Learn from hen, never boast about egg until after egg's birthday."

C.   Metaphors: "Question without answer like faraway water, no good for nearby fire." (*CHARLIE CHAN AT THE CIRCUS*)

The most common Chan sayings are metaphors which are usually constructed as the above quotation: "X like Y, (resembles) Z." The verb is generally understood and omitted in this arrangement. Almost every Chan film has at least one example. Some of Chan's metaphors are remarkably topical as well as amusingly outlandish, such as "Murder without bloodstain like Amos without Andy, most unusual," or "Mind like parachute, only function when open."

D. Observations: "If strength were all, tiger would not fear scorpion." (*CHARLIE CHAN'S SECRET*)

Examples of Charlie's poetic observations are also found in practically each film. They can range from the highly poetic to the rather commonplace. Some additional examples include: "Nut easy to crack often empty," "No poison more deadly than ink" and "When money talk, few are deaf."

E. Insults: "The wages of stupidity is hunt for new job." (*THE BLACK CAMEL*)

Charlie's put-downs are usually reserved for his offspring or Birmingham Brown. The insults are frequently used in the novels when Charlie becomes exasperated with Kashimo, his Japanese assistant. Chan's remark to Kashimo about stupidity is an example. Some of the insults also have a gentle side, such as "Eyes of kitten open only after nine days" or "My boy, if silence is golden, you are bankrupt." Keye Luke quoted one particularly clever insult that somehow wound up on the cutting room floor: "It is better to be quiet and thought stupid than to speak and remove all doubt."

F.   Jokes: "Chinese chimpanzee not interfere with monkey business of big baboon." (*THE CHINESE RING*)

Charlie's jokes occur more often than is usually thought. Sometimes the humor is highlighted by the actor's delivery of the line. Occasionally Charlie's jokes go over the head of the person to whom they are directed, but are picked up by the audience. Charlie is known to satirize himself with his comments at times, the most memorable being, "What Confucius say to this too terrible for even Charlie Chan to repeat!"

There are other Chan expressions that are also important. His politeness is legendary, and his courteous response, "Thank you so much" in any situation is unforgettable. Another popular phrase is "Contradiction please," when Charlie detects a mistake or flaw in the conclusion by a companion. Some of the weak points of Chan's sayings are his overuse of comments about hasty conclusions and alibis, as well as his tedious references to rotten eggs. Many of Chan's thoughts about women can easily be regarded today as sexist, particularly his comment, "Woman not made for heavy thinking, but should always decorate scene like blossom of plum." Considering Charlie's devotion to his wife, to whom he defers in all family decisions (as witnessed in *CHARLIE CHAN AT THE CIRCUS*), perhaps his old-fashioned attitude in these comments should be overlooked.

Chan's reliance on sayings seems to have been satirized as early as 1934 by Harold Lloyd in his Fox Studio film *THE CAT'S PAW*. Lloyd plays Ezekiel Cobb, the son of a missionary who grew up in China and returns to America to visit his old hometown. By an odd set of circumstances, he agrees to run for mayor and, by a fluke is elected. Cobb relies on the sayings of Ling Po (an obvious corruption of Li Po) to guide him in making decisions. Some of his Ling Po quotes sound like clever pastiches of Chan sayings, such as "Should the lark cease singing because winter is coming?" Lloyd's clever comedy was but the first to poke fun at Chan's sayings, and it is a measure of the influence of Chan on popular culture that many motion pictures and books have focused on Charlie's sayings as a fun target. Among the most unusual films to do this was *MESA OF LOST WOMEN* (1952), a hilarious, low-budget thriller with Jackie Coogan that included a character who spouted Chan-like quips.

ASIAN-AMERICAN CRITICISM OF CHAN

The harshest criticism of the Charlie Chan series arose during the Sixties and Seventies when several groups, such as the Association of Asian/Pacific American Artists, protested the image of Chan. In fact, boycotts were held in some areas to force Chan films off several television stations. This hostile attitude mellowed significantly after the initial protests. In 1986, the first recipient of the Lifetime Achievement Award by the Association of Asian/Pacific American Artists was none other than Keye Luke, who was the most passionate and vocal defender of the series.

The criticism of Chan by some Chinese groups was based on four points: Chan was a demeaning image; he spoke poor English; only non-Asians played the character; and racist elements are present in the films. The first argument is hard to understand, because the figure of Chan is highly positive. "You've got a Chinese hero!" Keye Luke would exclaim. In the films, Chan is usually the most intelligent character in each story and he is a man who is accorded respect around the world. Critics of Charlie Chan are usually not familiar with the films themselves, and sometimes confuse them with the "Yellow Peril" films of the early Thirties that were quite demeaning (such as the 1936 Bela Lugosi serial *SHADOW OF CHINATOWN*). If Chan came to be regarded as a stereotype, it was simply that his character was so appealing that it captured the imagination of the public at large and entered the popular culture. As a product of his times, Chan on all levels is a positive figure.

The second argument is also fairly weak. Chan never spoke broken English or pidgin English. His delivery is sometimes halting because he is thinking in his native language and then translating it into English. His English is perfect, with the exception that some pronouns and verbs are ommited. These words are intended to be understood by the listener. The Chan of the Biggers' novels (and the Winters series) also had an occasional syntax problem. Keye Luke also confronted Chinese activists when they made accusations that Chan used phrases such as "Me no savvy." In fact, in the first novel, *THE HOUSE WITHOUT A KEY*, the hero receives a phone call from someone posing as Chan, and he realizes the fraud when the fake Chan uses the phrase "savvy."

The third argument, that Chan was not performed by an Asian, has some validity. The first three Chans were Asian, but when Chan became the central figure of the films, it was because Warner Oland was such a convincing and charismatic presence. The series might never have been a success if Oland did not undertake the role. Perhaps no performer of Oriental descent could have carried the series in the Thirties or Forties like Oland or Toler. This is a regrettable but an accurate appraisal of the commercial market of those times. On the other hand, the other Oriental characters in the Chan films were regularly played by Asian-American actors, and their performances were highly positive and not stereotyped. Many excellent actors' careers were launched by the Chan series. A strong case can be made that later presentations of Chan should have been played by a performer of Asian descent. By the time Ross Martin played the part in the Seventies, it would have been more effective if Keye Luke or Khigh Dhiegh had assumed the role.

The final argument, unfortunately, is true. Occasional racist elements can be detected in the films. One of the most blatant examples is Sergeant Kelly (William Demerest) in *CHARLIE CHAN AT THE OPERA*. This shortcoming, however, is infrequent and genuinely atypical of the flavor of the entire series. A group of pictures from the Thirties and Forties that are referred to as "Yellow Peril" films contain frequent racist comments that are truly embarrassing and demeaning. The difference between these films and the Chan series is staggering. Author Fletcher Chan wrote an excellent article, **"Respecting Charlie Chan"** in *Classic Images,* Vol. 263 (May 1997) which places this issue in context and highlights the positive aspects of the portrayal of Asian-Americans in these films.

The same issue of racism also applies to Mantan Moreland, who is criticized as a black stereotype. His portrayal is closer to Eddie Anderson ("Rochester") than Stepin Fetchit. Mantan's wit, clever comebacks and obvious intelligence offset the situations when he reacts like Lou Costello in a haunted house. No one has ever called Costello's performance demeaning. The actual criticising then, is not of Moreland's performance, but that so few blacks characters were portrayed in a positive light during this era. That is a valid argument beyond the scope of this volume.

INFLUENCE AND APPEAL OF THE CHAN FILMS

Charlie Chan has always had a special appeal to audiences. Some of this can be attributed to America's fascination with the Far East. Another part concerns the family element in the series. Fans delight in watching the traditional Chan cope with his Americanized offspring and respond to the devotion that bonds their relationship. There are few scenes in the series between Chan and his wife, but the affection shown in those few scenes is essential to his character. Charlie's sayings, even when they sound like fortune cookie cliches, remain very popular. When these elements are added to a first-rate mystery, the result is pure magic. Even the movies with weaker stories were popular because of the basic strength of the formula.

The Chan films are quite enduring because of the appeal of the characters. The pictures certainly stimulated a respect and interest in Chinese culture. Other works in detective literature were certainly inspired by Chan, including John P. Marquand's "Mr. Moto" series (which succeeded Chan at *The Saturday Evening Post)* and Hugh Wiley's "Mr. Wong" series which started in 1935. Chan also influenced the creation of other diverse and unusual characters, such as Arthur W. Upfield's Aborigine detective Napoleon Bonaparte and Harry Kemelman's Rabbi David Small. Robert van Gulik based his memorable seventh century detective Dee Jen-Djieh, or Judge Dee, on an actual figure from Chinese history, but the character of the magistrate owes much to Chan.

It was clear that the character of Chan was absorbed into the national culture when numerous other films, such as the classic film noir *THE BIG SLEEP* (1946), had references to him. He was refered to quite often on radio programs in lines such as, "Who do you think you are, Charlie Chan?" Indeed, Chan himself became a popular shpw on radio in numerous series shows from 1933 through 1948. By the Fifties, the novelty of Chan began to wane, and the televion series based on him was rather weak. The main impact of Chan on television derived from broadcast of the films, and the influence upon other shows.

One of the most popular descendants of Chan on television is the series *KUNG FU* (1972-1975), which was revived during the Nineties. The storyline concerned Caine (David Carradine), a Chinese-American wanderer in the Old West who had been educated in a Shaolin Temple. An expert in the martial arts, Caine tried to embody the philosophical ideals he learned in his youth. The plot of each episode alternated between the American West and flashbacks to Caine's monastic training. Five veterans from Chan projects appeared in the pilot film, including Keye Luke, Victor Sen Yung, Benson Fong, Philip Ahn and James Hong. Keye Luke became a regular in the series, appearing as a blind teacher in the Chinese Monastery attended by Kwai Chang Caine. His performance at times was strongly reminiscent of Warner Oland, as he provided his young student with many philosophical sayings and insight. Luke's character was Master Po, perhaps another reference to Li Po. A feature film, *KUNG FU: THE MOVIE* (1986) also featured Luke and Fong.

Other projects showing a Chan influence include the exceptional television film effort called *JUDGE DEE AND THE HAUNTED MONASTERY* (1974) and the television series *KHAN* (1975). Both projects featured the remarkable Khigh Dhiegh, who is perhaps best known for his role as the villain Wo Fat on *HAWAII FIVE-O*. The Judge Dee film was crafted closely after the novel *THE HAUNTED MONASTERY* by Robert van Gulik, which was formatted on the style of seventeenth and eighteenth century Chinese detective novels, which traditionally combine three different mysteries in one narrative. The well-crafted film also featured Keye Luke as the villain of the story. In 1975, Khigh Dhiegh was given the lead in the television series *KHAN* in which he played a private detective in San Francisco's Chinatown. Khan's manner and style had many elements of an updated Charlie Chan. Khan was assisted by his two grown children, played by Irene Sun and Evan Kim. The series was never given a genuine chance to develop, as CBS pulled it from their schedule after only four episodes. The reverberations of Chan still continue. One can even detect an element of Charlie Chan in the popular character Yoda of the *STAR WARS* films.

Miramax has been considering reviving Charlie Chan for a new feature film. The focus would not be on Chan himself, but on his grandson who is a private detective. Actor Russell Wong, from the *VANISHING SON* television series, was among the performers considered for the leading role. Writer/producer David Mamet had been approached by Warner Brothers to develop another Chan project. Whether or not these particular endeavors pan out, there remains a growing interest in Earl Derr Biggers' detective.

Chan films have been frequently revived on cable television and video in recent years, and have garnered countless new fans. New viewers of the original series are sometimes surprised by the values and morals contained in the stories, above and beyond the mystery plot. The performers who brought Chan and his sons to life are now gone, but the dignity, affection and humanity they poured into these films will last forever. For all those who have been involved in the making of the Charlie Chan series over the years, film lovers can only repeat Chan's most frequent phrase, "Thank you so much!"

THE FILMS OF
CHARLIE CHAN

BEHIND THAT CURTAIN (1929)
Rating: *

FOX. Written by Sonya Levien and Clarke Silvernail; Adapted from the novel *BEHIND THAT CURTAIN* by Earl Derr Biggers; Photographed by Conrad Wells; Edited by Alfred De Gaetano; Produced by William Fox; Directed by Irving Cummings. 90 minutes.

ANNOTATED CAST LIST

E. L. Park......................Charlie Chan
Warner Baxter.................Col. John Beetham (Noted explorer)
Philip Strange................ Eric Durand (British playboy)
Lois Moran....................Eve Durand (Heiress wife of Durand)
Gilbert Emery.................Sir Frederic Bruce (Detective)
Claude King...................Sir George Mannering (Eve's uncle)
Montague Shaw..............Hilary Galt (Mannering's solicitor)
Boris Karloff.................. Sudanese servant (Beetham's attendant)
Jamiel Hassan.................Habib Hanna (Persian official)
Peter Gawthorne..............Bruce's Scotland Yard assistant
John Rogers...................Alf Pornick (Galt's night watchman)
Finch Smiles..................Clerk (Galt's secretary)
Mercedes De Valasco........Neinah (Durand's Indian mistress)

SYNOPSIS AND APPRAISAL

BEHIND THAT CURTAIN is perhaps Earl Derr Biggers' finest Chan mystery, set in a four day period in San Francisco, where Charlie solves the murder of Scotland Yard Inspector Sir Frederic Bruce. He does this by linking the killing to an old British murder case. This film eliminates the Bruce murder, and reduces Chan to a bit player. The writers take the "backstory" told by Eve Durand at the book's conclusion, and use it as the central plot instead. It completely destroys all the mystery element, since we learn the identity of the killer within moments of the crime. The picture is presented as a romance, about the tragic love story of Eve Durand and John Beetham. The screenplay opens with Sir George Mannering investigating the background and character of Eric Durand, who is romancing Eve, Mannering's heiress niece. Hilary Galt, his solicitor, tells Mannering he has found some damning evidence about Durand. Galt is also confronted by the explorer, Col. Beetham, who quarrels with him regarding a slanderous letter. Galt is murdered in his office that evening, and the night watchman follows and discovers the name of the murderer. He plans to black-mail him. Col. Beetham is in love with Eve Mannering, but she has fallen for Eric Durand and marries him in secret. They plan to move to India. Sir Frederic Bruce takes charge of the Galt murder, and the only clue is a pair of Chinese slippers that were found placed on Galt's corpse. Bruce contacts Charlie Chan in San Francisco, who identifies the slippers as a gift of the Chinese Emperor to Col. Beetham. By this time, Beetham is off on an expedition.

In India, Eve learns the true character of Durand. He is a complete scoundrel. She receives a letter from the night watchman. Durand has refused to give him more money, so he writes to Eve revealing her husband is a killer and demanding more money. Eve encounters Col. Beetham, and asks him to take her with him on his expedition. Later, Bruce turns up to question Durand. Together they track the Beetham caravan by plane, and finally locate their camp in the desert. They search, but fail to locate Eve. She has fled into the desert. Bruce questions Beetham about the slippers, and he says they were a gift to Eve before her mar-riage. Beetham meets with Bruce later in Teheran. He cannot locate Eve, and begs Bruce not to harass her. At this time, Eve is desperately trying to escape from her cold-blooded husband. Bruce agrees to act with restraint, after conclud-ing that Galt was murdered by Eric Durand.

A year later, Eve is located posing as an elevator girl in San Francisco by Charlie Chan. Bruce, Durand and Col. Beetham arrive in town. Chan has also obtained Eve's copy of the night watchman's letter. Sir Frederic and Chan confer on the problem. Durand tries to shoot Eve at a lecture presented by Beetham. He misses and slightly wounds Sir Frederic Bruce instead. Eve, with great reluc-tance, starts to answer Bruce's questions. Suddenly, a policeman arrives with news that Durand is dead, shot by Chan while resisting arrest. There is no long-er any need for her testimony. Bruce remarks, "How careless of Chan" as the film ends.

PERFORMANCES

E. L. Park appears as Chan only in the last ten minutes of the film, and he actually has only one genuine scene, a three minute cameo. All the rest of his activity is off-screen. Park reportedly was of Korean descent, and was employed behind the scenes at Fox Studios. He was recruited for this brief role because he was Asian and available. Half of his dialogue is in Chinese, and his few English sentences are delivered in an awkward, halting manner. This film is his only screen credit.

Most of the other performances in the film are poor as well. Almost all the dialogue is delivered in a stilted, artificial style, with a deliberate pause between each word. This is a common fault with a number of early talking films, but the problem is exaggerated here. Lois Moran and Warner Baxter have a few effective scenes, but they are few and far between. The most interesting aspect of the cast is the appearance of Boris Karloff in his first sound picture. He plays a turban-wearing servant. At first, his character seems mute in his scenes in the caravan, since he refuses to answer any questions. Later, in San Francisco, he has some brief dialogue as he attempts to comfort his master, Col. Beetham. His familiar-sounding voice seems the most natural one in the picture.

CHARLIE CHAN'S SAYINGS

There are no genuine Chan sayings in the script. The closest is a brief observation made by Chan to Sir Frederic Bruce, commenting on his plans to bring the case to a conclusion. He says, "It is the only way those who honorably love each other may find happiness."

THE BLACK CAMEL (1931)
Rating: ✱✱✱✱✱

FOX. Written by Barry Conners and Philip Klein; Story adapted by Hugh
Strange from the novel *THE BLACK CAMEL* by Earl Derr Biggers; Pho-
tographed by Joseph August and Daniel Clark; Edited by Alfred De Gaetano;
Musical direction by Emil Newman; Produced by Hamilton MacFadden and
William Sistrom; Directed by Hamilton MacFadden. 71 minutes.

ANNOTATED CAST LIST

Warner Oland..................Charlie Chan
Bela Lugosi....................Arthur Tarneverro (Fortune teller)
Dorothy Revier...............Shelah Fane (Glamorous film star)
Sally Eilers....................Julie O'Neil (Shelah's ward)
Victor Varconi................Robert Fyfe (Ex-husband of Shelah Fane)
William Post, Jr.............. Alan Jaynes (Wealthy bachelor)
Robert Young.................Jimmy Bradshaw (Hawaii tourism director)
Murray Kinnell............... Archie Smith (Artist and beachcomber)
Rita Rozelle...................Luana (Smith's girlfriend)
Otto Yamaoka................. Kashimo (Enthusiastic assistant to Chan)
Marjorie White............... Rita Ballou (Friend of Shelah)
Richard Tucker................Wilkie Ballou (Rita's husband)
C. Henry Gordon.............Huntley Van Horn (Actor and leading man)
Dwight Frye...................Jessop (Butler at the Fane Household)
Violet Dunn....................Anna (Fane's maid)
J. M. Kerrigan................ Thomas MacMaster (Friend of Tarneverro)
Mary Gordon..................Mrs. MacMaster (Friend of Tarneverro)
Robert Homans...............Honolulu police chief
Louise Mackintosh..........Librarian
Hamilton MacFadden....... Val Martino (Film director)

SYNOPSIS AND APPRAISAL

This film, the earliest of the traditional Chan series to survive, was entirely
filmed on location in Hawaii. The screenplay was patterned very closely to the
plot of the novel, with only slight modifications. Julie O'Neil was Shelah
Fane's secretary, not her ward, and Smith the beachcomber was not murdered.
Jessop the butler had no romantic interest in Anna the maid, and Val Martino's
role was practically eliminated. Other than that, much of the original storyline
and dialogue remained intact, resulting in an excellent picture, with crisp direction by Hamilton MacFadden. Several shortcomings, such as the lack of a genuine musical score, are easily overlooked.

The film opens with surfing footage as the soundtrack blares the tune, *On the Beach at Waikiki.* A motion picture is being shot at Waikiki Beach, but the leading lady, Shelah Fane, asks to be excused early. Millionaire Alan Jaynes has proposed to her, and the screen star has sent for her mystic advisor, Tarneverro, to ask his advice. At the *Royal Hawaiian Hotel,* Chan poses as a merchant and meets with Tarneverro. The mystic quickly penetrates his disguise, and Charlie gives him a friendly warning that fortune telling is frowned upon by the Honolulu police.

Shelah meets with Tarneverro, and they consult his crystal ball. He tells her the shadow of Denny Mayo, an actor murdered three years earlier, stands between her and any happiness. She tells Tarneverro about her involvement in Mayo's death as the scene fades out. Later, Shelah confides in Julie, her ward, that she will not marry. Anna, Shelah's maid, is very upset by something, and Jessop the butler asks to help. He is deeply in love with her, but she does not return his affection.

Alan Jaynes confronts Tarneverro at the hotel, upset that he will likely advise Shelah against their marriage, but Chan stops Jaynes from striking the mystic. Tarneverro alerts Charlie that he may be able to turn a murderer over to him later that evening. Kashimo, Chan's frenetic assistant interrupts their conversation, and his annoyed boss asks him to, "Spend more time looking for nothing to do."

Guests gather at Shelah's house for her evening dinner party. Julie and her boyfriend, Jimmy Bradshaw, find the actress stabbed to death in her beach-front pavilion. Julie begs Bradshaw to remove a ring from the corpse's finger before notifying the police. Chan is summoned from a hotel banquet, and he brings Tarneverro with him to investigate the crime. The mystic tells him that Shelah had witnessed the murder of Denny Mayo, but had kept silent until now. She also told Tarneverro that the killer is currently in Honolulu, but she did not reveal his name.

Chan and Tarneverro find a number of clues at the crime scene: crushed orchids pulled from Shelah's dress, her smashed wristwatch, and odd footprints from someone with a hole in his shoe. Julie hands Tarneverro a letter from the murdered actress. As Chan starts to read it, the lights are turned off and all but a fragment of the letter is stolen, which makes Chan furious. He intensely questions all the suspects: Julie; Jimmy Bradshaw; Alan Jaynes; Rita Ballou, former actress and close friend of Shelah; Wilkie Ballou, her husband; Huntley Van Horn, leading actor in the film; supporting actress Diana Dixon; and the servants Jessop the butler and Anna the maid. Jessop serves everyone coffee in the dining room. Chan discovers that Shelah was observed crying over a man's photograph that morning, and that the actress' emerald ring and diamond pin are missing. He also learns that the orchids were a gift from Robert Fyfe, Shelah's former husband, who is appearing in a stage play in Honolulu. Chan sends for him.

Arguments break out among the suspects when the Denny Mayo case is first mentioned. Kashimo locates pieces of a torn photograph in Shelah's room.

Both Tarneverro and Julie steal sections of the picture when the fragments scatter on the floor.

Robert Fyfe arrives, and Rita Ballou says she spotted the actor emerging from Shelah's pavilion earlier that evening. Fyfe explains that Shelah called him and they met only briefly since he was due to appear onstage. Kashimo arrests a beachcomber named Smith whose worn shoes correspond to the odd footprints. The hobo claims to have overheard Shelah and Fyfe arguing. At this point, Fyfe confesses to her murder, but Chan proves he is lying, since Shelah was seen alive by Wong the cook at 8:12 P.M., at which time Fyfe was on his way back to the theater to make his curtain call. Chan then releases all the suspects, much to the consternation of Tarneverro. Charlie finally locates the other piece of the missing letter, hidden under a rug, but it reveals nothing.

The next day, Smith the beachcomber tells his native girlfriend that he will earn some money by selling a painting, since the buyer wants him to remain silent. He sells it to Fyfe for $300. Later, Smith is mysteriously shot and wounded on the beach.

Charlie has breakfast with his family, who keep pestering him about the Fane case. He heads to the library where he discovers that all photos of Denny Mayo were cut out of the newspapers on file. He suspects Julie, but she shows Chan a note that prompted her to check the files at the library. After Bradshaw's urging, Julie admits that she removed Shelah's ring since Denny Mayo's name was engraved on it. She wanted to cover up Shelah's affair with Mayo. Chan then determines that Tarneverro sent Julie the note. He learns from two Australian tourists that the mysterious psychic is actually Arthur Mayo, the brother of Denny.

Smith's girlfriend accuses Fyfe of shooting the beachcomber. She brings Chan to her shack where Smith is dying. The beachcomber says he overheard Shelah confessing to the murder of Denny Mayo. Fyfe confirms this, adding that Shelah killed Mayo after learning he was already married. Fyfe made his false confession to preserve his ex-wife's reputation. Smith also hands over Shelah's diamond pin, which he stole from her pavilion. Chan deduces that the tip of the pin broke off and lodged in the heel of Shelah's killer. Charlie arrests Fyfe after the beachcomber dies.

The chief of police argues with Chan after he brings in Fyfe, demanding the arrest of Tarneverro, but Charlie insists the mystic is innocent. Searching Shelah's home, the police locate a number of pin scratches on the floor of the dinning room. A knife is thrown at Chan while he is searching, and the police chief suspects Jessop the butler. Chan then gathers the suspects to learn where they sat when coffee was served the night of the murder. Tarneverro sits in the incriminating chair, which convinces the chief of his guilt. Charlie then asks to see the right shoe of a different suspect, and he finally makes an accusation.

The killer confesses, and while giving an explanation, a second killer, the murderer of Smith, is uncovered. The picture ends with Kashimo rushing in with another clue, which Charlie tells him to save for the next case. The film comes to an abrupt close, as strains of *Aloha Oe* are heard over the closing title which proclams "THE END."

PERFORMANCES

This is the earliest surviving performance of Warner Oland as Charlie Chan, and his characterization is fully realized. He is somewhat sharper and more volatile than in his later readings, provoked no doubt by the assault on him while reading Tarneverro's letter. The scene of Charlie at the breakfast table with his family is marvelous, as he humorously reflects on the Americanization of his children. His interaction with other cast members, Lugosi in particular, is first rate. The only weak element is his rapport with Kashimo, his assistant. Although conceived by Biggers himself, the character of Kashimo is a disaster. He runs around madly and is as childish as a ten year old. By comparison, all of the Chan offspring who assisted Charlie in the later movies seem like geniuses. There is also no affection or even understanding between Charlie and Kashimo, the element that makes his relationship between Chan and his sons so meaningful in later films. Otto Yamaoka is unbearable to watch as Kashimo, and he does nothing but irritate the audience with his antics.

This was the first role for Bela Lugosi after the major box office success of *DRACULA* (1931). He is masterful as Tarneverro, although his accent is a bit preposterous when his character turns out to be Irish. The interaction between Oland and Lugosi is unique in the Chan film series, particularly with their mutual respect and admiration. The plot also fully exploits the logical reason for Tarneverro's attempt to hinder Chan. Their lighter moments are excellent, particularly when Chan transports Tarneverro to the murder scene. Lugosi observes Charlie's eccentric driving, and asks, "Have you been driving long?" "No," Chan replies. "At first I am pretty bad driver, but now me and road turn corner same time." The comic timing of both players in the scene is indeed perfect.

The performances of the other supporting players are mixed, suffering from stilted stage bound acting often present in early talking pictures. Robert Young, in his screen debut, comes off best as the light romantic lead. His breezy, informal style is quite charming even when his dialogue is hokey. Dorothy Revier (Shelah), Sally Eilers (Julie) and Murray Kinnell (Smith) are also laudable. On the other hand, Victor Varconi (Fyfe) and William Post, Jr. (Jaynes) are simply dreadful. Hamilton MacFadden himself is good as the director of Shelah's film, but this part, which is rather significant in the novel, is a mere cameo in the screenplay. The unnamed Oriental actor who plays Wong, Shelah's cook, is very striking in his small role. Dwight Frye, best known as the flamboyant madman Renfield from both the stage and screen versions of *DRACULA* is a true delight as Jessop, notably when he gets to rant and chew the scenery at the climax of the film. Dwight Frye later appeared in *INSPECTOR CHARLIE CHAN*, the stage production derived from Biggers' final Chan novel, *THE KEEPER OF THE KEYS*.

CHARLIE CHAN'S SAYINGS

◇ Wages of stupidity is hunt for new job.

◇ Mouse cannot cast shadow like elephant.

◇ Always harder to keep murder secret than for egg to bounce on sidewalk.

◇ Very few after-dinner speeches equipped with self-stopper.

◇ All foxes come at last to fur store.

◇ Sometimes very difficult to pick up pumpkin with one finger.

◇ There is old saying, "Death is a black camel that kneels unbidden at every gate." Tonight black camel has knelt here.

◇ Alibi have habit of disappearing like hole in water.

◇ Even bagpipe will not speak when stomach is empty.

◇ Way to find rabbit's residence is to turn rabbit loose and watch.

◇ Always happens, when conscience tries to speak, telephone out of order.

◇ Even wisest man sometimes mistake bumble bee for blackbird.

◇ Soap and water can never change perfume of billy goat.

◇ Only very clever man can bite pie without breaking crust.

◇ Learn from hen, never boast about egg until after egg's birthday.

◇ Can cut off monkey's tail, but he is still monkey.

BLACK MAGIC (1944) Alternate title: *MEETING AT MIDNIGHT*
Rating: ✳✳✳

MONOGRAM. Written by George Callahan; Photographed by Arthur Martinelli; Edited by John Link; Music by Alexander Laszlo; Produced by Philip N. Krasne and James S. Burkett; Directed by Phil Rosen.   67 minutes.

ANNOTATED CAST LIST

Sidney Toler	Charlie Chan
Frances Chan	Frances Chan (Charlie's daughter)
Mantan Moreland	Birmingham Brown (Bonner's new butler)
Joseph Crehan	Mathews (Police sergeant)
Helen Beverly	Nancy Wood (Norma Duncan in disguise)
Jacqueline De Wit	Justine Bonner (Wife of psychic)
Geraldine Wall	Harriet Green (Blackmailed by Bonner)
Ralph Peters	Rafferty (Police detective)
Frank Jacquet	Paul Hamlin (Blackmailed by Bonner)
Edward Earle	Dawson (Chemist working with Chan)
Claudia Dell	Vera Starkey (Bonner's assistant)
Charles Jordan	Tom Starkey (Bonner's assistant)
Richard Gordon	William Bonner (Murdered psychic)
Harry Depp	Charles Edwards (Manufacturer of magic supplies)

SYNOPSIS AND APPRAISAL

This is the most popular film of the Monogram series, even if it is not the finest one. Part of the appeal lies in the subject matter which relies upon supernatural elements as in the popular *CHARLIE CHAN AT TREASURE ISLAND* and *DEAD MEN TELL.*   Here the story centers on the world of psychics and phony mediums, with clever development and snappy dialogue. The solution of the mystery is classic, in the style of the original Biggers novels. The film is plagued by a cartoon-like music score and an overabundance of comic relief.

The film opens with Birmingham Brown assuming the job of butler at the home of the psychics William and Justine Bonner. William is killed while holding a seance attended by Harriet Green, Charles Edwards, Paul Hamlin, Nancy Wood and Frances Chan. Frances determines Bonner was shot and the police are notified. They are baffled, and when they learn that Frances is Charlie Chan's daughter, they quickly send for the famous detective.

In his hotel suite, Charlie is testing and playing with the large number of toys, gifts for his children in Honolulu. He goes to police headquarters to vouch for Frances and Birmingham. Sergeant Mathews tells him that Bonner was shot in the heart, but no gun was found on anyone at the seance, nor was one found in the house. In addition, no bullet was located in Bonner's body, despite the lack of an exit wound. Chan is on his way home to Hawaii, but he agrees to help when Mathews threatens to detain Frances. A rather silly sequence follows, where Chan demonstrates how phony psychics operate. He produces "spirit rappings" by using Mexican jumping beans and levitates a handkerchief behind his back.

Chan reviews the statements of all the suspects and concludes that Nancy Wood is an impostor. Daughter Frances ("Beauty of Chan family") noticed that Nancy's handbag was monogrammed with the initials "N. D." Her real name turns out to be Norma Duncan, whose late father had been a client of Bonner. She believes the Bonners were responsible for his suicide, and she lied about her name and attended the seances to investigate the pair. She also admits to Chan that she uncovered no useful evidence against them.

At the mansion, Justine Bonner tries to placate Tom and Vera Starkey, employees who work out of a hidden room. They operate the special effects and also portray ghosts during the Bonner seances. They want to flee before the police learn of their presence during the murder. Birmingham overhears Justine talking to the couple, and thinks they are ghosts. Charlie and Frances arrive to investigate the seance parlor, and locate the hidden room loaded with devices that could fake the presence of spirits.

Chan gathers and questions the suspects, who all seem to have motives. Norma Duncan recalls that during the seance Bonner was asked, "What happened in London on the night of October 5th, 1935?" just before he was shot. The voice wasn't that of any of the suspects, but it definitely sounded familiar to her. Chan visits a chemist, who is working on a theory Chan has about the mystery bullet. Receiving a message from his hotel that Nancy Duncan is waiting to see him, Chan finds her in a trance when he returns to his room to talk with her. The lights go out and a man shoots at Nancy and runs off. Chan revives the woman, but she remembers nothing.

Paul Hamlin and Harriet Green, blackmail victims of Bonner, are seen conferring with Justine. She agrees to meet them at the Berkely Building. Chan appears, and asks her about the date mentioned at the seance, but she continues to be evasive. Birmingham and Frances overhear Justine planning a getaway with Tom and Vera.

The police are notified that Charles Edwards has been observed acting strangely on the seventh floor of the Berkely Building. Francis and Birmingham track justine Bonner to the same location, where she walks off the building's ledge, urged on by a hypnotic voice, and falls to her death. Chan finds a chemical stain on Justine's dress. He has it analyzed, and learns it is a drug that leaves its victim powerless to resist any suggestion. The chemist provides Chan with a pill that can render the drug harmless.

His captor hypnotizes the detective, using the drug, but Charlie manages to take the antidote, and is saved from leaping to his death when the medication takes effect. He is unable, however, to identify the killer who escapes. Chan is delighted when he receives a cable from Scotland Yard about the mysterious date, and he proclaims, "Tonight, Charlie Chan will hold seance!"

Tom and Vera are caught by Charlie while they are trying to make their escape. He questions them, and then gathers all the remaining suspects together for his seance, which turns out to be a word association test. Chan utters a word, and shines a light on each suspect who says the first word that comes into their mind. This continues until the killer makes a slip. The lights are shut off, and a strange sound, like a spring uncoiling, is heard. The lights were turned off on purpose by Frances, and a bullet hole has appeared in the chair where Chan had been sitting. Chan then reveals the secret of October 5th, 1935. A famous magician named Chardo the Great was injured in a serious auto crash while pursuing his wife, Justine, who was running away with his assistant, William Bonner. Chardo was thought to have died, but he actually recovered his face altered by plastic surgery. He is the murderer, out for revenge, now disguised as one of the suspects. He is also a ventriloquist, and when he asked Bonner the fatal question, Norma Duncan recognized Chardo's stage voice. The magician killed Bonner with a spring gun using a bullet made of frozen blood. This device is concealed in a trick cigar case. Chan names the killer, who threatens Chan with this weapon, but is distracted by Chan's trick handkerchief. The culprit is taken into custody, and Charlie praises Frances for her fine assistance in solving the mystery.

PERFORMANCES

Sidney Toler shows a number of different sides of Charlie in this film. He was practically blackmailed by Mathews into solving the case, and he taunts and baits the dim-witted sergeant throughout the film. He refuses to share information with him, and he teases him with his handkerchief trick on three occasions. He also overrules him when he tries to make an arrest. On the other hand, Chan shows his delight in playing with the toys he has bought for his children. He is very proud of his daughter, and is shown doting on her, mocking the wolf whistles she will draw from the boys with her new outfit. He offers Frances little criticism, but neither does he provide her much instruction, so this film has very few Chan sayings.

The actress Frances Chan appeared in a number of films in the Forties, including *GOD IS MY CO-PILOT* (1945). The producer decided to cast this role with Frances using her actual name. She is presumably Charlie's "Number one daughter," and she is bright, spunky and intelligent. At one point, Charlie refuses her assistance, and she throws a brief tantrum in Chinese. Frances provides a refreshing change of pace, and it is a shame that this was her only appearance in the series.

Mantan Moreland's performance seems forced and strained throughout. His role is on the furthest fringes of the plot, and few of his diversions are funny, with the exception of his dialogue with the original Bonner butler, where the usual Moreland charm and timing are apparent. Most of the time, he is left muttering to himself about his fear of spooks, or swallowing Mexican jumping beans thinking they are vitamins.

Joseph Crehan, Sergeant Mathews, gives an outlandish performance as the policeman-in-charge. He seems totally out of his depth, and he never realizes how little regard Charlie has for him. Claudia Dell and Charles Jordan are fine as Tom and Vera Starkey, and they make excellent red herrings. Their escape attempt in black robes is actually one of the film's highlights. Richard Gordon is ideal as the medium, William Bonner. It is a shame he has so little screen time.

Helen Beverly is commendable as Norma Duncan. She seems the typical Chan heroine, except the script oddly provides her with no boyfriend. One dangling thread in the plot is her phone call to the police noting Edwards' strange behavior. The motivation for this call is never resolved. It seems the writer just wanted to get the cast over to the Berkeley building, and used Edwards as an excuse. Jacqueline De Wit is also quite effective as Justine Bonner. Her performance during the opening seance is quite memorable, as well as the scenes where her nervous deterioration when her world closes in upon her. An editing gaff can be detected during her suicide leap. Her murderer is seen speaking to her, peering through a curtain, but he then is seen a second later in the street seven stories below.

CHARLIE CHAN'S SAYINGS

⋄ Shady business do not make for sunny life.

⋄ Spirits always have a very long way to come.

CASTLE IN THE DESERT (1942)
Rating: ✳✳✳✳

TWENTIETH CENTURY FOX. Written by John Larkin; Photographed by
Virgil Miller; Edited by John Brady; Musical direction by Emil Newman;
Produced by Ralph Dietrich; Directed by Harry Lachman.   62 minutes.

ANNOTATED CAST LIST

Sidney Toler....................Charlie Chan
Victor Sen Yung..............Jimmy Chan (Number two son)
Douglass Dumbrille.........Paul Manderley (Eccentric and wealthy author)
Lenita Lane....................Lucy Manderley (His wife, formerly Lucy Borgia)
Richard Derr...................Carl Detheridge (Medieval historian)
Henry Daniell.................Watson King (Sculptor)
Edmund MacDonald.........Walter Hartford (Manderley's lawyer)
Arlene Whelan.................Brenda Hartford (His wife)
Ethel Griffes...................Lizzie Saturnia (Fortune teller)
Milton Parsons...............Arthur Fletcher (Private detective)
Stephen Geray.................Dr. Retling (Manderley's physician)
Lucien Littlefield.............Professor Gleason (Genealogist)
Paul Kruger....................Guard on Manderley estate
George Chandler..............Bus driver
Oliver Prickett................Wigley (Mojave Wells hotel manager)

SYNOPSIS AND APPRAISAL

This is the last Twentieth Century Fox Chan picture and it ends the series on
a high note, being a very strong, offbeat film. The plot moves swiftly, with
many twists and turns and the comic relief is blended well into the general storyline. A supernatural element is added as the weird psychic, Madame Saturnia,
proves very accurate with her mystic observations. The drawbacks to the film
are several plot threads that are still left dangling when the story abruptly ends.
It seems that a longer explanation from Chan at the conclusion was needed but
never provided.

The film opens at the extravagant home of Paul Manderley, a castle located
in the Mojave Desert. Manderley is an eccentric author who wears a black cloth
mask across half of his face, hiding a hideous scar from a chemical explosion.
He is writing a biography of Cesare Borgia, the notorious 16th century Italian
warlord and power broker. His wife. Lucy, is a direct descendant of Lucrezia
Borgia, whose reputation as a poisoner was legendary. Professor Gleason, a genealogist, visits Manderley Castle, and is apparently poisoned after being served
a drink by Lucy. Two of Manderley's guests, Dr. Retling and Walter Hartford,
his doctor and lawyer, conspire to transfer the body to the hotel in the nearest

town, Mojave Wells.

Jimmy Chan has a one week leave from the army, and is visiting his father at a hotel when Charlie receives an urgent letter from Lucy Manderley asking for his help. Charlie borrows a carrier pigeon entrusted to Jimmy for communication purposes, since Manderley Castle has no electricity or telephone. He names the bird Ming Toy, "daughter of happiness."

Chan is treated rudely when he arrives by bus in Mojave Wells, since the residents all seem to bear a grudge against the Manderleys. Lizzie Saturnia, an elderly fortune teller, warns Chan that she sees death reaching for him. When the Manderley car arrives, Chan is joined by sculptor Watson King for the drive.

Both Manderley and his wife seem perplexed by Chan's visit, and Lucy claims the letter from her is a forgery. Dr. Retling explains that Manderley is terrified of scandal because he would lose control of his twenty million dollar estate if he becomes involved in any notoriety. Chan also chats with Carl Detheridge, a medieval scholar who once helped him on a case. Walter Hartford and his wife are also guests. Wilson, Manderley's butler, reveals that the car has been deliberately disabled and the distributor cap is missing. Now everyone is stranded at the castle for the near future. Watson King starts to mold a bust of Mrs. Manderley.

Meanwhile, Jimmy shows up in Mojave Wells, and hires the bus driver to take him to the castle. Madame Saturnia asks to come along, and the driver drops them off two miles short of the estate. They walk to the castle where Jimmy falls through an opening into the basement and the fortune teller follows. They explore a chamber of horrors and a lab filled with various poisons. A private detective named Fletcher comes to the castle on foot after his car breaks down. He is investigating the death of Professor Gleason.

At supper, Fletcher collapses after drinking a toast, and Chan determines his drink has been drugged. Jimmy emerges from the basement , and gives his father a warning letter that was delivered after he left on the case. Dr. Retling takes charge of Fletcher's body. Manderley and Chan discover that a quantity of poison is missing from his basement chemical lab. Lizzie Saturnia urges them to destroy all the poison before someone is killed. When Chan informs her that somebody has already been poisoned, she claims that no one has ever died on the estate. She also tells Chan to beware of arrows.

Dr. Retling urges Manderley to have his wife committed to an asylum, but Chan insists there is no evidence that Lucy is responsible for the poisonings of Gleason and Fletcher. The writer considers giving his lawyer power of attorney to manage his fortune. Chan saves Manderley from consuming a drink laced with poison, and he later finds his carrier pigeon, Ming Toy, dead from poison. While standing at a window examining Ming Toy, Chan is almost struck by an arrow launched from outside. This upsets Jimmy, who is then ordered by his father to guard the body of Fletcher.

Charlie tries to comfort the fretful Lucy Manderley, who speaks about her stepbrother, who was once accused of poisoning. She claims he was killed in the Spanish Civil War, but Saturnia insists he is still alive. Jimmy bursts onto the scene with news that Fletcher's body has been stolen, but this does not surprise Charlie. He brings Dr. Retling and Brenda Hartford to Lucy's room, and announces that Mrs. Manderley is the victim of a conspiracy. The original letter received by Chan was a forgery written by Walter Hartford. Together with Dr. Retling, the Hartfords have been scheming to gain control of the Manderley estate. Gleason and Fletcher were paid accomplices who weren't poisoned, only drugged to appear dead. The fake murder plot was devised to frighten Manderley into signing a power of attorney over to his lawyer. Chan was summoned by them as a witness to confirm Manderley's suspicions about his wife, but the detective instead saw through their strategy. Chan then cautions them about another plot far more serious than their fraud. Someone is trying to kill Paul Manderley.

Brenda Hartford insists that Lucy's brother is still alive, and that he wrote her husband asking for money. Lucy is startled, still believing he was killed in action in Spain. Jimmy dresses in a suit of ornamental armor to watch the events from a secret vantage point. Unknown to him, Fletcher has also donned armor for the same reason, and pushes Jimmy down a flight of stairs into the cellar.

Watson King helps Jimmy back to his feet. The sculptor tells Chan and his son that he actually is a private investigator hired by Lucy Manderley. They search for Walter Hartford who is missing, and finally locate him cowering in a corner of the dungeon. He says he will remain in hiding because someone is trying to kill him. As Charlie and Jimmy start to climb back upstairs, Hartford collapses, struck by an arrow. With the help of King, they try to determine from which direction the arrow was fired.

Chan summons everyone to meet in the castle's main hall. Jimmy is seized by an unseen assailant who steals his crossbow. While waiting for the suspects, Chan is again almost hit by an arrow that barely misses him. Manderley appears moments later, and Chan alerts him that his wife's stepbrother is in the castle, probably disguised as one of his guests, since his face has been altered by plastic surgery. Chan rips the mask from Manderley's face, and reveals that he has no scars. The writer claims he wore the mask so that people would not be curious about his extreme reclusiveness.

After the suspects gather, Chan explains the motive for the murder of Hartford. He stood in the way of Lucy's stepbrother, who was planning to kill Manderley and gain control of his fortune. Chan tricks the killer into revealing his identity, who then pulls a gun and threatens the others. Fletcher, still in armor, jumps the gunman, and Chan takes him into custody. He then uncovers the hiding place of the missing distributor cap.

Lizzie Saturnia helps Jimmy up from the cellar. Charlie congratulates her on her perfect record with her predictions. Jimmy's helmet closes, and moments later he is overcome by smoke when one of the guests walking by tosses a cigarette into the armor.

PERFORMANCES

Sidney Toler concludes his last Fox Chan film in high style. There are even a few innovations, including some rare and interesting location footage as Chan is seen arriving by bus. The photographic composition of Toler when he firsts encounters Ethel Griffes (Lizzie Saturnia) is very well framed and quite breathtaking with a magnificent clouded sky visible in the background. Toler has to fend off some racist comments by the hotel operator, which he totally disregards. His cooing to the carrier pigeon and his tender concern for Lucy Manderley are two of his many highlights in the film.

Victor Sen Yung plays Jimmy as slightly more mature, perhaps consciously in light of his character's recent military training. It would have been interesting to see how this would have developed if the Fox series had continued. Most of his comic highlights involve his misadventures while wearing the suit of armor.

Ethel Griffes comes close to stealing the film as she did in *DEAD MEN TELL*. Her eccentric stargazer, Lizzie Saturnia, shows perfectly that the best comic relief in a Chan picture comes from richness of character, not slapstick or distracting physical humor.

The remaining members of the supporting cast are quite strong with veterans Douglass Dumbrille (Manderley), Henry Daniell (King) and Milton Parsons (Fletcher) leading the way. Lenita Lane (Lucy) is both fragile and compelling. One of the biggest unexplained moments in the plot is why she refers to Watson King as "Jim" in one scene. Was this a deliberate gaffe to show Watson King was not who he pretended to be? It is also never made clear if she actually hired Watson King as her own private investigator as he later asserts to Chan. One other loophole is why Manderley and Lucy couldn't recognize her stepbrother even with plastic surgery. Wouldn't his distinctive voice give him away? There are other loose ends involve the fraud plot by their doctor, lawyer and his wife. Apparently, their cruel and heartless scheme is allowed to go unpunished at the end of the picture.

CHARLIE CHAN'S SAYINGS

⋄ Man who walk have both feet on ground.

⋄ Man without enemy like dog without fleas.

⋄ Man who fear death die a thousand times.

⋄ To study Eskimo or African pygmy, anthropologist must make their home his home.

⋄ Caution sometimes mother of suspicion.

⋄ Practical joke sometimes disguise for sinister motive.

⋄ Lovers use element of surprise...also criminals!

◇ Guilty conscience like dog at circus, many tricks!

◇ Sometime solution to murder problem does not require scandal.

◇ Theory like thunderstorm, very wet.

◇ Sharp wit sometimes much better than deadly weapon.

◇ Timid man never win lottery prize.

CHARLIE CHAN AND THE CURSE OF THE DRAGON QUEEN (1981)
Rating: *

WARNER BROTHERS. Written by Stan Burns and David Axelrod after a story by Jerry Sherlock; Photographed by Paul Lohman; Edited by Walt Hannemann and Phil Tucker; Music by Patrick Williams and Ambrose Thomas; Produced by Jerry Sherlock; Directed by Clive Donner. 97 minutes.

ANNOTATED CAST LIST

Peter Ustinov............. Charlie Chan
Richard Hatch.............Lee Chan, Jr. (Charlie's grandson)
Lee Grant...................Sylvia Lupowitz (Lee, Jr.'s grandmother)
Angie Dickinson.........The Dragon queen (Notorious poisoner)
Brian Keith................ Chief Baxter (San Francisco police chief)
Roddy McDowall........ Gillespie (Lupowitz family butler)
Rachel Roberts........... Mrs. Dangers (Lupowitz family housekeeper)
Michele Pfeiffer.......... Cordelia (Lee Jr.'s fiancee)
Paul Ryan..................Masters (Baxter's assistant)
Johnny Sekka.............. Stefan (Lupowitz family chauffeur)
David Hironane...........Lee Chan (Number one son)
Karlene Crockett......... Brenda Lupowitz Chan (Lee's wife)
Paula Ustinov.............Maid (Killer on screen in movie theater)

SYNOPSIS AND APPRAISAL

This film is a total misfire, due largely to the writer's ambivalent approach. A straight, historical treatment, with tongue planted firmly in cheek, could have worked far better. Even a broad satire, used to good effect in *MURDER BY DEATH* (1976) or *THE ADVENTURE OF SHERLOCK HOLMES' SMARTER BROTHER* (1975), would have been preferable, because these films based their exaggerations on actual conventions of the genre. This film, however, bases its humor almost entirely on physical slapstick and prolonged chase sequences, elements that have absolutely no reference to the conventions of a typical Chan film. Most of the humor, therefore, is pointless, irrelevant and ill-conceived.

The plot begins in Honolulu in the Forties, when Chan solves the murder of Bernard Lupowitz and proves he was murdered by his mistress, known as the "Dragon Queen." Her motive was Lupowitz's decision to return to his wife, Sylvia. He solves the case based on the unusual clue of a fork left in a tea cup. His son, Lee, saves Charlie when the Dragon Queen tries to shoot him. As she is taken away, she places a curse on Chan and his descendants. Chan believes the curse may be real after Lee starts to romance Brenda Lupowitz, daughter of the murdered man. This background is dramatized in a short opening sequence and flashbacks, all of which are filmed in black and white.

The story then shifts to the Eighties. Lee Chan, Jr. is Charlie's grandson, half-Jewish and half-Oriental. He lives with his maternal grandmother, Sylvia Lupowitz, in an elaborate mansion in San Francisco. This household is filled with eccentric servants, including a sinister butler in a wheelchair, a paranoid housekeeper and an elegant black chauffeur. Lee, Jr. is a total klutz, who continually knocks things over and leaves total chaos in his wake. He is engaged to Cordelia, a lovely, bubble-headed heiress who adores him. Lee, Jr. wants to be a detective, and he has started a business as a private eye. Meanwhile, the Dragon Queen has finished her lengthy prison sentence, and is seen lurking around the Lupowitz estate.

A series of weird murders have struck San Francisco, such as a killing in the acupuncture clinic where the victim was staked with a giant spike. The blustery and foul-tempered Police Chief Baxter has called in his old friend, Charlie Chan, to help catch this fiend, dubbed in the newspapers as the "Bizarre Killer." Charlie arrives by helicopter, and Lee, Jr., of course, wants to assist him with his investigations. A matchbook clue leads them to the *Shanghai Club* where they witness the electrocution of the saxophone player on stage with the band.

When Chan visits Lee, Jr.'s office, a wounded man appears at his door with a note stuck in his back with a knife. The man dies, and the message tells Chan to head to the park, where the Dragon Queen throws a knife at him. A ltedious and involved chase scene follows with horse drawn carriages, and the Dragon Lady escapes.

On the day of Lee, Jr.'s wedding, he and his bride are called by the Dragon Queen who tells them she has Charlie Chan as a prisoner in the loft of the *Eltinge* theater which is showing a retrospective festival of Charlie Chan films. She is lying, of course, and the young couple fall into her trap. Chan, the police and the wedding party learn about this ploy, and madly rush off to rescue them. They succeed, but then the Dragon Queen pulls a gun on Chan and threatens to fulfill her curse. Lee, Jr. knocks the gun out of her hand, and Police Chief Baxter arrests her. Chan then reveals that, while the Dragon Lady did indeed try to kill him, she wasn't the "Bizarre Killer," and that he will now reveal the identity of the murderer.

Chan's suspects are all members of the Lupowitz family household: Gillespie, the butler; Mrs. Dangers, the housekeeper; Stefan, the chauffeur; and Mrs. Lupowitz herself. Chan reveals astounding secrets about each of the suspects before naming the killer. In the stunned pause after Chan's revelation, the "Bizarre Killer" then bolts from the scene and another chase begins. The killer is trapped in the movie theater where a Charlie Chan film is being shown, and the killer is caught after arguing with the figure of Chan on the screen. The story ends with the wedding of Lee Jr. and his bride.

The film is burdened with too much emphasis on Lee, Jr.'s clumsy pratfalls, the long musical number at the Shanghai Club and dull, elaborate chase scenes scored with the music of the *Zampa Overture* by Ambrose Thomas. Very few of the sight gags are actually funny. The cleverest one is when Charlie walks by a group of pimps, who are impressed with his attire. "White on white is all right!" one of them exclaims. A few days later, Chan is driving by in a car, and he notices all the pimps are now dressing exactly like him. This picture may be mildly entertaining to kids, but it is a painful experience for any Chan devotee to watch.

PERFORMANCES

Peter Ustinov is one of the most distinguished talents of the twentieth century, as an actor, author, director, musician and commentator, but his rendition of Charlie Chan is absolutely dreadful. This is all the more disappointing, since Ustinov is brilliant as Hercule Poirot, Agatha Christie's Belgian sleuth in a series of lavish, all-star productions. Ustinov's Chan, however, has no warmth, no intelligence and no charisma. None of his lines is delivered with any zest, and worse, he speaks in a grotesque, forced accent. Even in satirical terms, Ustinov seems to miss the entire point. Peter Sellers, in Neil Simon's spoof *MURDER BY DEATH* (1976), played Sidney Wang, a send-up of Chan. His presentation was amusing and pertinent, but there is little relevant humor in Ustinov's characterization. All his Chan manages to do is look on disapprovingly at his fumbling grandson. If only some of the legendary Ustinov wit could have emerged into his reading of the part. His performance is flat, tired and bland. For much of the film he is disengaged, merely filling space on the screen. His involvement is somewhat better in the black and white flashbacks, and in the film-within-the-film on screen during the theater sequence. But it is all too little to save this empty performance.

Richard Hatch has very little appeal as the awkward Lee, Jr. His character resembles Jerry Lewis in *THE BELLBOY* (1960) more than any of the traditional Chan offspring. Neither his appearance nor attitude reflect any of his supposed "half-Oriental" background. His performance is totally lacking in charm. His endless pratfalls are poorly done and irritating to the viewer. His finest moment is in the *Club Shanghai* when he orders a "Captain Apollo" on the rocks, an inside joke referring to his role as Captain Apollo on the television series *BATTLESTAR GALLACTICA*.

Angie Dickinson is also unimpressive in her performance as the Dragon Queen. This role called for a genuine camp approach and over-the-top villainy, but she merely walks through the picture, and is she hardly noticed at all. Roddy McDowall gives the most successful portrayal in the film, as the scowling and ill-tempered butler, Gillespie, who madly glides through the film on a motorized wheelchair. He continually tips his cigarette ashes into the urn of the late Bernard Lupowitz. Soon, the doting Sylvia Lupowitz lifts the urn and remarks, "Bernie, you are gaining weight." McDowall's performance with his grotesque facial gestures and impeccable timing manage to steal every scene in which he appears. His reaction is priceless when Chan shows that Gillespie can walk. "Of course I can walk!" he exclaims, "I just don't like to."

Brian Keith is fairly successful as the excitable police chief, but his swearing and ranting become overdone and predictable by the mid-point of the film. Keith is at his best in his exchanges with Chan, when he sidesteps from his outbursts to a few seconds of warmth before he has another blow-up. His finest line is during a chase scene in the police car, when his assistant, Masters, asks if he should follow the suspect. Keith suddenly drifts into a wistful reverie, sighing, "It is such a beautiful day, I'd love to drive to the beach!" Masters turns to him in disbelief when Keith resumes his normal screaming, "Of course, follow them!" Both Keith and McDowall provide the finest satirical moments in the picture.

Lee Grant gives a cloying and overdone reading to her role as the dowager, Sylvia Lupowitz. Her housekeeper, played by Rachel Roberts, is also unsatisfying as the fearful and fretful Mrs. Dangers. Michelle Pfeiffer is wasted in her role as the addlebrained fiancee of Lee, Jr. She is radiant as always, but there is just nothing written into her part for her to do.

Johnny Sekka, on the other hand, hits the nail on the head in his minor role as the African prince-turned-chauffeur. The huffy dignity he instills in the role is quite effective. He is a character who seems almost normal, but as you observe him you realize that there is a screw loose somewhere in his psychological make-up. It is really quite clever.

Finally, in the theater sequence, Chan is seen in a movie on screen, denouncing a murderess. This cameo is played by Ustinov's actual daughter, Paula. It is a nice touch, but it also tends to highlight yet another problem. In the scenario for this picture, how could Charlie Chan be both a real life detective and a fictional screen detective at the same time?

CHARLIE CHAN'S SAYINGS

⋄ Hasty departure outward manifestation of guilty minds.

⋄ Clues often speak to detective with as clear a voice as murderer making confession.

⋄ Kind words most appreciated, but fear that mirror is more accurate.

⋄ Process of aging never agreeable, but better than alternative.

⋄ Experience is good school, but sometimes fees are high.

⋄ Many times catching a cat more difficult than solving murders.

⋄ Every journey seem long at the beginning, but every step taken bring you closer to goal.

◇ Mud of bewilderment will soon be dredged from pool of thought.

◇ Absence of suspicion often denote presence of danger.

◇ Modern times difficult for young couples. Observe that most ceremonies today last longer then marriage.

◇ Worry does not enhance appearance of beautiful woman.

◇ Doctor tell me climbing stairs add years onto life. He not wrong. I feel ten years older already.

CHARLIE CHAN AT MONTE CARLO (1937)

Rating: *

TWENTIETH CENTURY FOX. Written by Charles Belden and Jerry Cady; Story by Robert Ellis and Helen Logan; Photographed by Daniel B. Clark; Edited by Nick De Maggio; Musical direction by Samuel Kaylin; Produced by John Stone; Directed by Eugene Forde. 71 minutes.

ANNOTATED CAST LIST

Warner Oland.............. Charlie Chan
Keye Luke................... Lee Chan (Number one son)
Harold Huber...............Jules Joubert (Monte Carlo police chief)
Sidney Blackmer.......... Victor Karnoff (Wealthy financier)
Kay Linaker.................Joan Karnoff (His wife)
Robert Kent.................Gordon Chase (Karnoff's private secretary)
Edward Raquello.......... Paul Savarin (Financier & enemy of Karnoff)
Virginia Field..............Evelyn Gray (Monte Carlo playgirl)
George Lynn................Al Rogers (Bartender)
Louis Mercier..............Taxi driver
George Davis.............. Pepite
John Bleifer................ Ludwig (Karnoff's chauffeur).
George Renavent..........Renault (Bank messenger)
George Sorrell............Gendarme

SYNOPSIS AND APPRAISAL

This film is the last completed film of Warner Oland's career. Unfortunately, it is his weakest Chan entry, a misfire after a remarkable string of outstanding successes. The picture is disappointing on many levels. The plot is muddled, the writing is boring and the acting is mechanical and lackluster. Even so, there are still a handful of excellent moments that save the film from being a total loss.

Charlie and Lee are stopping over at Monte Carlo on their way to an art show in Paris where Lee is exhibiting a painting. Monte Carlo police chief Joubert attempts to roll out the red carpet for them. Lee plays and loses at the roulette table. Charlie watches two wealthy rivals, Victor Karnoff and Paul Savarin, compete during a game of chemin de fer, a form of baccarat. At the bar, Mrs. Karnoff confers with her brother Gordon Chase, who is her husband's secretary. He warns her that Karnoff plans to sell some bonds that night. Mrs. Karnoff had appropriated a number of them, and they have to be replaced at once. Chase then chats with Evelyn Gray, his girlfriend.

Mrs. Karnoff heads to a hotel bar, where she tells the shifty barman, Al Rogers, begging him to return the bonds she gave to him. He will only hand them back in exchange for cash. Charlie and Lee leave the casino in a taxi that breaks down on the road. At home, Mrs. Karnoff slips the bonds to Gordon, who is able to replace them just in time. Karnoff completes his transaction with Renault, a bank messenger. Ludwig, Karnoff's chauffeur, informs someone by telephone that the bonds will be sent to Paris that night. He then drives Renault to the airport.

On foot, Charlie and Lee sight a Rolls Royce racing away from a parked car. They discover the body of Renault in the back seat. Chan notes that several footprints were obliterated by a cane. He also finds a rhinestone on the ground. Lee flags down the police, and tries to explain the situation in French. They arrest the Chans, believing Lee has confessed to murder.

Joubert sets them free as soon as he arrives at the police station, and asks Charlie's help with the case. Karnoff, when informed of the murder, says Renault was transporting a fortune in bonds. Joubert orders a search for Ludwig, the Karnoff chauffeur. While heading to the hotel, Lee recognizes the Rolls Royce that fled the crime scene. Joubert discovers it belongs to Evelyn Gray, who is entertaining Paul Savarin in her suite. Chan questions Savarin about his cane, and notices a rhinestone is missing from one of Evelyn's fancy shoes. Gray confesses that she discovered the body in the car, but fled from the scene, not wishing to become involved. Karnoff arrives at police headquarters, where he and Savarin hurl accusations at each other. Al Rogers, the bartender, is also picked up, based on a report that he tried to peddle the same type of bonds earlier in the evening. The police find Ludwig's body in a marsh off the road. Rogers returns to his hotel room, where he finds his bonds are missing. Karnoff visits Rogers and demands to know how he got the bonds, but the bartender reveals nothing.

The next morning, Lee has trouble trying to order waffles for his father. Charlie draws a sketch of them for the waiter. Joubert shows up, confused by the case. They notice Evelyn and Gordon Chase conferring over breakfast. The waiter returns, bringing Chan a book of crossword puzzles. Jimmy says, "I hope you enjoy the breakfast you drew for yourself." Meanwhile, Evelyn has trouble persuading Chase that she isn't interested in Savarin. Lee follows Evelyn, who reports directly to Savarin. He overhears Savarin telling her to learn the exact relationship between Rogers and Mrs. Karnoff. Evelyn heads to the hotel bar and tries to worm information out of the bartender. She is interrupted when Rogers receives a phone call from Mrs. Karnoff, and he arranges to meet her at his hotel. Lee also heads there.

Joubert learns about the bartender's shady background, and that Mrs. Karnoff has just pawned an expensive piece of jewelry. Lee tries to enter Rogers' room from a second-story window, but he has to run away when gendarme becomes suspicious of him. Chan and Joubert arrive at Rogers' hotel and find him dead. The murder scene is clumsily arranged to look like suicide. They also find the stolen bonds in the room, but Chan doubts Rogers stole them.

Joubert and Chan go to Karnoff's house where they unexpectedly find Evelyn and Savarin. Mrs. Karnoff confesses that Rogers is blackmailing her. She is his ex-wife, and he is pressuring her for money to keep quite about her past. She admits she gave the bonds to Rogers, and later stole them from his room when alerted by Chase, her brother. She arranged to meet him at his hotel to pay him off, but instead found him murdered.

After clever questioning by Chan, the killer is revealed. He quickly flees through an open window and is struck by a car while running across the road. Later Charlie and Lee leave for Paris, but are hesitant about taking the same taxi that broke down the previous night. The driver boasts that he now has new spark plugs, and the cab sputters as it heads off.

PERFORMANCES

At times in this film, Warner Oland is reduced to a bystander who merely observes Joubert's investigation. This is largely the fault of the writers. The breakfast scene, however, is a unique gem, where Charlie tries to outwit Lee, and ends up outwitting himself. It it interesting to note that in the byplay between father and son, Lee occasionally wins. One cannot imagine Jimmy or Tommy being as successful.

Keye Luke is good, even if his material is rather weak. His fractured attempts to speak French becomes wearing, as do his escapades on the trail of Evelyn. On the other hand, Luke's scene at the roulette table is effective and not overdone.

Harold Huber, so excellent in *CHARLIE CHAN ON BROADWAY* is atrocious as Joubert, the Monte Carlo police chief. He is tolerable for the first few minutes, where his interaction with Oland is fairly balanced. This changes during his first scene with the taxi cab driver when he starts to bellow wildly in French. His malapropisms, such as "I am slowly confusing," are delivered in a ham-handed manner that robs them of any humor. Since the writers chose to showcase Joubert throughout the entire middle of the film, it becomes very tedious for Chan fans.

The performance of Louis Mercier as the comic taxi driver is almost as disruptive as that of Huber. The suspects, however, are rather good and help to redeem the film when the spotlight is on them. Sidney Blackmer (Karnoff) and Robert Raquello (Savarin) are superb as the two wealthy rivals, each determined to destroy the other. Both were splendid character performers. Blackmer specialized in playing Teddy Roosevelt in three films, and in his later years he practically stole the show in *ROSEMARY'S BABY* (1968) as Roman Castevet. Kay Linaker is poignant as Mrs. Karnoff, and Virginia Field is sparkling as the cold, heartless Evelyn. George Lynn is persuasive as the slimy bartender. The fine acting of Robert Kent (Chase) helps to round off an interesting collection of characters.

CHARLIE CHAN'S SAYINGS

- ◇ Humble presence of no more importance than one drop of rain in cloud-burst.

- ◇ (Describing Lee after his casino losses) Chip off ancient block.

- ◇ Honorable ancestor once have large holdings in fan-tan house.

- ◇ (On Lee as an artist) If paintings as full of imagination as detective work, he will be Chinese Rembrandt.

- ◇ Illustrious ancestor once say, destination never reached by turning back on same.

- ◇ Actions speak louder than French...French very difficult language.

- ◇ Assassination of French language not serious crime.

- ◇ Tongue often hang man quicker than rope.

- ◇ Present case like too many cocktails, make very bad headache.

- ◇ One picture still worth ten thousand words.

- ◇ Very doubtful petty larceny mouse attack millionaire lion.

- ◇ Questions are keys to door of truth.

- ◇ Truth cannot be insult.

- ◇ Car with new spark plug like flea on new puppy dog, make both most active.

CHARLIE CHAN AT THE CIRCUS (1936)

Rating: ✳✳✳✳

TWENTIETH CENTURY FOX. Written by Robert Ellis and Helen Logan; Photographed by Daniel B. Clark; Edited by Alex Troffey; Musical direction by Samuel Kaylin; Produced by John Stone; Directed by Harry Lachman. 72 minutes.

ANNOTATED CAST LIST

Warner Oland..................Charlie Chan
Keye Luke......................Lee Chan (Number one son)
George Brasno ....Tiny Tim (Midget dancer)
Olive Brasno..................Lady Tiny (His wife and partner)
Francis Ford...................John Gaines (Circus co-owner)
Paul Stanton..................Joe Kinney (Murdered circus owner)
John McGuire.................Hal Blake (Animal trainer)
Maxine Reiner................Marie Norman (Trapese artist)
Shirley Deane.................Louise Norman (Marie's sister)
J. Carrol Naish...............Tom Holt (Snake charmer)
Booth Hayward...............Dan Ferrell (Assistant animal handler)
Drue Leyton...................Nellie Farrell (Dan's sister)
Wade Boteler..................Lt. Macy (Police detective)
Shia Jung......................Su Toy (Circus acrobat)
Francis Farnum...............Mike (Ticket taker)
John Dilson...................Dr. Leed (Circus physician)

SYNOPSIS AND APPRAISAL

This is a particularly enjoyable entry in the series, with a colorful setting and a leisurely but interesting plot. The picture has a number of unusual aspects, including several long segments that feature the entire Chan family. The script is also graced by an extraordinary number of Chan sayings. The cinematography and direction by Harry Lachman is very atmospheric with an effective use of shadows. The scenes with the gorilla are also very well executed. The entire circus ambience is very well maintained.

The picture opens at the sideshow, with blaring circus music. Charlie, his wife and twelve children are attending the circus as guests of one of the owners, Joe Kinney, who wants Charlie's advice about some threatening letters. Kinney introduces Charlie to Tiny Tim and Lady Tiny, a married dance couple who are both midgits. They ask Charlie for his autograph. He signs their book with meticulous Chinese calligraphy. Lee becomes fascinated with Su Toy, a beauti-

ful acrobat and contortionist. With the main show starting, Charlie agrees to
meet Kinney at the business wagon at nine o'clock.

Circus box office receipts has been inadequate lately, and co-owner John
Gaines is being threatened by Kinney, who plans to take sole ownership if his
partner is late in repaying his loan. Caesar, the show's ape, is acting up, and
Kinney attempts to whip him. He is stopped by animal trainer Hal Blake, who
threatens to quit the show. A fistfight breaks out among Kinney, Blake and the
animal handlers, during which the key to Caesar's cage is dropped and stolen.
Gaines intervenes and tries to restore order. Blake goes to the tent of his girlfriend, Louise Norman, and tells her he has decided to leave the circus and wants
her to leave with him. Meanwhile, her sister Marie, the trapese artist, tries to
calm Joe Kinney, whom she intends to marry. Joe's old flame, wardrobe mistress Nellie Farrell, is furious that Kinney is carrying on with Marie in her presence. Her brother Dan is one of the animal trainers, and he tells her that he will
take care of Kinney in his own way.

As Marie begins her trapese act, Charlie leaves the main tent to meet with
Kinney, but finds the wagon locked, bolted from the inside. Tiny Tim manages
to gain entrance after being hoisted to the roof by the circus giant, and opens the
door for Chan, Lee and Gaines. They uncover the body of Kinney, throttled to
death, and Chan sends Lee to telephone the police.

Hal Blake discovers that the ape was released, and alerts all hands to track
him down. The animal breaks into Su Toy's tent, and then frightens Lee. Su
Toy is knocked down by the paniced Lee, who then locks her in an animal cage
"for safety." When his son arrives to alert him, Charlie is not surprised, because
he discovered animal hairs at the murder scene. They explore outside the wagon,
and discover ape tracks on the ground. Caesar leaps upon Chan, but sna-
kecharmer Tom Holt holds the beast off until Hal Blake and Dan Farrell are able
to subdue the gorilla and return him to his cage.

Lee briefs Lt. Macy on developments, and they work on the theory that the
ape could have strangled Kinney through the bars of the window in the business
wagon. Charlie tells Macy that Kinney was concerned about threatening letters
which are now missing. As Chan leaves to escort his family back to their hotel.
Lee finally remembers that Su Toy is still locked in a cage, and he releases her.
She is furious, and backs Lee into another cage.

The Chan family are about to leave their hotel the next morning when Lady
Tiny comes to see Charlie to plead for his help. Macy is planning to delay the
circus tour, which would mean financial ruin. Charlie's children beg him to take
the case, prompting him to say, "Jury seem to render verdict without retiring,
final decision in hands of judge." He defers to his wife, who also consents, and
the Chans delay their intended tour of the Grand Canyon.

At headquarters, Macy is astonished at the hostility that everyone felt against
Kinney, and he arrests the entire company. Chan plants a suggestion with Macy
that he soon regards as his own idea, namely to let the circus continue and ask
Chan to travel with them. Later that night, Charlie and Lee join the circus

train, and are given Kinney's compartment. Holt, working as night porter, prepares the room, and Charlie goes to bed early. Moments later, a deadly snake slithers into his compartment through a ventilator. Chan sees the serpent, and turns on Lee's phonograph, which plays an Oriental dance record. His son, hearing the music, enters the room and shoots the snake after grabbing a gun from his father's coat pocket. Macy, Gaines and Holt are alerted by the shot. Since Holt is in charge of the snakes, he says that someone is trying to make him look guilty.

Next morning, Chan breakfasts with Tim and Lady Tiny, and they watch as the animals are unloaded. Macy learns someone filed open the lock to the business wagon while it was traveling on a flat car, and tried but failed to crack the safe. Macy finds Kinney's insurance policy, with Marie Norman as beneficiary. He also finds a certificate of marriage beteen Kinney and Nellie Farrell.

Lee and Tim dress in an outlandish guise as a nanny with a baby. They spy on Nellie Farrell as she visits a lawyer, and later meets Dan, her brother. Su Toy spots Lee dressed as a woman, and starts to tease him. Meanwhile Chan, finding some filings inside the safe, deduces that the safe had actually been opened.

Before showtime, Nellie Farrell decalres she is actually Kinney's widow, as well as co-owner of the circus. Marie Norman says the marriage certificate is a phony. Moments later, Marie falls and is seriously hurt while performing her trapese act. From a bullet hole in the canvas big top, Chan determines that the trapese rope was severed by a rifle shot. He also comes to the conclusion that Kinney's signature on the marriage document is not genuine.

While searching through Marie's scrapbook, Chan finds a clipping that places Joe Kinney as a witness to an unsolved shooting in an El Paso casino on the exact night Nellie Farrell claims he married her in Mexico. The doctor annouces an emergency operation must be performed to save Marie's life. Her tent is turned into an operating room, and Chan warns everyone that quiet is essential for the success of the delicate surgery.

Lee phones the police in El Paso for information about the shooting. Later, both Caesar's keeper and Lee are knocked out, as the ape is released again. The animal smashes into the operating tent and is shot. The entire set-up, however, is a trap, and Marie is actually recovering at the hospital in town. Charlie reveals that the attacking ape is actually the killer in disguise, and the real Caesar is found gorging himself on a bunch of bananas. Chan explains that the assassin released the ape as camouflage whenever he planned to strike. The culprit was Kinney's partner in a gambling scam in El Paso, where he shot a deputy. Although uninvolved in the murder, Dan and Nellie Farrell are also arrested for their forgery scheme to claim Kinney's estate.

The film ends as Charlie is given a lifetime pass to the circus for himself and his entire family. When asked how many passes he would need, Charlie says, "Think fourteen quite sufficient." Then after spotting Lee with Su Toy, he coyly adds, "Maybe more later."

PERFORMANCES

Warner Oland's interaction with the Chan family is the real milestone in this film. The family has a wonderful introduction, as each member passes by the ticket-taker in correct order of height until Oland appears at the rear, holding an infant, with everyone tickets tucked in his hat band. Even more impressive is his scene in the hotel room when Lady Tiny appeals for him to save the circus. Charlie gently defers to his wife's decision in the matter, and this glimpse into his domestic life is both warm and engaging. His breakfast with the midgets and his bedtime encounter with the snake in the train compartment are his two most memorable scenes. Chan films are often set aboard ship, but train settings are far more infrequent.

Keye Luke's part is more frenetic than usual in this film, foreshadowing the typical way Jimmy is regularly portrayed. Luke's performance retains the genuine warmth and sincerity that is his trademark. His comic byplay with Shia Jung (Su Toy) is a very amusing subplot. Shia Jung plays a smart, assertive and sassy Su Toy, with a temper that is evident when she locks Lee in a cage. There is also some interesting exchanges between Wade Boteler (Lt. Macy) and Lee. In one scene, Macy chokes Lee with a little too much enthusiasm in order to demonstrate the murderer's attack. Moments later, Lee knocks Macy off a circus barrel to explain a different point. Was this actually a subtle or subconscious revenge on Lee's part? Since both Macy and Lee are both very likeable characters, it seems more like some light-hearted tit-for-tat that came off more forceful than originally intended. Luke's best instant in the film is his exchange with Oland immediately before the snake attack, one of the rare verbal exchanges in which Lee tops Charlie.

Some critics have denigrated the performances of George and Olive Brasno, the dancing midgets. A few of their lines may sound awkward, but their scenes have a natural charm and innocence that can rival that of any professional. In one wild scene, George dresses like a baby in a perambulator pushed by Keye Luke disguised as his female nanny. This scene, later satirized in *WHO FRAMED ROGER RABBIT* (1988), probably had its origin in the two Lon Chaney renditions of *THE UNHOLY THREE* (1925 and 1930). It may be silly, but the scene works, particularly when Su Toy catches them in their charade.

Francis Ford, older brother of director John Ford, plays the sympathetic Gaines with a great amount of shrewdness, smoothly coloring this character with enough shades of grey that the audience is never quite sure how to regard him. J. Carrol Naish (Holt) is laudable in his character role. Oddly enough, this versatile actor himself later played Charlie Chan on television for thirty-nine episodes. Paul Stanton was also most effective as the offensive Joe Kinney. Except for Shia Jung (Su Toy), most of the actresses turn in adequate but unmemorable performances. The unbilled stuntman who played Caesar was far more effective and realistic than the typical gorilla portrayals on film.

CHARLIE CHAN'S SAYINGS

⋄ Free ticket to circus like gold ring on merry-go-round, make enjoyment double.

⋄ Size of package does not indicate quality within.

⋄ Wise precaution to accept apple sauce with large pinch of salt.

⋄ Curiosity responsible for cat needing nine lives.

⋄ More than one way to remove skin from cat.

⋄ Jack had no trouble sliding down beanstalk.

⋄ Much evil can enter through very small space.

⋄ One ounce of experience worth ton of detective book.

⋄ Man who seek trouble, never find it far off.

⋄ Frightened bird very difficult to catch.

⋄ Give man plenty rope, will hang self.

⋄ Guilty conscience only enemy to peaceful rest.

⋄ Circus performer like detective, must be johnny of many trades.

⋄ Ancient adage say, "Music soothe savage breast."

⋄ (Spoken by Lee Chan) You know what you always say, Pop. If you want to understand men, study women.

⋄ Question without answer, like faraway water, no good for nearby fire.

⋄ Enemy who misses mark, like serpent, must coil to strike again.

⋄ Very wise to know way out before going in.

⋄ Facts, like photographic film, must be exposed before developing.

⋄ Trouble rain on man already wet.

⋄ Too soon to count chickens until eggs are in nest.

⋄ One grain of luck sometimes worth more than whole rice field of wisdom.

⋄ Cannot tell where path lead until reach end of road.

⋄ Good tools shorten labor.

⋄ Inquisitive person, like bear after honey, sometimes find hornet's nest.

◇ Best to slip with foot than with tongue.

◇ Silent witness sometimes speak loudest.

◇ Magnifying female charms very ancient optical illusion.

◇ Even if name signed one million times, no two signatures exactly alike.

◇ Not always wise to accept simplest solution.

◇ Mind, like parachute, only function when open.

◇ Unloaded gun always cause most trouble.

◇ No use to hurry unless sure of catching right train.

CHARLIE CHAN AT THE OLYMPICS (1937)
Rating: ✳✳✳✳

TWENTIETH CENTURY FOX. Written by Robert Ellis and Helen Logan; Story by Paul Burger; Photographed by Daniel B. Clark; Edited by Fred Allen; Musical direction by Samuel Kaylin; Produced by John Stone; Directed by H. Bruce Humberstone. 71 minutes.

ANNOTATED CAST LIST

Warner Oland	Charlie Chan
Keye Luke	Lee Chan (Number one son)
Layne Tom, Jr.	Charlie Chan, Jr. (Son on fishing trip)
Katherine DeMille	Yvonne Roland (International spy);
Allan Lane	Richard Masters (Pilot and pole vaulter)
Pauline Moore	Betty Adams (Olympic athlete)
C. Henry Gordon	Arthur Hughes (Munitions dealer)
John Eldredge	Cartwright (Inventor)
Jonathan Hale	Hopkins (Cartwright's partner)
Morgan Wallace	Charles Zaraka (Spy mastermind)
Frederick Vogeding	Strasser (Berlin police inspector)
Andrew Tombes	Scott (Honolulu police chief)
Howard Hickman	Dr. Burton (Honolulu police doctor)
Edward Keane	Colonel observing test flight
Selmer Jackson	Navy commander
Don Brodie	Radio announcer
George Chandler	Ship's radio operator
Emmett Vogan	Ship's officer
Minerva Urecal	Olympic village matron and spy

SYNOPSIS AND APPRAISAL

This Chan film is one of the most unusual and richest of the series, one that works on various levels. The picture is a genuine "slice of history" that highlights actual events, as well as the first Chan spy drama. The film most impressively splices in documentary footage from the Berlin Olympics, including the hero of the event, Jesse Owens. Hitler is not shown, but soldiers can be seen giving the Nazi salute at the games. Events in the film have a genuine dark side, as the coming world war is clearly foreshadowed in some conversations. Chan also faces a personal crisis when Lee is kidnapped and becomes a pawn in the deadly game of international intrigue. The writing itself is excellent, and the story structure is different, as the paths of Lee and Charlie don't cross until the second half of the story. The only shortcoming is the revelation of the killer at the conclusion, which is artificial, unsatisfying and not quite logical. This is also the only film which includes the character of Charlie Chan, Jr.

The picture opens with a stirring reprise of the opening music from *CHARLIE CHAN AT THE CIRCUS*. Dr. Burton is giving Charlie his yearly physical at police headquarters, prior to Chan's fishing trip with his son, Charlie, Jr. Chief Scott lends Charlie his fishing tackle.

Overhead, a plane is testing a new remote control device. Scott, Chan and his son watch from the window. Many people are watching this flight from different locations. Cartwright, the inventor, and Hopkins, his financier, are demonstrating the device for the military. Richard Masters, original test pilot for the flight, is nursing a slight injury and preparing to leave for the Olympic games. Yvonne Roland, Richard's friend, is actually a foreign agent. Arthur Hughes, an international arms merchant, wants to steal the device. On the plane, the test pilot, Edwards, is knocked out by an intruder who takes control of the flight and heads out to sea. An emergency search is organized from the naval base at Pearl Harbor.

While on their fishing trip two days later, Charlie, Jr. and his father discover the plane on an isolated stretch of beach. Chan finds the pilot's body and notices the remote control device is missing. The authorities are notified, and Chan tries to track down the hijacker. He deduces that the identity of the culprit is Miller, an employee of the Hopkins Aviation Company, whose timecard has been altered. With Cartwright, Hopkins and Chief Scott, Chan searches Miller's room, and find his body hidden in the closet. Evidence is also uncovered that Miller's last visitor wore a white fox fur.

Chan and Chief Scott believe the invention was stolen to sell to a foreign government, perhaps in Berlin. They examine the passenger list of the *Flying Clipper*, which left Honolulu the day after the theft. Hopkins is suspicious of Arthur Hughes, a passenger on the flight. Richard Masters, on his way to the Olympic games in Berlin, was also on the flight accompanied by Yvonne Roland. The ticket salesman recalled Roland wore a white fox fur. Scott sends Chan to Berlin to pursue her. Charlie plans to beat her there by using an all-air route, including the famous dirigible *Hindenburg*[1] from Lakehurst, New Jersey. Later he learns that Hughes was poisoned while on the *Flying Clipper*, but quickly recovered.

Lee Chan is also on the steamer *Manhattan*, sailing from New York to Hamburg. On the same ship are Richard Masters and the rest of the U. S. Olympic team. Lee is friendly with Betty Adams, Masters' regular girlfriend. Arthur Hughes missed the ship's departure from New York, but was able to rendezvous with the vessel at Sandy Hook. Hopkins and Cartwright are traveling with Chan on the *Hindenburg*, and at one point they fly directly over the *Manhattan*.

Betty confides in Lee that she is jealous of Yvonne Roland, who seems to be

---

[1] *The Hindenburg exploded over Lakehurst, New Jersey on May 6, 1937, ten months after Chan's trip in July 1936.*

playing up to Masters. Lee thinks she is an adventuress, and also notices that Hughes is spying on Roland. Yvonne borrows Betty's camera to take some snapshots. Hughes steals Roland's radiogram, which Lee manages to steal back. The message, dated July 29, 1936, is supposedly from Roland's husband, which makes Betty even more furious. Lee convinces her to keep the this information secret.

The *Hindenburg* flies over the Olympic stadium in Berlin. In Germany, Charlie works with Inspector Strasser, an old-fashioned, pompous official who does not seem to be a Nazi. He orders the *Manhattan* detained until he and Chan can board the ship and uncover the invention apparently stolen by Roland. Her cabin, however, has been ransacked and the woman is missing. They question Hughes, who knocks at her door a few minutes later. Strasser plans to arrest him, but Chan convinces the inspector that Roland simply fled the ship. Alone, Charlie catches an intruder who slips into Roland's cabin by easing feet first through the porthole, and discovered that it is Lee. His son is astonished to find Charlie in the room, and shows him the radiogram. Chan interprets it as code, giving Roland instructions when to slip off the ship and get picked up by another boat.

On the train to Berlin, Hughes overhears Lee telling his father that Yvonne borrowed Betty's camera. The arms dealer enters Charlie's compartment to thank him for his assistance. A rifleman in a car speeding alongside the train takes a shot at Charlie, but Hughes knocks him down, saving his life.

The reception of the athletes in Berlin is intercut with historic footage of the actual parade. Betty's camera is stolen when a bystander snatches it from her hands as she rides in a bus. In a nearby automobile, Hughes is disappointed to find the camera is empty. At the Olympic village, a matron rummages through Betty's luggage as soon as she leaves her quarters, but Chan and Strasser catch the matron in the act when she removes a package. Chan opens it, and Cartwright and Hopkins identify the remote control device in the box. The matron shouts a warning from the window, and while everyone is distracted, Chan replaces the device in the box with a book. Betty returns, and is questioned. She reports that Roland insisted on helping her pack, which explains the presence of the device in her luggage. Hopkins believes Masters is the thief, and that Betty was helping him.

Masters is upset when Betty tells him about Hopkins' accusation. He storms off, saying he will settle with him. Betty asks Lee to head him off. At the hotel, Hopkins and Cartwright argue over possession of the device. Hughes shows up, and pulls a gun on Hopkins.

When Chan arrives at the hotel, Cartwright claims that Hopkins ran off with the box after arguing with Hughes. Lee reports that he saw Hopkins speed off in a car with two other men. Masters declares that he saw Yvonne Roland in the hotel lobby while on his way to see Hopkins.

Yvonne Roland reports to her sponsor, the wealthy Charles Zaraka. Expecting to find the remote control device in the box, they open it and find a book instead. Zaraka says that only Charlie Chan could have the device now. He then sends an invitation to Charlie to sit with him in his reserved box during the opening ceremonies of the Olympic Games.

Charlie correctly surmises that Zaraka is the master spy, and accepts the invitation. The pageantry of the Olympic ceremony is intercut with Zaraka and Chan discussing the present world situation Their conversation clearly prefigures the coming world war. Yvonne Roland is also in the box, and Hughes spies on them using a lip reader with binoculars. Chan refuses to hand over the device, and Lee is kidnapped a few minutes later.

Strasser sincerely tries to comfort Chan and offers his complete support. Charlie receives a message telling him to return to the same box on the following day. Richard Masters competes in the pole vaulting event, urged on by a cheering Betty. Chan is handed a message to report to the Brandenburg gate at six o'clock that evening with the remote control device.

Cartwright agrees to let Chan take the device, after Charlie appeals to him "as a very humble father." That night, Charlie is taken to Zaraka's headquarters, and Yvonne gently chides him. Chan pushes a lever on the device, which sends out a broadcasting signal to the police. Hopkins is brought in to identify the secret invention, but it is unclear whether he is an accomplice or a prisoner. After Hopkins authenticates the device, the master spy releases Lee. As father and son embrace, Zaraka tells them they will both die. Suddenly, Hughes storms the headquarters with armed men. He seizes the device, only to pronounce it is a fraud. Instead, it is actually a transmitter. Hughes demands that Chan disclose the location of the actual invention, but he keeps silent. Strasser's men close in and take control of the building, overcoming the forces of both Hughes and Zaraka. After Hopkins is shot, Chan discloses the identity of the culprit who worked with Roland in the murder of Miller.

The next day, Chan is overjoyed as Lee wins the gold medal in the 100 meter freestyle swimming competition.[2] The film ends as Charlie shows Lee a paddle, similar to the one he used when teaching Lee to swim. He shows it to his son, saying, "Very lucky, was prepared for emergency."

PERFORMANCES

This is one of Warner Oland's finest films as Charlie Chan. His mastery of the role is most impressive, especially when he is torn between his duty and love for his son. This is the most serious personal crisis in the entire series for Charlie, and Oland is able to convey his anguish quite subtly and effectively.

Keye Luke is also quite convincing in this entry. In the scenes with Betty, he often quotes his father's sayings, but the writers spoil the effect by having him add "...or something like that." to each quote. Layne Tom, Jr. does well in the first of three appearances as different children in the Chan household. The character of Charlie, Jr. was eliminated, and instead became "Number two son" Jimmy in *CHARLIE CHAN IN HONOLULU*.

---

[2] *The actual winner was Ferenc Csik of Hungary.*

Allan Lane is excellent as Masters. Not long afterward, Lane became a serial and western star with Republic pictures as "Rocky" Lane. In the Sixties, he became the voice of the talking horse on television program *MR. ED.*

Katherine DeMille, the adopted daughter of the celebrated director Cecil B. DeMille, is quite effective as the lovely spy Yvonne Roland. The same year as this film, Katherine married a young actor who was just getting started named Anthony Quinn, a marriage which lasted twenty-eight years.

Frequent Chan character actor C. Henry Gordon has one of his best parts as Arthur Hughes. Morgan Wallace underplays Zaraka, a role which could have used greater menace. Frederick Vogeding is perfect as the stuffy Inspector Strasser, and he shows flashes of genuine humanity towards the end of the film. Two other Chan veterans, John Eldredge (Cartwright) and Jonathan Hale (Hopkins), are merely adequate in this production.

CHARLIE CHAN'S SAYINGS

⋄ Good fisherman like clever merchant, know lure of bright colors.

⋄ Would be greatest blessing if all war fought with machinery instead of human beings.

⋄ Fish in sea like flea on dog, always present but difficult to catch.

⋄ Truth, like football, receive many kicks before reaching goal.

⋄ Race not always won by man who start first.

⋄ Good hunter never warn tiger of trap.

⋄ (Spoken by Lee) Man who stretch neck looking up, very apt to break neck falling down.

⋄ (Spoken by Lee) When a woman play with fire, man get burned.

⋄ (Spoken by Lee) Sugar catch more flies than hamburger steak.

⋄ Useless to sprinkle salt on tail of time.

⋄ Suspect husband, like toupee on bald head, used for coverup.

⋄ All play and no work make Charlie Chan very dull policeman.

⋄ Last step ease toil of most difficult journey.

⋄ Hasty accusation like long shot at race, odds good but conclusion doubtful.

⋄ (Spoken by Lee) Don't rub sore finger with sandpaper.

⋄ When all players hold suspicious cards, good idea to have joker up sleeve.

⋄ Envelope, like skin of banana, must be removed to digest contents.

⋄ I have never met Santa Claus either, yet accept gift from same.

⋄ Could not be more clear if magnified by two hundred inch telescope.

⋄ Players sometime disregard even most excellent coaching from sidelines.

⋄ Ancient Chinese philosophers say, "Hope is sunshine which illuminate darkest path."

⋄ Wise philosopher once say, "Only foolish man will not acknowledge defeat."

⋄ Better for Oriental to lose life than lose face.

⋄ Perhaps good idea not to accept gold medal until race is run.

CHARLIE CHAN AT THE OPERA (1936)
Rating: *****

TWENTIETH CENTURY FOX. Written by Scott Darling and Charles S. Belden; Story by Bess Meredyth; Photographed by Lucien Androit; Edited by Alex Troffey; Musical direction by Samuel Kaylin; Opera *CARNIVAL* by Oscar Levant, with libretto by William Kendall and orchestrations by Charles Maxwell; Produced by John Stone; Directed by H. Bruce Humberstone. 66 minutes.

ANNOTATED CAST LIST

Warner Oland..................Charlie Chan
Keye Luke.....................Lee Chan (Number one son)
Boris Karloff.................Gravelle (Demented opera singer)
Tudor Williams...............Gravelle's singing voice.
Margaret Irving...............Lilli Rochelle (Diva, ex-wife of Gravelle)
Zarubi Elmassian............Rochelle's singing voice.
Charlotte Henry..............Kitty Gravelle (Daughter of Lilli)
Thomas Beck..................Phil Childers (Fiance of Kitty)
Frank Conroy.................Whitely (Lilli's current husband)
Gregory Gaye.................Enrico Barelli (Foppish baritone)
Enrico Ricardi...............Barelli's singing voice.
Nedda Harrigan...............Anita Barelli (His wife and singer):
Zarubi Elmassian............Anita Barelli's singing voice.
Guy Usher.....................Regan (Los Angeles police inspector)
William Demarest...........Sergeant Kelly (Detective)
Maurice Cass.................Arnold (Opera stage manager)
Tom McGuire.................Pop Morris (Stage door attendant)
Fred Kelsey...................Duggan (Gray-haired policeman)
Selmer Jackson..............Hudson (L.A. photowire technician)
Emmett Vogan..............Smitty (Chicago photowire technician)
Benson Fong.................Extra in opera chorus

SYNOPSIS AND APPRAISAL

This film is a clear favorite of many Chan enthusiasts. No doubt the presence of Boris Karloff in his second Chan film is partially responsible, but the picture is compelling and crisply dramatic on its own terms. The plot is unusually tight, taking place in one day. The opera sequences, composed specifically for this film by the brilliant celebrity Oscar Levant, are quite good, and combine elements of Charles Gounod's *FAUST* with a vibrant flair reminiscent of the operas of Puccini. This film was no doubt influenced by *THE PHANTOM OF THE OPERA* (1925), but in turn the film seems to have inspired some elements of the plotline of Andrew Lloyd Webber's popular musical based on the story. In the Chan film, Karloff overpowers and substitutes for Enrico Barelli onstage in the opera, just as the phantom kills and substitutes for Ubaldo Piangi in the Webber version. There is no corresponding event in the Gaston Leroux novel or any other version of *THE PHANTOM OF THE OPERA*.

H. Bruce Humberstone's direction has exceptional energy and sweep, and the film is particularly well edited. Only one ingredient spoils this picture from being a perfect Chan film, and that is the characterization of William Demarest as a comic police detective. He is too rude and demeaning to be funny, and his comments have a racist edge to them on occasion that is offensive. Without this blemish, *CHARLIE CHAN AT THE OPERA* could have rated as the pinnacle of the series.

As the opening credits roll, the soundtracks erupts with the dramatic baritone aria from Levant's opera *CARNIVAL*. The music continues unbroken into the first scene of the picture at the Rockland State Sanitarium where a nameless amnesia patient is playing the piano and singing the stirring aria. A violent thunderstorm is raging as an attendant brings in the evening paper. The patient's memory is suddenly restored when he reads an article about opera diva Lilli Rochelle, who is returning to sing in Los Angeles with the San Marco Opera Company after a long absence. He subdues the attendant and escapes from the asylum. The next day's newspaper headlines are displayed onscreen, calling the escapee a dangerous madman.

At police headquarters, Inspector Regan is working on the case when Charlie Chan arrives, and he congratulates Charlie for solving the case depicted in *CHARLIE CHAN AT THE RACE TRACK*. Regan introduces him to a member of his staff, Sergeant Kelly, a fast-talking cop with a sour disposition. Suddenly, soprano Lilli Rochelle barges into Regan's office, alarmed by a death threat she received in a basket of flowers. She invites Chan to come to the opera that evening to hear her sing. Regan connects the threat with the newspaper article that prompted the escape from the asylum, and agrees to provide police protection to the diva. Later, a private eye calls Lilli's husband, Mr. Whitely, and reports that she has been seen in the company of Enrico Barelli.

Charlie meets Lee at the florist, where he learns from the proprietor that the only bouquet ordered for the opera house was by Barelli to be delivered to his wife, another singer with the troupe. Lee offers to assist with the case, and Charlie arranges for him to pose as a member of the chorus that evening.

At the opera house, Sergeant Kelly refuses to allow Kitty Gravelle and Phil Childers, to go backstage and confer with Lilli Rochelle. They later sneak in. Anita Barelli is upset that her husband has been seeing too much of Rochelle. The wardrobe mistress is frightened by an intruder hiding among the backstage props. Kelly chases Lee, who is costumed as a medieval soldier, thinking he may be the intruder. Lee lowers the visor of his helmet and mixes with the other members of the chorus. Kelly demands they all remove their headgear, and is surprised to discover that they are all Chinese. Regan and Chan arrive, and begin their own search for the intruder. Meanwhile, Whitely, orders Barelli to stay away from his wife.

In her dressing room, Anita Barelli encounters the stranger whom she identifies as Gravelle, Lilli's first husband. He tells her that he plans to sing in the opera that night in the role of Mephisto, his favorite part. He relates that years earlier, someone locked him in his dressing room during a theater fire. His mind has been clouded since that night, and it was believed that he had died in the fire. Barelli interrupts this conversation when he enters the dressing room, and Gravelle hides. Barelli introduces his wife to Charlie Chan. Anita says she never received her husband's floral gift. Chan notices a burned card from the flower shop in her wastebasket. She claims she never saw it before. After Charlie leaves, she searches for Gravelle, who disappeared through an overhead crawl space in her closet.

The opera begins, as a village girl does an energetic dance during a colorful carnival. Lee confers with his father, turning over personal items with fingerprints that he swiped from the suspects during his undercover work. Chan discovers the fingerprints on the burned card are not those of Madame Barelli.

In his dressing room, Barelli is costumed in the elaborate garb of Mephisto, when Gravelle confronts him wearing the same wardrobe. Moments later, Gravelle, masked as Mephisto, appears onstage and delivers a fiery duet with Lilli. The soprano quickly realizes that the baritone is not Barelli, and she faints in the climax of the scene when Mephisto stabs her. It is the end of the first act, and Gravelle hurries off. He knocks Kelly out when the sergeant tries to follow him, and returns to Barelli's dressing room.

The police break down the door, and find Barelli's body, stabbed to death. An examination of the room reveals a trap door in the closet ceiling, which Kelly explores. He discovers a maze of passageways and falls though another trap door into Lilli's dressing room, where he encounters Phil Childers standing over the diva. Whitely then enters the room and tries to revive his wife, but she is dead, stabbed in the heart. He tells Chan that he left her alone for a short period in order to call a doctor. Whitely discovers a knife hidden in a floral bouquet, but in by touching it, he smears any fingerprints on the handle.

The opera continues, however, as Arnold the stage manager uses understudies to replace of the murder victims. Phil Childers explains that he and Kitty Gravelle wanted to see Lilli to ask her permission for their marriage. Kitty is Lilli's daughter from her first marriage, about which Whitely was never told. Kitty doesn't remember her father, whom she thinks was killed in an opera house fire in Chicago in 1923. Gravelle overhears the questioning. Chan sends for a photograph of Gravelle, which is identified by the wardrobe mistress as the intruder. He tells Lee they must work fast if they are to catch the midnight boat back to Honolulu.

As the second act concludes, Gravelle visits Kitty while she waits in a dressing room. He tries to stimulate her memory of him by playing the piano for her, as he did when she was a little girl. She passes out as Gravelle tries to embrace her. Chan enters the room and calmly speaks with the desperate man, whose mood slowly changes from hostility to trust. Charlie implores him to sing the role of Mephisto again, and Gravelle agrees.

Kelly is doubtful of Charlie's plan. Arnold tells everyone that they are testing a new baritone, and Chan persuades Anita Barelli to sing Lilli's role. He asks all other persons to position themselves as they were during the original rendition of the dramatic duet. The suspense becomes very intense during this reconstruction, and Gravelle, as Mephisto, sings with even more fervor than earlier. Madame Barelli screams when Mephisto pulls out his knife from his scabbard, and a policeman fires at him from the wings. Gravelle collapses, and he is carried off for medical attention.

Backstage, Charlie reveals what he has learned. Gravelle was not responsible for the two murders. The knife in Gravelle's possession was not used, since it is still coated with oil applied by the prop department. Chan then reveals who penned the death threat on the bouquet card. The murderer, however, is another individual who used Gravelle's presence in the theater to camouflage the crimes. The killer confesses after Chan presents his clever chain of evidence.

Gravelle will recover from his wounds if he can be kept quiet on the way to the hospital. Chan recruits Kitty to comfort him, and tells Regan to reveal the fact she is actually his daughter only when his survival is certain. Lee finally reappears with a clue that implicates the actual murderer, but Charlie tells him it is no longer needed. Reagan provides a police escort so Charlie and Lee (still dressed in his opera costume) can catch their boat to Honolulu.

PERFORMANCES

Warner Oland's performance is refined, well-modulated and masterful. It is plain that Chan's motivating factor is primarily to do good, not punish evil. In this regard, his behavior clearly reflects the philosophy of Confucius, with its emphasis on virtue and humility.

Boris Karloff is admirable as the deranged mental patient. His over-the-title billing in the film (Warner Oland vs Boris Karloff) is misleading, because Chan and Gravelle are not really adversaries. In fact, his presentation is derived in part from a picture filmed earlier in 1936, *THE WALKING DEAD.* He treads a fine line between being a figure of menace and of pathos. His lip synching of the operatic arias is not well done, but his stage presence in the opera sequence is magnificent. The rich and powerful baritone voice who recorded Gravelle's singing voice belonged to Tudor Williams. The highlight of the picture remains Karloff's extended scene with Oland, where Chan wins his confidence and gains his cooperation.

Keye Luke described this as his all time favorite Chan film, even though his own part is somewhat diminished compared to other entries in the series. Part of the reason might be that Luke injured his ankle while filming one of his chase scenes. His absence during the climatic restaging of the duet and the unmasking of the killer is never explained.

William Demarest (Kelly) appeared with Warner Oland in *THE JAZZ SINGER* (1927), and the actor later received an Oscar nomination for *THE JOLSON STORY* (1946). Demarest may be best remembered as Uncle Charley on the television series *MY THREE SONS* after he replaced William Frawley. In this Chan film, his comic part has a hostile edge that is repugnant. He keeps referring to Charlie as "Chop Suey" and "Egg Foo Yong," and at one point, he blurts out, "Ha! I get it...he's hitting the pipe again!" which clearly suggests all Orientals have an opium habit. The character of Kelly is one instance where the complaints of Chinese groups who protested Chan films may have sound justification. The blame for Kelly's depiction must be laid at the feet of the writers for also promoting the stereotype of a race-baiting Irish cop.

The other supporting actors are top-notch. Margaret Irving (Lilli), Nedda Harrigan (Madame Barelli) and Charlotte Henry fill their performances with fire and character. Gregory Gaye (Barelli) had a long and fascinating career as a utility actor, ranging from the Martian invader in the popular serial *FLYING DISK MAN FROM MARS* (1951) to the edgy Soviet Premier in *METEOR* (1978). The vocal doubles for Rochelle and the Barelli's were truly exceptional performers who brought an extra edge to the operatic scenes.

By a happy circumstance, Benson Fong, destined to play Chan's Number three son Tommy, made his earliest screen appearances in this film as one of the soldiers in the chorus. He was merely an extra, and it was several years before he seriously undertook an acting career. Decades later, Benson Fong and Keye Luke had wonderful back-to-back death scenes in the original feature version of *KUNG FU* (1972). Victor Sen Yung (Jimmy Chan) and James Hong (television's Barry Chan) were also in the film, making it a unique collaboration of Chan alumni.

CHARLIE CHAN'S SAYINGS

⬦ Honorable father once say, politeness golden key that open many doors.

⬦ Confucius say, "Luck happy combination of foolish accidents."

⬦ Small things sometimes tell large stories.

⬦ Madame's voice like monastery bell, when ringing, must attend.

⬦ Puppy love very expensive pastime.

⬦ (To Lee) Graceful as bamboo shoot, beautiful as water lily...long time ago use same description for honorable mother.

⬦ Roses in romance like tenor in opera, sing most persuasive love song.

⬦ The bouquet like summer tourist on wrong train, evidently suffer switch in destination.

⋄ Disloyalty of husband sometimes ample provocation for revenge.

⋄ Dead hands cannot hide knife.

⋄ Humility only defense against rightful blame.

⋄ Voice from back seat sometime very disconcerting to driver.

⋄ Man who ride on merry-go-round often enough finally catch brass ring.

⋄ Very old Chinese wise man once say, "Madness twin brother of genius because each live in world created by own ego. One sometimes mistaken for other.

⋄ Unwise officer who eat apple not yet ripe get official tummy

⋄ (To Kelly) Old Chinese proverb say... (at which point Chan continues in Chinese. At the end of the film, he translates for Kelly) Ancient proverb meaning, "When fear attack brain, tongue wave distress signal.

⋄ Excellent clue, but like last rose of summer, bloom too late.

CHARLIE CHAN AT THE RACE TRACK (1936)
Rating: ***

TWENTIETH CENTURY FOX. Written by Robert Ellis, Helen Logan and Edward T. Lowe; Story by Lou Breslow and Saul Elkins; Photographed by Harry Jackson; Edited by Nick De Maggio; Musical direction by Samuel Kaylin; Produced by John Stone; Directed by H. Bruce Humberstone. 70 minutes.

ANNOTATED CAST LIST

Warner Oland	Charlie Chan
Keye Luke	Lee Chan (Number one son)
Jonathan Hale	Warren Fenton (Horse breeder)
Helen Wood	Alice Fenton (His daughter)
George Irving	Major Kent (Breeder of Avalanche)
Gloria Roy	Catherine Chester (Kent's daughter)
Alan Dinehart	George Chester (Her husband and horse owner)
Thomas Beck	Bruce Rogers (Kent's secretary)
Gavin Muir	Bagley (Avalanche's trainer):
G. P. Huntley, Jr.	Denny Barton (Sophisticated gambler)
Frank Coghlan, Jr.	Eddie Brill (Injured jockey)
Frankie Darro	Tip Collins (Crooked jockey)
John Rogers	Mooney (Chief steward of *Oceanic*)
John H. Allen	Streamline Jones (Stable hand)
Lollipop	Streamline's monkey
Harry Jans	Al Meers (Race track camera operator)
Robert Warwick	Honolulu police chief
Jack Mulhall	Assistant purser of *Oceanic*
Paul Fix	Lefty (Gangster)
Charles Williams	Reporter at L.A. Harbor
Sidney Bracey	Waiter aboard *Oceanic*

SYNOPSIS AND APPRAISAL

This is a very entertaining film that is weakened somewhat by enormous plot loopholes. The gangsters are plotting to trigger the best odds, but their schemes work at cross-purposes. The threats against the front runner, Avalanche, make no sense in light of their plans to switch him with another horse, Gallant Lad. The threats against Avalanche would increase the odds against Gallant Lad. On another occasion, Charlie and Lee escape from a mob's hideout on foot. They then show up moments later at the race track with a laundry truck, but the film provides does not explain how they were able to do this. All detective films rely on overlooking several weak points in the plot, but this picture has so many of them that they are hard to ignore. What saves this film is the pure sense of fun with the characters and the execution of the story. Many viewers have pointed out that the film no doubt inspired elements of the action in the Marx Brothers' *A DAY AT THE RACES* (1937) which went into production shortly after this film.

The picture opens at police headquarters in Honolulu, where Chan is instructing other detectives on the proper interpretation of bloodstains and the meaning of certain patterns of these stains. His lecture is interrupted by Lee, declaring the Melbourne Sweepstakes race is about to begin. The radio is tuned in, and Lee collects bets from all of them to bring to the bookie! Even Charlie places a bet when he learns the front runner, Avalanche, is owned by his friend Major Kent.

At the Melbourne racetrack, George Chester is proud of Avalanche, a gift from his father-in-law, Major Kent. A rival horseman, Warren Fenton, is a friend of Catherine, Chester's wife. Alice Fenton, Warren's daughter, is engaged to Bruce Rogers, Kent's secretary. They all place last minute bets with racing enthusiast Denny Barton.

During the race, Avalanche is disqualified due to a blatant foul by jockey Tip Collins, who is later suspended from racing for two years. In private, Avalanche's trainer, Bagley, berates Collins for being obvious in throwing the race, and Collins is disappointed at his meager cash payoff for his misdeed. Chester is planning to run Avalanche in the Santa Juanita handicap in California. Major Kent believes gamblers were responsible for corrupting Collins, and he cables Charlie Chan to meet their boat, the *Oceanic*, in Honolulu.

When the ship arrives, however, Kent is dead, killed presumably by Avalanche in the hold of the ship. The Major was found dead in the horses's stall, his head covered in blood. The Honolulu police chief assigns the case to Chan. Aboard the *Oceanic*, the ship's doctor informs Chan that hoof marks were discernible on Kent's skull. Charlie questions various suspects including Bagley, Fenton, Rogers and Barton, the last person to see Kent alive. Fenton is transporting a number of horses on the *Oceanic*, and Kent's body was first discovered by his black stable hand, Streamline. After learning the position of the body, Chan declares that Kent was murdered. The location of the bloodstains in the stall prove that Avalanche couldn't have killed him. Charlie also learns that Avalanche reacts wildly when approached by Streamline's pet monkey. Fenton explains that his predominant horse Gallant Lad is emotionally bonded to the monkey.

Unknown to the other passengers, Tip Collins is aboard the ship. Captain Blake appeals to the police chief not to impound his vessel. Chan demonstrates to them that the murder weapon is a winch, which can produce an impression similar to a horseshoe. The winch on the cargo deck had been stolen. The police chief proposes that Chan travel to Los Angeles aboard the *Oceanic* and continue his investigation.

As the ship resumes its voyage, Chester receives a typed note warning him not to enter Avalanche in the Santa Juanita handicap. Chan observes that the letters in the note had several unique characteristics. Lee joins the ship's crew as a cabin boy, and his father asks him to search for the typewriter on which the note was typed. Fenton makes an offer to buy Avalanche, promising to use him only for breeding purposes.

Bruce tells Alice that he is going to gamble all his earnings on Avalanche so they will have enough money to get married. Lee identifies Fenton's typewriter as the one used to prepare the note. The ship's steward becomes suspicious of Lee, and plans to throw him in the brig. Charlie asks his son to type and deliver phony letters threatening the principals in the case.

A suspicious fire breaks out on the cargo deck, which Chan observes was deliberately set right under a sensor alarm. This conflagration was intended merely as a distraction. He discovers that a matchbook was rigged with a fuse to start the blaze. Streamline is sent to retrieve Bagley's gun, which accidentally fires when Chester examines it. The bullet grazes Chan's leg, and Lee comforts him as he rests in his stateroom.

Barton shows up, believing Chan was behind the latest series of notes, but Charlie refuses to confide in him. The steward catches Lee, and locks him in the brig for the rest of the voyage. When the *Oceanic* docks in Los Angeles, Chester is met by Eddie Brill, an injured jockey who once rode for him. Brill insists he is ready to ride again. The threats against Avalanche are the topic of the day, and the odds on the race are shifting wildly. Chan and Lee are puzzled when Gallant Lad seems terrified by his mascot monkey on the dock. When Avalanche appears friendly towards the monkey, Chan deduces that the horses were switched, probably during the fire. The two horses are identical, except for the white spot on Avalanche's nose.

Bagley is approached by Tip Collins, who also has figured out the horse switch, and the trainer takes him to meet with the members of the gambling ring. The gangsters explain that the horses were switched to take advantage of higher gambling odds if Gallant Lad wins the race. Collins wants to join the gang, but Bagley arranges to have him killed instead. At the Santa Juanita racetrack (obviously a pseudonym for Santa Anita), Chan observes the trial runs. Al Meers, the race track camera operator, explains to Charlie the workings of photography system with automatic sensors that are positioned around the track. Lee sneaks into the stables, and finds white dye on the nose of Avalanche, proving he is really Gallant Lad.

A gunman tries to shoot Chan at his hotel room, but is foiled when the window shade abruptly snaps up, a booby trap arranged by Charlie. When the hit man reports to Bagley, he develops a new plan to kidnap the detective. Meanwhile, Bagley bribes Al Meers into replacing one of the sensors with a dart-shooting tranquilizer gun. This would prevent any other horse but Gallant Lad (Avalanche in disguise) from winning the race.

Chester receives another threatening letter on the day of the race. Avalanche's jockey withdraws, and Chester hires an enthusiastic Eddie Brill to ride the horse. Charlie dresses Lee as a laundry truck driver, and instructs him to create a diversion on Charlie's signal. On their way to the track, they are seized by two thugs who imprison them in the kitchen at mob headquarters. The crooks are placing bets on Gallant Lad across the nation by telephone. Charlie and Lee use a distraction to trick their guard, overpower him and make their escape.

At the race track, Lee sets off fireworks in a laundry truck, allowing Charlie to slip into the heavily guarded stables. He switches Avalanche and Gallant Lad back to their proper stalls, rubbing off the dye on their noses. Working with the authorities, Chan arrests Bagley outside of the stable, and a police squad raids the gangsters' headquarters.

The race begins, and since Avalanche leads, Al Meers shoots him with a tranquilizer dart. Avalanche is thrown off stride, but Brill helps him to recover and win the race before collapsing from the drug. Chan orders all the suspects brought to the office of the racing association. Barton is angry at being detained. Meers and Bagley refuse to name their ringleader. A photo of the finish of the race reveals the dart in the side of Avalanche. After the end of the race, this dart was removed by one of the suspects. Chan orders everyone searched, and the dart is found in the pocket of one of the suspects, who claims it was planted there. The murderer then makes a mistake, mentioning the winch that killed Kent. Since only the police and Captain Blake knew this was the murder weapon, Kent's killer and leader of the gambling ring is revealed. As the film ends, Lee rushes in with a hot clue, which Charlie tells him he can save for another case.

PERFORMANCES

Warner Oland's delivery is atypical and offbeat in a number of areas. For instance, in the stables he punches and knocks out a security guard. Chan could have switched the two horses without resorting to secret means, since he was working closely with the authorities at the race track. Chan's actions seemed both elliptical and illogical at times in the story. Keye Luke also reported that Oland was fuzzier than usual while making this film due to his heavy drinking. In one crowd scene, Oland was reportedly weaving, unable to stand still, and the extras on either side of him propped him up and steadied him for the shot.

This film provides Keye Luke with one of his busiest scripts. He goes undercover twice in the story, and his comic pidgin English is quite amusing. He frequently lapses into Chinese in order to pass important information on to his father. One unexplained bit is Lee's gambling bet collecting from the detectives to place with a bookie. Even Charlie participates in this apparently illegal activity, which is another of this film's annoying plot loopholes.

The supporting players are adequate but not very impressive. The most effective ones are Thomas Beck (Rogers), Helen Wood (Alice) and Jonathan Hale (Fenton). Robert Warwick (Chan's supervisor) was an extraordinarily active character actor whose parts ranged from the reliable Detective Raymond, hero in the very entertaining serial *THE WHISPERING SHADOW* (1933) to Lord Montague in *ROMEO AND JULIET* (1936). Gavin Muir (Bagley) was actually an American actor although he specialized in playing soft-spoken British villains on the stage and screen. Frankie Darro (Collins) was best known for playing jockeys or troubled youths. Years later, he was the actor in the suit of the famous Robby the Robot in *FORBIDDEN PLANET* (1956). Frank Coghlan, Jr. is one of the most interesting of screen personalities. His career dates back to appearances as a baby after his birth in 1916. He was a memorable child performer in the late silent and early sound era, billed as "Junior" Coghlan. His role as the injuried jockey, Eddie Brill, is almost peripheral to the main storyline, but Coghlan makes a good impression as always. John H. Allen's Streamline is rather embarrassing and degrading, particularly when observed by modern viewers. It is a black caricature upon which Hollywood was too reliant in the Thirties.

CHARLIE CHAN'S SAYINGS

⋄ Record indicate most murder result from violence, and murder without bloodstains like Amos without Andy, most unusual.

⋄ Smart fly keep out of gravy.

⋄ When player cannot see man who deal cards, much wiser to stay out of game.

⋄ Suspicion often father of truth.

⋄ Easy to criticize, more difficult to be correct.

⋄ Frequent spanking while young make rear view very familiar.

⋄ Confucius say, "No man is poor who have worthy son."

⋄ Hasty conclusion like toy balloon: easy blow up, easy pop.

⋄ Surprise attack often find enemy unprepared.

⋄ Long road sometimes shortest way to end of journey.

⋄ Foolish to seek fortune when real treasure hiding under nose.

⋄ Rabbit run very fast, but sometime turtle win race.

⋄ (After being shot) Happy bullet in leg rather than heart.

⋄ Ocean have many fish.

⋄ Foolish rooster who stick head in lawn mower end in stew.

⋄ Innocent grass may conceal snake.

◇ Man who flirt with dynamite sometimes fly with angels.

◇ Roots of tree lead in many directions.

◇ Man with gun like lightning, never strike twice in same place.

◇ Useless talk like boat without oar, get nowhere.

◇ Cold-blooded murder no joke.

◇ Truth sometimes like stab of cruel knife.

◇ Good wife best household furniture.

CHARLIE CHAN AT THE WAX MUSEUM (1940)
Rating: ✶✶✶✶

TWENTIETH CENTURY FOX. Written by John Larkin; Photographed by Virgil Miller; Edited by James B. Clark; Musical direction by Emil Newman; Produced by Walter Morosco and Ralph Dietrich; Directed by Lynn Shores. 63 minutes.

ANNOTATED CAST LIST

Sidney Toler...................Charlie Chan
Victor Sen Yung.............Jimmy Chan (Number two son)
C. Henry Gordon.............Dr. Cream (Owner of wax museum)
Marc Lawrence................Steve McBirney (Convicted murderer)
Joan Valerie...................Lily Latimer (Dr. Cream's assistant)
Marguerite Chapman........Mary Bolton (Newspaper reporter)
Ted Osborne...................Tom Agnew (Radio announcer)
Michael Visaroff............. Dr. Otto Von Brom (Criminologist)
Charles Wagenheim......... Wille Fern (Museum night watchman)
Archie Twitchell............. Carter Lane (Mrs. Rocke's lawyer)
Edward Marr...................Grenock (McBirney's bodyguard)
Joe King.......................O'Matthews (Police inspector)
Harold Goodwin..............Edwards (Radio engineer)
Hilda Vaughn................. Mrs. Rocke (Wife of hanged man)
Charles Trowbridge..........Judge
Stanley Blystone.............Court clerk
Emmett Vogan............... District Attorney

SYNOPSIS AND APPRAISAL

A tight plot and a clever setting combine to make this picture a genuine audience pleaser, despite its relatively low budget. The atmosphere of the film is particularly successful, combining a stormy night, an unknown killer and the moody surroundings of a wax museum with its chamber of horrors. Even Chan enjoys the museum exhibits of Jack the Ripper and Henri Landru, better known as Bluebeard. Ever since Paul Leni's *WAXWORKS* (1924) and the classic scary Lionel Atwill thriller *MYSTERY OF THE WAX MUSEUM* (1933), this setting has been ideal one for eccentric mysteries. The various elements of the motion picture link up like clockwork to provide both a brisk pace and a stimulating light melodrama

The film opens in a New York courtroom as Steve McBirney is sentenced to death for robbery and murder. The criminal fulminates against Chan, whose testimony convicted him. This threat becomes more significant when McBirney makes a daring escape moments later. That night the criminal and his cohort, Grenock, go to Dr. Cream's Wax Museum, where they observe the owner playing chess with an automaton that is operated by his protege, Lily Latimer. Cream maintains a hideout in the cellar of his museum, where he also performs plastic surgery. McBirney asks Cream to give him a new face at once, but he is told that recovery would take some time.

Three weeks later, Chan is approached by reporter Mary Bolten and Dr. Cream, who hosts a weekly radio show from his waxworks. They invite Charlie to join Dr. Otto Von Brom in discussing the case of Joe Rocke, a hanged criminal whom Chan has maintained was innocent. Von Brom provided the evidence that convicted Rocke. Inspector O'Matthews of the police is surprised at Chan's acceptance, but Charlie suspects Cream's underworld connections. He believes that Dr. Cream might have performed plastic surgery on Butcher Degan, the actual killer in the Rocke case. Chan is wary that the show might be a trap set by McBirney.

McBirney, covered in bandages, plots with Cream to murder Charlie during the broadcast by wiring his chair with electricity. They plan to blame Willie Fern, the feeble-minded custodian, for committing the crime. After the museum closes, Fern smuggles in Joe Rocke's widow to watch the broadcast. Jimmy also sneaks in to watch the broadcast.

A thunderstorm breaks out as Dr. Cream gives a tour of his waxen images and the "chamber of horrors." Tom Agnew, the radio announcer, is upset that the broadcast topic was changed to the Rocke case, claiming he has no notes on it. Chan explains his theory to Von Brom that Rocke was innocent and was framed by Butcher Degan, a confederate of McBirney. Degan was assumed to be later killed by McBirney, but Chan is dubious. Von Brom is fascinated with Chan's theory. Mrs. Rocke's attorney, Carter Lane, shows up and tries to stop the broadcast. Von Brom insists the show must proceed, because he now understands what actually happened. Dr. Cream seats his guests for the broadcast, but Von Brom asks Chan to switch chairs with him as the show progresses, and Charlie has no problem accomodating his wish.

Grenock convinces Fern to throw an electrical switch. The lights go out and sparks fly behind Von Brom's chair. The German detective stands with a quizzical expression, and then collapses, dead. Chan determines that Von Brom was killed by a poison dart, not electrocution. Someone in the room committed the crime, either Carter Lane, announcer Tom Agnew, radio engineer Edwards, reporter Mary Bolton, Dr. Cream or his assistant Lily Latimer. Chan believes Lily had severed the electrical wire attached to the chair, rendering it harmless.

As Chan spots a hollow quill toothpick on the floor, Dr. Cream's automaton suddenly moves, and Jimmy steps out. His father questions him, and then finds the toothpick is missing. Charlie believes that it might be the murder weapon. After sending the suspects to Cream's office, Chan discovers Mrs. Rocke sleeping in one of the tableaux, but she is incoherent when he talks to her.

Jimmy telephones the police, but McBirney and Grenock intercept the call from their basement hideout. They are surprised by the news that Von Brom was the victim. Jimmy seeks out Charlie to tell him about a figure he saw in the basement, but is startled to find that he is talking to a waxen image of his father instead. Carter Lane talks to Mrs. Rocke, whose confusion is only an act. She is convinced that Butcher Degan is in the museum.

Chan determines that Willie Fern threw the electrical switch, after being instructed by "the warden." Cream insists that such instructions were imaginary. Jimmy tells his father about two other individuals he spotted in the museum when he sneaked in. This information leads Charlie to discover the secret hideaway, where he locates a paper with cut-out figures, a hobby of McBirney. Cream concedes that he operated on the criminal. McBirney plans to kill Chan from a hidden room, but stops when he overhears Chan say that Von Brom was killed by Butcher Degan because the German detective penetrated his disguise. Degan is also McBirney's enemy, so he decides to spare Chan until he identifies the Butcher.

Tom Agnew and Carter Lane overhear Charlie's theory about Degan. All the suspects debate the issue as Chan tries to phone the police. The lights are turned off, and a knife is thrown at the figure of Chan in the museum office. When the power is switched back on, Dr. Cream has vanished. Jimmy is shocked when he sees his father's body, but it is only the waxen image which Charlie used to bait a trap.

Jimmy is sent to fetch the police in person, but he stumbles upon the body of Steve McBirney, and Chan concludes he was killed by Butcher Degan. Inspector O'Matthews arrives, puzzled by the interruption of the radio broadcast. He stopped Dr. Cream who was in the act of fleeing the building. Jimmy tells his father that he thought Lane had switched off the lights before the attack on Charlie. Grenock, hidden in the automaton, tries to shoot Chan, but is stopped by Mrs. Rocke. Chan demonstrates how a quill toothpick can be used as a weapon, blowing a dart at a wax dummy. The figure, however, is the killer, Butcher Degan, posing as a dummy. His actual identity exposed, Degan confesses and begs for the antidote, but learns that he was only hit by a match stick.

Mrs. Rocke thanks Chan for clearing her husband, and Charlie discusses the clues by which he discovered Degan's identity. The picture ends as Jimmy exclaims that he is getting irritated by all the wax dummies. He gives the dummy of his father a boot in the rear, only to discover it is actually Charlie. Inspector O'Matthews explodes in laughter as he watches Chan's reaction.

PERFORMANCES

Sidney Toler gets to deliver a large number of pithy one-liners in this film. The wax double of Chan is exceptionally good, particularly in the film's last moments when the entire audience assumes that Charlie is the figure standing next to the inspector. His friendly rivalry with Von Brom is also very well played, especially since both characters have genuine respect for each other. It is also the only film which ends with Charlie groaning in pain, being the butt of the screenwriter's joke.

Victor Sen Yung comes off a little too juvenile in the story, but he has one magnificent scene when he believes his father has been stabbed. Even his father is moved by his genuine distress which Sen Yung plays very well.

The supporting players are well cast and deliver credible assignments except for Edward Marr (Grenock), whose character is just not believable. As written, Willie Fern is another unbelievable role, but Charles Wagenheim's gentle loony is so finely crafted, that he manages to be convincing. The same is true with Hilda Vaughn's excellent performance as Mrs. Rocke. The exceptional Marc Lawrence (McBirney) delivers another one of his classic gangster portrayals. Fifty-eight years later, Lawrence is still an active performer, working on the popular televison drama *ER*. He always manages to be convincing with his smooth delivery.   Marguerite Chapman (Mary Bolton) removes enough of the hard edge from the role of the inquisitive reporter to make her seem fresh and interesting. Marguerite was featured in many staring roles in B pictures during the Forties, and she later had a nice supporting part in the Marilyn Monroe comedy, *THE SEVEN YEAR ITCH* (1955).   Michael Visaroff is somewhat exaggerated and larger than life as the pompous criminologist Otto Von Brom, but even this works well, particularly when he is persuaded by Chan's arguments. Their byplay is a sheer delight to watch becuase it is unconventional and without any rancor whatsoever.

C. Henry Gordon (Dr. Cream) is masterful as usual as the creepy museum owner. Gordon was one of the most memorable and consistently good performers who appeared in numerous Chan films dating back to *CHARLIE CHAN CARRIES ON*.   He also was noted for playing the villainous Khan who was speared by Errol Flynn at the climax of *THE CHARGE OF THE LIGHT BRIGADE* (1936). This was his final Chan film, because Gordon died shortly after the the completion of this film from complications resulting from a leg amputation.

CHARLIE CHAN'S SAYINGS

◇ Always prefer to utilize element of surprise, never to be victim.

◇ Only very foolish mouse makes nest in cat's ear.

◇ Any powder that kills flea is good powder.

◇ Will imitate woman and change mind.

◇ Knowledge only gained through curiosity.

◇ Mice only play when cat supposed to be in bed.

◇ Old solution...sometimes like ancient egg.

◇ Justice can be brought to dead man.

- ◇ Truth speak from any chair.

- ◇ Every bird seek his own tree, never tree the bird.

- ◇ Suspicion is only toy of fools.

- ◇ Filial grief honorable music to ancient heart.

- ◇ Sometimes better to see and not tell.

- ◇ Fear is cruel padlock.

- ◇ Justice, like virtue, brings its own reward.

CHARLIE CHAN AT TREASURE ISLAND (1939)
Rating: *****

TWENTIETH CENTURY FOX. Written by John Larkin; Photographed by Virgil Miller; Edited by Norman Colbert; Musical direction by Samuel Kaylin; Produced by Edward Kauffman; Directed by Norman Foster. 75 minutes.

ANNOTATED CAST LIST

Sidney Toler...............Charlie Chan
Victor Sen Yung.........Jimmy Chan (Number two son)
Cesar Romero.............Fred Rhadini (Stage magician)
Pauline Moore............Eve Cairo (Mind reader)
Douglas Fowley..........Pete Lewis (Newspaper reporter)
June Gale...................Myra Rhadini (Wife of magician)
Douglass Dumbrille.....Thomas Gregory (Insurance detective)
Sally Blane................ Stella Essex (Widow of Paul Essex)
Billy Seward...............Bessie Sibley (Society lady)
Wally Vernon.............Elmer (Rhadini's comic assistant)
Donald McBride.......... Kilvaine (Deputy Police Chief)
Charles Halton............Redley (Essex's business manager)
Trevor Bardette...........The Turk (Zodiac's henchman)
Gerald Mohr...............Image of Dr. Zodiac
Louis Jean Heydt.........Paul Essex (Blackmailed novelist)

SYNOPSIS AND APPRAISAL

Many fans and critics consider this the best of all Chan films. It is extremely well written and includes a powerful and mysterious adversary. The supernatural element is well handled, and the pacing of the conclusion is a masterpiece of suspense. Director Norman Foster keeps this production on track throughout, creating an extraordinarily rich film that may equal or surpass even Oland's best efforts. It is also one of those rare films that seems to improve with repeated viewings.

The film opens with Charlie, Jimmy and novelist Paul Essex among the many passengers enjoying a flight to San Francisco to visit the Exposition at Treasure Island. Chan becomes curious about another passenger, Tom Gregory, an insurance actuary who befriended Essex during his visit to Hawaii. Essex completed his latest mystery novel during his stay, and he seems to be satisfied with the manuscript that he just completed. An obscurely worded radiogram (merely signed "Zodiac") arrives which greatly troubles Essex, and later he is found dead when the plane lands. Charlie concludes that it was suicide, probably triggered by the threatening note.

Paul's wife Stella and buisness manager Redley are waiting for the plane to disembark. Charlie sees them, and reluctantly but gently breaks the terrible news to them. Charlie is then whisked away in a cab moments later by two heavy-set men. They make some ominous comments, but Charlie simply laughs, calling them "brother officers." They are really police detectives who have been sent to escort Charlie by his old friend Deputy Chief Kilvaine of the San Francisco police department.

At headquarters, Charlie meets another old friend, newspaperman Pete Lewis. With the Paul Essex tragedy on his mind, Charlie learns from his police friends about a series of suicides, all clients of a mysterious local psychic who is known under the name Dr. Zodiac. Chan is joined in these suspicions by another casual acquaintance, stage magician Fred Rhadini, who is out to expose Dr. Zodiac as a charlatan and fraud.

Charlie and Pete set out to pay a visit to Dr. Zodiac, and Rhadini joins them wearing a disguise. The group is graciously received at Dr. Zodiac's mansion, and a delightfully spooky seance follows, which ends when Pete Wilson learns that Dr. Zodiac has been poisoning the mind of his girlfriend, Eve Cairo, against him. Dr. Zodiac produces a gun as he leaves the room after Wilson's temper flares and after he sees through Rhadini's feeble disguise. As they leave the premises, Chan is approached by Dr. Zodiac's servant to pay a twenty dollar fee for his consultation.

That evening, Chan attends a party given by Rhadini at Treasure Island, where he meets a number of unusual people, including Eve Cairo, a stage performer and telepath who has genuine mind reading ability. Gregory mysteriously shows up at the party (invited by Jimmy, who suspects him regarding Essex's death).

Eve Cairo's mind-reading act impresses Charlie, who discovers that she is particularly able to tune in to his own thoughts. Eve warns Charlie that someone is thinking of murder seconds before a knife is thrown at him, missing by inches.

Chan plans a midnight raid on Dr. Zodiac's headquarters, and he is joined again by Wilson and Rhadini. Jimmy, wearing a grotesque disguise, also invades Dr. Zodiac's stronghold. Charlie discovers that the image of "Dr. Zodiac" is itself an elaborate pretense, and he believes that Dr. Zodiac may be different people at different times. He breaks into Dr. Zodiac's secret vault, where he uncovers numerous files of people whom the masquerading psychic is blackmailing. Charlie learns his friend Paul Essex was covering up an old stock fraud case in which he was involved. Charlie nobly burns all these files, even if they contained evidence of past crimes by many individuals who had become victims of Dr. Zodiac.

Back at his hotel, Charlie reads the manuscript of Essex's last book, *THE SECRET OF THE PYGMY ARROW*, that was retrieved by Jimmy during his undercover work. The novel appears to be a thinly disguised expose of

Dr. Zodiac's blackmailing scheme, but the last page with the final solution, is missing. Tom Gregory shows up, and tells Charlie that he is really an insurance investigator working on the Zodiac case. Chan does not trust him, and foils his attempt to steal the manuscript of Essex's final novel.

Chan persuades Rhadini to issue a public challenge to Dr. Zodiac to appear at his stage show. The mystic's acceptance is later posted one of the doors at Rhadini's Temple of Magic, and is written on the back of the last page of Essex's manuscript. Charlie hopes to trap Dr. Zodiac during Rhadini's magic show and extravaganza that night.

Besides Tom Gregory, Chan's main suspects include: Bessie Sibley, a socialite who had frequent contact with Dr. Zodiac; Mr. Redley, Essex's business manager; The Turk, a henchman working with Dr. Zodiac; Myra Rhadini, the magician's jealous wife, and Rhadini himself. The confrontation occurs on stage at Rhadini's show at Treasure Island. This sequence is outstanding, one of the best set pieces in any mystery film. The editing, lighting, sound effects and acting are simply unsurpassed.

During one of Rhadini's main illusions, a levitation trick, the figure of Rhadini appears and is murdered, killed by a pygmy arrow appropriated from one of Rhadini's exhibits. Removing his mask, Chan uncovers the Turk behind Dr. Zodiac's disguise. Charlie tries to reconstruct the crime before the entire theater audience, and has Jimmy take the place of the girl in the levitation trick. This time, Rhadini himself is the victim of an attack while the theater lights are dimmed.

At the climax of this sequence, Chan decides to use Eve Cairo to help expose the identity of the real Dr. Zodiac. The melodramatic close-up of the killer's eyes during this terrific sequence can still make an audience gasp even today. The tension is finally eased as Jimmy steps in to prevent the killer from shooting his father. Chan then explains to solution to all parties, including the theater audience, and in the finally shot of the picture, he takes a curtain call for the audience in the theater as well as the film's audience. This motion picture is as thrilling, as it is captivating, and as much fun as any entertainment can be.

PERFORMANCES

Sidney Toler is at the top of his form in this entry. He moves like quicksilver through various roles...as father, concerned friend, heart-broken comforter, suspicious detective and world-renowned celebrity. It is hard to cite a single highlight, since the entire film is nothing but a series of highlights, but his interaction with Eve Cairo is definitely the most intense moments in the entire film.

Sen Yung is quite charming as Jimmy. He is most convincing in the plane scenes when the thunderstorm strikes with a terrible fury. His fear is genuinely portrayed, particularly in the touching moment when he lays his head on Charlie's shoulder. He looks ridiculous in his disguise in the middle section of the picture, but this outlandish costume makes a fitting parallel to the clever disguises employed by Dr. Zodiac throughout the picture. Jimmy also is a genuine hero when he deflects the gun carried by Dr. Zodiac, and assists in his capture during the remarkable apex of the picture.

Cesar Romero is fabulous on all counts as Rhadini, a charming and calculating figure, who sometimes sports a flimsy disguise when he accompanies Charlie's investigation of Dr. Zodiac. His stage technique is smooth and clever. His performance in the final sequence adds immeasurably to the overall success of the picture.

Pauline Moore is also essential to the dynamic realization of the film. Her ethereal moments in a trance are compelling and highly dramatic. At those colorful instances, no music is heard on the soundtrack. Instead, the loud ticking of a chronometer adds to the intensity of these scenes. The interplay between Eve Cairo, Chan and Dr. Zodiac is one of the best milestones in the entire series of Chan films.

Gerald Mohr is not really a character in the film. He stands in for the figure of Dr. Zodiac whenever anyone wears the disguise. In one brief scene, it is actually Charlie Chan himself in the Zodiac costume. But it is Mohr, however, who makes Dr. Zodiac's brief scenes so effective.

June Gale is commendable in her very brief role as Rhadini's jealous wife. Interestingly, June married Oscar Levant during the year this picture was released. Levant had earlier composed the memorable opera sequence from *CHARLIE CHAN AT THE OPERA.*

CHARLIE CHAN'S SAYINGS

◇ One scholar in family better than two detectives.

◇ Unhappy news sometimes correct self the next day.

◇ Impossible to miss someone who will always be in heart.

◇ Sometimes black magic very close relative to blackmail.

◇ Do not challenge supernatural unless armed with sword of truth.

◇ If request music, must be willing to pay the fiddler.

◇ To destroy false prophet, must first unmask him before eyes of believers.

◇ Little mouse lucky his clothes do not fit elephant.

◇ Great happiness follows great pain.

◇ (Saying read from Chan's mind by Eve Cairo) Favorite pastime of man is fooling himself.

◇ If befriend donkey, expect to be kicked.

⋄ Swelled head gives criminal more trouble than indigestion.

⋄ (Quoted by Jimmy Chan) Swelled head sometimes gives police more cooperation than criminal mistake.

⋄ (To son Jimmy) Recommend you imitate excellent example of Sphinx and keep silent.

⋄ Obvious clues, like tricks in magic, usually prove deceptive.

CHARLIE CHAN IN CITY IN DARKNESS (1939)

Rating: *

TWENTIETH CENTURY FOX. Written by Robert Ellis and Helen Logan based on a play by Gina Kaus and Ladislaus Fodor; Photographed by Virgil Miller; Edited by Harry Reynolds; Musical direction by Samuel Kaylin; Produced by John Stone; Directed by Herbert I. Leeds. 75 minutes.

ANNOTATED CAST LIST

Sidney Toler..................Charlie Chan
Douglass Dumbrille.........B. Petroff (Corrupt businessman)
Richard Clarke................Madero (Secretary fired by Petroff)
Lynn Bari......................Marie Dubon (Madero's wife)
Harold Huber..................Marcel Stivarg (Prefect's secretary)
Pedro de Cordoba.............Antoine (Petroff butler)
Dorothy Tree..................Charlotte Ronnelle (Munitions smuggler)
C. Henry Gordon.............J. Romaine (Paris prefect of police)
Noel Mason...................Belescu (French Maritime official)
Leo G. Carroll................Louis Santelle (Locksmith & forger)
Lon Chaney, Jr...............Pierre (Santelle's assistant))
Louis Mercier.................Max (Jewel thief)
George Davis..................Alex (Max's accomplice)
Barbara Leonard...............Lola (Lookout for Max)
Adrienne d'Ambricourt......Owner of Hotel des Voyageurs
Frederick Vogeding..........Holst (Captain of the Medusa)
Alphonse Martell............Gendarme (Blackout patrol)
Eugene Borden................Gendarme (Guard at Petroff's house)
Ann Codee....................Complaining woman at prefecture
Gino Corrado..................Cafe owner
Rolfe Desan...................Baptiste (Hotel employee)

SYNOPSIS AND APPRAISAL

This is without question the weakest of the Twentieth Century Fox series of Chan films, and it is ironic that it was made directly after *CHARLIE CHAN AT TREASURE ISLAND* which many consider the best Chan film. Some critics blame Toler for not fitting into a European setting, which is ridiculous. Chan has simply very little screen time without the character of Marcel, who rants, raves, mugs and bellows in a most irritating fashion. This character renders the film a complete mess. Toler just stands back and tries to keep out of his way. The title of this film has also been the subject of some confusion.

It has often been mistakenly called *CHARLIE CHAN IN THE CITY IN DARKNESS* as well as *CHARLIE CHAN IN CITY OF DARKNESS*.

The rich "slice of history" plot built around the war panic over Hitler's demands concerning Czechoslovakia is well chosen. But the writers, director and actors let it all go to waste by their spotlighting of the manic Marcel to the detriment of the rest of the cast and plot. Remarkably, this is the only Toler film without any of his offspring, and Jimmy is sorely missed because he might have softened the non-stop comic relief invested in the character of Marcel. The basic story is awkwardly grafted from a play by Gina Kaus and Ladislaus Fodor, which doesn't mesh well with the Chan formula. After all, the spies are never even captured, but killed instead in an airplane accident. In the end, the murderer is practically feted as a hero, which is very odd indeed.

The film has a very promising opening with a Walter Winchell-style narrator describing the critical events of September, 1938 during the Czechoslovakian crisis. A montage of news footage shows Neville Chamberlain, Benito Mussolini and Adolf Hitler, as the war scare is vividly described. On September 28th, Paris is to be totally blacked out, making the historic "City of Light" instead a "city in darkness."

On that night, Chan is attending a twentieth reunion with World War One comrades in the Intelligence service, hosted by Romaine, the Parisian prefect of police. Marcel Stivarg, the prefect's hyperactive godson, serves as his secretary. Marcel is visited by Antoine, the butler of an important businessman named Petroff. Antoine hands over a threatening letter from Tony Madero, an employee whom Petroff fired for embezzlement. Marcel brings the letter to Romaine at the reunion. Chan notes that the letter was opened and resealed.

Elsewhere in Paris, foreign agent Charlotte Ronnelle is planning to smuggle munitions onto a ship with the help of Belescu, a maritime official. They argue about money, which is supposed to be paid to him by Petroff, Belescu's business partner.

Chan is unable to book passage out of France at the shipping office. He is approached by Louis Santelle who offers to sell him a ticket to Panama at an inflated price, but Chan defers to Marie Dubon, a woman desperate to leave the country. She is actually buying the ticket for her husband, Tony Madero, and Santelle also offers to procure a phony passport for him. We learn the forger is working for Petroff, who is setting a trap for Marie.

Antoine accompanies his son to the train depot as he departs with his military regiment. A gang of thieves plan to break into Petroff's house after the butler leaves, and Belescu also has a meeting with Petroff.

After midnight, Marcel is notified by Antoine that Petroff has been shot and killed. The prefect is busy working with the Department of Public Safety, so he asks Marcel to handle the case himself. In turn, Marcel begs Chan for his help. The excitable secretary makes a complete mess of the investigation, but Charlie advises him on proper procedure. After examining the crime scene, Charlie alerts Marcel that burglars had broken into Petroff's house. They visit underworld hangouts, and arrest Max and Alex, the two thieves involved in the crime. They confess to robbery, but admit no knowledge of the murder. Max claims that a woman entered the house as they escaped.

Chan locates Petroff's address book, and suggests to Marcel that he inquire into the last entry in the book, "M.D." at the Hotel des Voyageurs. They detain Marie Dubon and Tony Madero, and quickly discover his phony passport. Madero claims Petroff framed him for embezzlement because he had learned that Petroff had undercover dealings with the Nazis.

Charlie finds locksmith Louis Santelle's business card in Madero's hotel room, and goes to his shop. He asks him about the forged passport. Pierre, Santelle's assistant, overpowers Chan and ties him up. They plan to torture him for information, but Chan manages to turn on the outside light, which alerts the police enforcing the blackout. They free Charlie and capture the locksmith. At the prefecture, Chan questions all the suspects. Belescu says he visited Petroff on business and left at midnight. Santelle claims he asked a huge sum for the forged passport because Petroff wanted to force Marie Dubon to come to him for the funds. Marie says Petroff gave her the money, but threatened to turn her husband over to the police unless she agreed to become his mistress. Antoine claims that Marie could not have killed Petroff, and that he learned that his employer and Belescu were aiding the Nazis. The thieves relate that Petroff's safe was already open when they tried to rob it. There is an alert when planes are heard overhead, but Chan identifies them as French army planes, not a sneak German attack. Belescu flees during this distraction.

A manhunt is initiated for Belescu. Marcel learns that Petroff was killed precisely at 12:06 AM while dictating a telegram to the Medusa to clear their cargo. Chan suggests that the Medusa be detained. Belescu sneaks into his apartment where Charlotte Ronnelle is waiting for him. He accuses her of murdering Petroff for the clearance papers, and she shoots him when he threatens to tell the police everything. Chan and Marcel hear the shots while on their way to search the apartment, and they chase her by car. She escapes to a private airfield where she and the other smugglers perish when their plane crashes on take-off.

The next day, Romaine toasts Chan for tracking down the spy ring, but he replies that the murderer of Petroff is still free. He then reveals the name of the killer, but suggests that he not be prosecuted because his motive was to stop the munitions shipment. The film ends as news arrives of Hitler's invitation to a peace conference to be held in Munich. Everyone seems happy and relieved except Chan, who issues a dark, prophetic warning about the spider who invites a fly into his parlor.

PERFORMANCES

Harold Huber, a fine character actor, was excellent in *CHARLIE CHAN ON BROADWAY* anumerous other films, but here, as in *CHARLIE CHAN IN MONTE CARLO*, he ruins the picture almost single-handedly. His caricature of a manic Frenchman is absurd, especially when the plot reveals

Marcel isn't even a Frenchman but Rumanian instead. He overwhelms Sidney Toler, and everyone else, in all of their scenes together, and Toler has no choice but to yield him the floor.

Sidney Toler is sufficient as Charlie in his scenes without Huber. He is excellent at the opening banquet and in the scene where he is captured at Santelle's store. His final comments, with his warning about Hitler, are laudable. Some critics proposed the idea that Toler's Chan was not suited to foreign settings like Warner Oland. This is really not a fair comment, since the European backdrop was basically denied him due to the war. Toler could have functioned very well in foreign settings with an adequate script, but this film failed to provide him with one.

Leo G. Carroll is memorable as the smarmy locksmith and forger, Santelle. His henchman is played by Lon Chaney, Jr. in a very minor role without dialogue. Chaney's very next film would be Lenny in *OF MICE AND MEN* (1939) that launched him into major roles. In fact, his teamwork with Burgess Meredith in the poignant John Steinbeck story was of Academy Award caliber. In many ways, this role was the most important of his career, even considering his other major triumph as Lawrence Talbot in *THE WOLFMAN* (1940).

Pedro de Cordoba (Antoine), Douglass Dumbrille (Petroff) and C. Henry Gordon (Romaine) also deliver competent and sound performances, but the rest of the cast are swamped in the wake of Huber's histrionics.

CHARLIE CHAN'S SAYINGS

⋄ Have not prepared for emergency, like man who buy suit with only one pair of pants.

⋄ First war profiteer, like early bird, look for big fat worm.

⋄ Birds never divide worm until safe in nest.

⋄ In every city there are roosts where birds of feather congregate.

⋄ Patience big sister to wisdom.

⋄ Quite evident sugar daddy attract many butterflies.

⋄ Confucius has said, "A wise man question himself, a fool others."

⋄ Acid very poor oil to loosen stubborn tongue.

⋄ To describe bitter medicine will not improve it's flavor.

⋄ Very difficult to drive car forward while looking backward.

⋄ Wise man has said, "Beware of spider who invite fly into parlor."

CHARLIE CHAN IN EGYPT (1935)

Rating: ✳✳✳

FOX. Written by Robert Ellis and Helen Logan; Photographed by Daniel B. Clarke; Edited by Alfred De Gaetano; Musical direction by Samuel Kaylin; Produced by Edward T. Lowe; Directed by Luis King. 65 minutes.

ANNOTATED CAST LIST

Warner Oland..................Charlie Chan
George Irving.................Professor Arnold (Head of expedition)
Pat Paterson..................Carol Arnold (His daughter)
Thomas Beck..................Tom Evans (Archaeologist)
Rita Hayworth................Nayda (Exotic servant)
James Eagles..................Barry Arnold (Carol's crippled brother)
Jameson Thomas.............Dr. Anton Racine (Carol's doctor)
Frank Conroy.................John Thurston (Arnold's brother)
Nigel de Brulier..............Edfu Ahmet (Thurston servant)
Paul Porcasi..................Soueidia (Luxor police inspector)
Arthur Stone.................Dragoman (Egyptian guide)
Stepin Fetchit................Snowshoes (Evans servant)
Frank Reicher.................Dr. Jaipur (Egyptian Physician)
Anita Brown..................Snowshoes' girlfriend
John Davidson................Daoud Atrash (Chemist)
John George..................Egyptian dwarf

SYNOPSIS AND APPRAISAL

This interesting film is a mixed bag with numerous positive and negative elements. On the plus side, the exotic setting is well chosen and well handled. The fervor resulting from the discovery of Tutankhamen's tomb in 1922 provides much of the inspiration, with a sideplot of ancient curses and hidden treasure. The moody setting and exceptional photography create a unique atmosphere. On the negative side, the mystery is transparent and quite weak. Few attentive viewers will miss identifying the guilty figure within the first twenty minutes. The use of Stepin Fetchit also dilutes the story, and the soundtrack in virtually every print is muddy and almost unlistenable.

The credits appear with the silhouette of the three great pyramids at Giza in the background. The story depicts the Arnold Archaeological Expedition as they explore the tomb of High Priest Ahmeti. One of the native workers collapses and dies after helping remove a small chest positioned in an alcove. Later that night, someone secretly explores the tomb alone, presumably to plunder it.

Six months later, Charlie Chan arrives in Egypt being flown in a primitive open-air biplane, and his pilot flies him directly over the pyramids. Eventually,

Charlie has to travel by donkey to reach the expedition, and he topples off the animal after an unexpected gust of wind.

At the headquarters of the expedition, Charlie encounters Snowshoes, an unusual and eccentric servant who says he was brought to Egypt after being won in a crap game by explorer Tom Evans. Snowshoes believes he is of Egyptian descent, and he is looking for the tomb of his ancestors. Charlie meets Evans and Carol Arnold, explaining he was hired by the French Archaeological Society to investigate the possibility of theft from the Ahmeti tomb. Chan is troubled when he learns of the absence of Professor Arnold, head of the expedition. His brother, Egyptologist John Thurston, is left in charge.

Thurston is unaware of the theft when Chan produces a photograph of Ahmeti's necklace and ring, recently purchased by a museum in Berlin. Carol is worried about her father, working at a remote site, who has not been answering her letters for some time. Chan is shown some Ahmeti treasures in Thurston's laboratory. Thurston explains that the mummy case itself has not been opened, but Chan finds evidence of tampering. When an X-ray of the sarcophagus reveals a bullet in the heart of the mummy, they open the case and find the body of Professor Arnold. In another room, Carol screams, overwhelmed by a terrible premonition, and Dr. Racine is summoned to treat the troubled young woman. Her brother, Barry Arnold, injured in a tomb opening ten years earlier, claims they are all victims of an ancient curse. Chan notes that Carol's cigarette has been laced with a drug.

At this point, Thurston confesses to Chan that he sold the ring and necklace to repay funds Arnold borrowed from Dr. Racine to complete his work. Evans offers to share his accommodations with Chan while he works on the case. Charlie discovers that the last note received from Professor Arnold was typed on Evans' typewriter. Evans admits that he was fired by Professor Arnold, but Thurston rehired him. He points out that everyone had access to his typewriter, even Thurston's servant Edfu Ahmet who claims to be a direct descendant of Ahmeti. Evans also relates that Ahmeti was known to have amassed a large treasure, but it was not found in the tomb. Chan asks to see the tomb at once, in the middle of the night. Snowshoes accompanies them on their visit.

Charlie is intrigued by an unfinished passageway in the tomb. The generator powering the lights in the tomb fails, and they see a figure glowing in the dark, masquerading as the goddess Sekhmet. Someone then rolls a boulder down upon them as they leave the tomb.

The next day, Charlie has Carol's cigarette analyzed by a chemist before attending the autopsy on the body of Professor Arnold. Inspector Soueidia of the Luxor police welcomes Chan's help in solving the murder. Arnold died from a blow to the skull, and the blood was also drained from his body by an incision to his jugular vein. The bullet lodged in Arnold's body was received during an earlier incident in a confrontation with some natives. Not satisfied with Dr. Racine's conclusions, Chan examines the body himself.

Carol is worried that her brother is becoming unhinged by recent events.

Charlie asks Dr. Racine about the hallucinatory drug found in Carol's cigarette. He decides to question Barry, who is playing the violin in his room. As Charlie enters, the man clutches his throat and collapses. Dr. Racine pronounces him dead. Edfu Ahmet says it is the vengeance of the ancient gods of Egypt, and Chan asks him about Carol's cigarettes. Ahmet draws a gun and asserts all members of the household are marked for death. The Egyptian then runs off into the night.

Evans is asked by Charlie to again visit the tomb. They plan to search for the secret exit through which the intruder escaped the previous night. Pushing two stones carved with the hieroglyph of the symbol of "life," Chan and Evans open a secret room with a reflection pool filled with water. Charlie recalls a comment by Barry about a hidden river in the tomb, and he floats a piece of paper on the pool, revealing a current. Evans discovers the treasure chamber after swimming underwater through the pool. Among the artifacts is the mask of the goddess Sekhmet. He also finds a neatly folded pile of clothing belonging to Professor Arnold.

Evans is shot while exploring the room. While falling, the archaeologist bumps into a statue on the wall which opens another passage to the main tomb. Snowshoes and Charlie rush in and carry the unconscious man back to Thurston's house and alert Dr. Jaipur, a local physician. Nayda is very worried about the condition of Evans. She explains that Thurston and Racine went to Luxor to get the police. Chan investigates Barry's room, and examines his violin While playing it, Chan immediately feels faint. Nayda spies on Charlie as he opens the violin and discovers a tube containing gas. When Soueidia arrives with Thurston and Racine, Carol, frantic over the attack on Evans, considers Chan a failure and asks him to leave. Thurston agrees, but first Chan demonstrates how Barry was killed by poison gas. He explains about the treasure room containing Arnold's clothes, and then hands the case over to Soueidia, with the hope that Evans will name his attacker when he revives. The inspector assumes that Edfu Ahmet is the guilty party. Dr. Jaipur departs, leaving Evans in the hands of Dr. Racine.

Later that night, a figure slips into the sick room to kill Evans, but is caught by Chan in the act. Charlie's departure was a ploy to allow the killer an opportunity to attack the young explorer. Chan accounts for the motive of the killer, the control of the priceless treasure of Ahmet. The film ends as Snowshoes puzzles over one of Charlie's sayings.

PERFORMANCES

Warner Oland is exceptional, providing an entertaining one-man show from his preposterous donkey ride to his unusual midnight explorations. The film features one of Chan's earliest references to Confucius. His reflections while scrutinizing Ahmeti's tomb are actually quite poetic. He works very well with Thomas Beck (Evans), who is ideal as the young archaeologist. The scene in which Beck dives into the "river of life" to locate the hidden treasure chamber is masterful, heightened by effective lighting and fine acting. The motivation for Chan undertaking this case is weak, since it usually takes a serious situation to persuade Charlie to undertake a case so far from home. It seems that he must have owed someone at the French Archaeological Society a favor to undertake the initial investigation. After all, Charlie had to undertake a flight in a hazardous open-air plane, as well as attempt to mount and ride a donkey. It is fun watching Oland play Charlie in his struggle to maintain his dignity in such humorous situations.

Unfortunately, most of the other supporting characters are weak, poorly written caricatures who squander their opportunities in this exotic setting, with the exception of Nigel de Brulier (Edfu Ahmet). His role may be a conventional one, but he adds a lot of zest to it.

Pat Paterson is plainly unsympathetic as the heroine, and James Eagles overacts needlessly as Barry. Rita Hayworth, billed as Rita Cansino, is given very little opportunity except to watch the proceedings. There are numerous admirers of Lincoln Perry, who as Stepin Fetchit was noted for his portrayals of a slow-thinking black comic. Others regard him as the epitome of a racist stereotype. Most viewers, however, will find his performance unwatchable, not because it is unfashionable but because it is simply unfunny. His acting is an annoying distraction from the story. By comparison, the later addition of Mantan Moreland to the series is sophisticated, with very clever asides. Moreland always seems to rise above the poor material with which he was sometimes provided. Oddly enough, Fetchit keeps referring to Chan as "Mr. Chang," just like Inspector Thacker in *CHARLIE CHAN IN LONDON*.

CHARLIE CHAN'S SAYINGS

⋄ Drop of water on thirsty tongue more precious than gold in purse.

⋄ Reverence for ancestors always most commendable.

⋄ Inconspicuous molehill sometimes more important than conspicuous mountain.

⋄ Waiting for tomorrow waste of today.

⋄ Cannot read printing in new book until pages are cut.

⋄ Theory, like mist on eyeglasses, obscures facts.

⋄ Impossible to prepare defense until direction of attack is known.

⋄ Story of man very short...Am reminded of ancient sage, Confucius, who write, "From life to death is reach of man."

⋄ Hasty conclusion easy to make, like hole in water.

⋄ Kind thoughts add favorable weight in balance of life and death.

⋄ Admitting failure like drinking bitter tea.

⋄ Courage greatest devotion to those we love.

⋄ Journey of life like feather on stream, must continue with current.

CHARLIE CHAN IN HONOLULU (1938)

Rating: ✳✳

TWENTIETH CENTURY FOX. Written by Charles Belden; Photographed by Charles Clarke; Edited by Nick De Maggio; Musical direction by Samuel Kaylin; Produced by John Stone; Directed by H. Bruce Humberstone. 65 minutes.

ANNOTATED CAST LIST

Sidney Toler...................Charlie Chan
Victor Sen Yung.............Jimmy Chan (Number two son)
Layne Tom, Jr................Tommy Chan (Number three son)
Phyllis Brooks...............Judy Hayes (Legal secretary)
Eddie Collins.................Al Hogan (Animal custodian)
John King.....................George Randolph (Ship's chief officer)
Claire Dodd...................Carol Wayne (Widow)
George Zucco................. Dr. Cardigan (Eccentric psychiatrist)
Robert Barrat..................Johnson (Freighter Captain)
Richard Lane.................. Arnold (San Francisco police detective)
Marc Lawrence...............Johnnie McCoy (Arnold's prisoner)
Philip Ahn....................Wing Fu (Son-in-law of Charlie Chan)
Paul Harvey.................. Inspector Rawlins (Homicide detective)
Dick Alexander.............. Bulky sailor
James Flavin.................Police dispatcher

SYNOPSIS AND APPRAISAL

This is the first film in the Toler/Fox series, and the production values are modest, as if Fox did not want to risk too much in case Toler didn't succeed as Chan. In fact, the film was conceived as a one-shot deal. The audience response was positive, so the series continued with *CHARLIE CHAN IN RENO* which nailed the formula down. One drawback to this picture is the structure of the film. Charlie is not permitted to take over the case until later in the picture, so the introduction to the mystery is left in the awkward hands of Jimmy. The story never really gets back on track after this stumbling introduction. There is also too much padding with the comic animal keeper and his pet lion, Oscar. At times, the plot is static, and limited to the confines of the ship. Yet despite these flaws, the film proved that the character of Charlie Chan did not perish with Warner Oland.

The picture opens at the Chan home on Punchbowl Hill. Charlie, his wife and eleven children are gathered at the dinner table, eating a meal of lo mein with chopsticks. A servant is pouring tea as Charlie tries to quiet the lunchtime commotion. Jimmy talks about his desire to become a detective. "Now that brother Lee is in the New York Art School, I can take his place." Tommy adds that he is as good a detective as Jimmy. Wing Fu, Chan's son-in-law, arrives to proclaim that his wife is about to give birth. The Chans are thrilled with the prospect of their first grandchild. Charlie tells his wife, "You have had same experience thirteen times. There is no cause to worry!" But Charlie seems as nervous as she is as he rushes his family to the maternity hospital.

Tommy answers the phone, and gets a message from the Homicide Bureau for Charlie to investigate a murder on the freighter *Susan B. Jennings*, on its way from Shanghai to San Francisco. Tommy tells his older brother, but instead of trying to catch his father, Jimmy decides to tackle the case himself. Unknown to his brother, Tommy also decides to tag along.

Aboard ship in the harbor, Judy Hayes and Captain Johnson are discussing the crime. When Jimmy arrives on a transport boat, the Captain assumes he's Charlie Chan, although he is surprised by his youth. While they are talking, Tommy sneaks on board, having hidden out on the same transport. Jimmy begins to question the six passengers on the *Susan B. Jennings*. Dr. Cardigan, a partially deaf scientist, arouses his suspicions. Judy Hayes, a legal secretary, witnessed the murder. She was transporting a package of $300,000 to be delivered upon receipt of a special ring. An unknown man came aboard with the ring, but was shot and killed before Judy could hand over the package. Other passengers include: Al Hogan, in charge of a shipment of wild animals for the San Francisco zoo; Carol Wayne, a recent widow; Arnold, a detective from San Francisco and Johnny McCoy, a criminal in his custody.

When Jimmy views the victim's body, he finds that all identification has been removed from the body. Tommy wanders around the ship, observing the passengers. One of Al Hogan's animals, Oscar the lion, is loose and frightens Jimmy. Meanwhile at the hospital, Charlie calls Inspector Rawlins of Homicide and learns not only about the murder case, but that the ship radioed that he was on board. Chan sets off at once for the ship.

Jimmy runs into difficulties while trying to interview the crew, a tough group of a dozen men who are hostile and unresponsive to his questions. Charlie comes aboard and watches Jimmy's predicament, intervening when they try to toss his son overboard. He tells Randolph, the chief officer, "Honolulu police frown on choking bay with bodies!"

Taking charge, Charlie approaches Dr. Cardigan. Jimmy explains the man is deaf, which Charlie quickly disproves by tossing a coin on deck that catches the doctor's attention. Al Hogan catches Tommy around his animal cages, and Charlie sends the boy home with one of his policemen, but allows Jimmy to stay. After Chan examines the body, Jimmy hands him the wedding ring that the dead stranger gave to Judy Hayes. The ring's engraving reads "E.H. to R.H." Dr. Cardigan enters the cabin, claiming he wants to see if the eyes of the victim contain any images. He explains that he is writing a book, and pretended to be deaf to gain an advantage while observing people. He propounds various theories, and Chan hands him a button from his coat, which proves the scientist had already been in the room earlier.

While talking with the detective, Judy Hayes says her employer is lawyer John Emery of Shanghai. Randolph is very protective of Judy, and asks Chan to let her rest. Carol Wayne asserts she was in her cabin at the time of the murder, but Judy claims she was the first one on deck after the shot. While interrogating Arnold and his prisoner Johnnie McCoy, Chan is alerted that Judy's package of $300,000 has been stolen from her room. The ship finally docks, but Chan orders the freighter sealed, with no cargo, or passengers allowed to leave the vessel.

Carol Wayne taunts Randolph about a gun she saw handed to Judy Hayes by him before the murder, but he defies her attempt at blackmail. Al Hogan brings Oscar the lion down the gangplank for exercise, scaring away the guards. The lion runs off, chasing a pet monkey belonging to one of the dock workers. During a lengthy sequence, Hogan wrestles the lion and gets him under control. Meanwhile, Judy Hayes flees the ship, and Jimmy tries in vain to catch her.

Chan, assisted by Arnold, undertakes a search of the cabins on the ship. They discover a weird apparatus in Dr. Cardigan's room containing a living brain of the criminal Chang Ho Ping. The eccentric doctor claims he has kept it alive for six months, and that he has even more specimens in his home. Charlie also finds a paper money band from the National Bank of Shanghai in the doctor's room.

Johnnie McCoy is missing from the room in which Arnold locked him. He returns moments later, and Chan discovers he has a passkey, at which point Arnold punches out his prisoner. Jimmy alerts his father about Judy's escape, and he leaves Arnold, who in private is scolded by McCoy for acting like a real cop. The man posing as Arnold is really Mike Hannigan, McCoy's criminal ally.

Chan telephones Inspector Rawlins to report about Judy Hayes, but the operator also patches in a call from Wing Fu from the maternity hospital. This results in a very humorous three-way conversation that totally befuddles the Rawlins, who confuses the name of the suspect with proposed names for the new baby. Finally, the phone call ends when a policeman arrives with Judy and the other suspects.

Captain Johnson accuses her of going ashore to stash the missing money, which Judy denies, saying she only left the ship to call her employer in Shanghai. Carol mentions her gun, and Judy hands it over to Chan. Randolph says he gave her his own gun for protection while she was handling the money package, and claims Carol tried to blackmail him into allowing her to go ashore. She refuses to answer when Chan asks her about it. He dismisses everyone with a sarcastic remark, "So grateful for cooperation."

On deck, Randolph advises Judy to tell Chan the entire truth, and shows her $10,000 that he found hidden in her room. Judy believes the money was planted in her room by Carol Wayne. Chan and Jimmy search Carol's room, and discover her watch, engraved "R.H. to E.H." which duplicates the initials on the murdered man's ring. They proceed back to their cabin. Through the open door of Judy's cabin, Jimmy spots Carol Wayne's body, strangled with a scarf.

Later a fire alarm blares on the ship, causing general confusion. By the time Captain Johnson and the crew trace the fire, it has been extinguished by Chan. Privately, Jimmy tells his father he lit the fire in a bathtub to catch the criminal who would instinctively retrieve the money. Jimmy spies a gun aimed at his father which appears in a porthole. He knocks Charlie out of the way as the gun is fired. He is unharmed, and grateful to Jimmy for his quick response.

Randolph catches McCoy removing the cash package from a lifeboat. They fight, and the officer brings the criminal to Chan on deck. McCoy asserts he found the package by accident. Arnold claims custody of the criminal, and handcuffs himself to McCoy. However, Chan takes the detective's keys and arrests both men. He is aware of the masquerade of Mike Hannigan from a recent wanted flyer. The body of the genuine Arnold had been discovered in China. Al Hogan turns in a gun that was just dropped down a pipe into the cargo hold. Chan tells the Captain to gather the passengers in his cabin, and then asks Dr. Cardigan to help him prepare a trap using a hidden camera.

At his meeting, Chan asks the Captain for Carol Wayne's passport, and learns her real name was Elsie Hillman. The Captain explains that she wanted her anonymity protected. Judy reveals that Hillman was the name of the man to whom she was to deliver the money. He was trying to protect his assets in a divorce case. Chan then announces that Mrs. Hillman has been murdered, and that the gun turned in by Hogan would reveal the identity of the killer.

Charlie plans to take the fingerprints of each suspect. He is interrupted by another call from Wing Fu. Abruptly, someone turns off the lights and seizes the gun. Chan, however, had prepared for this, since the camera was set to photograph anyone who touched the weapon. Dr. Cardigan quickly develops the photograph, and Charlie hands it to the guilty party without checking it. The culprit murdered Hillman and later stole the money and hid it in the lifeboat after planting false clues. The cash was accidentally discovered by McCoy. The killer murdered Mrs. Hillman when she began to suspect him, and then tried to shoot Chan. The prints on the weapon were smudged, so Chan forced the murderer into his trap with the camera and the gun. McCoy, Hannigan and the killer are then carted off to jail.

Finally, Tommy and Wing Fu call with the news of the birth of Charlie's grandson. Chan hands the receiver around as everyone hears the sounds of the newborn crying. The film ends with Charlie cooing "Kootchie, kootchie" into the telephone.

PERFORMANCES

In his debut as Charlie Chan, Sidney Toler clearly shows that his reading is not a carbon copy of Warner Oland's approach. His Chan lacks the placidity and some of the warmth of Oland, but he has more bite and sarcasm. In one aspect, his performance surpasses Oland, and that is with his facial expressions. Sidney Toler is a master of the double-take, and it becomes one of his Chan trademarks. A good example is when Jimmy tries to persuade his father to allow him to stay on the case. He tells Charlie, "Two heads are better than one!" Toler's facial response is an incredible double-take that is both hilarious and totally in character. On the other hand, Toler seems less in control of each situation than Oland. He finds it difficult, in the film's opening to even exercise control over his children at lunch. Not all elements of Toler's reading seem fully in place for this film. This will not happen until the next picture, but Toler makes an excellent start, rendering an effective and credible Chan who could easily carry on the series of films.

Victor Sen Yung has a few rough moments in his debut as Jimmy Chan. It is cumbersome to have Jimmy in the position of impersonating his father, and it actually alienates the audience to some degree. He is unable to win them over until late in the picture, when he saves his father's life. His comic scenes with the lion seem contrived, and overall he has a difficult time taking over from Keye Luke.

Layne Tom, Jr. plays Tommy Chan, pioneering a role later assumed by Benson Fong. There is one clear mistake in the script. When we see the entire Chan family, Tommy is clearly the eldest son at the table after Jimmy. Chan has thirteen children, so all of them are at the table except for Lee at art school, and his daughter married to Wing Fu. However, when Charlie sees him at the ship, he calls him the fifth of his nine sons, when he should have called him his third son.

George Zucco plays one of the most striking and effective of all "red herring" roles in the series as Dr. Cardigan. He is bizarre, sinister and thoroughly entertaining. His "living brain" experiment, however, makes it seem more like he belongs in a Monogram horror film than a Chan murder mystery. Zucco breathes such life and color into his part, that the film brightens whenever his character appears on the scene. His verbal duels with Toler are memorable. At one point, while setting the trap with the camera, Zucco pulls a gun on Toler with insane glee, pleased at catching the detective in a mistake. But he is deflated a moment later when Chan advises him the gun is empty. This little byplay is just a sample of how Zucco manages to enrich the film.

Eddie Collins (Al Hogan) prefigures the technique and style of Lou Costello in many scenes. He can be quite amusing, but both he and Oscar the lion become more of a distraction than anything else. Marc Lawrence and Richard Lane are good as the criminal team posing as a detective and his prisoner.

The actresses, Phyllis Brooks (Judy Hayes) and Claire Dodd (Carol Wayne) are very sharp as the female leads. Philip Ahn, a superb actor, is wonderful as Wing Fu, and it is a shame that his character never appears again in the series. The other players are adequate but not exceptional.

CHARLIE CHAN'S SAYINGS

◇ As mind is fed with silent thought, so should body absorb its Fud.

◇ Bills sometimes more difficult to collect than murder clues.

◇ Hospital is for the sick, not playground for the healthy.

◇ When money talk, few are deaf.

◇ Opinion like tea leaf in hot water, both need time for brewing.

◇ Making bedfellow of serpent, no guarantee against snake bite.

◇ Must compliment sparrow with eye of eagle.

◇ Caution very good life insurance.

◇ Bait only good if fish bite on same.

CHARLIE CHAN IN LONDON
(1934)
Rating: ✱✱✱

FOX. Written by Philip MacDonald; Photographed by L.W. O'Connell; Edited by Alfred De Gaetano; Musical direction by Samuel Kaylin; Produced by John Stone; Directed by Eugene Forde.   79 minutes.

ANNOTATED CAST LIST

Warner Oland..................Charlie Chan
Ray Milland....................Neil Howard (Gray's lawyer)
Douglas Walton..............Paul Gray (Prisoner on death row)
Drue Leyton...................Pamela Gray (His sister)
Alan Mowbray................Geoffrey Richmond (Gray's employer)
Mona Barrie...................Lady Mary Bristol (Richmond's fiancee)
Murray Kinnell...............Phillips (Richmond butler)
Walter Johnson...............Jerry Garton (Old friend of Lady Mary)
George Bernard................Major Jardine (Horseman and Richmond guest)
John Rogers...................Lake (Richmond horse groom)
E. E. Clive.................... Thacker (Stuffy police detective)
Paul England..................Bunny Fothergill (Tipsy guest of Richmond)
Madge Bellamy...............Becky Fothergill (His wife)
David Torrence................Sir Lionel Bashford (Home Secretary)
Perry Ivins....................Kemp (Sir Lionel's private secretary)
Helena Grant.................. Judson (Kemp's assistant)
Claude King...................Commandant (Head of Farnwell Aerodrome)
Reginald Sheffield........... Commander King (Friend of murdered officer)
Montague Shaw..............Doctor
Phyllis Coghlan..............Nurse
Margaret Mann............... Alice Perkins (Richmond maid)

SYNOPSIS AND APPRAISAL

This was the first original Chan story written directly for the screen and not based on a Biggers novel. It is also the start of a series of traveling Chan films, so from London he proceeds directly to Paris, then to Egypt and Shanghai. At 79 minutes, this is the longest film in the Fox and Monogram series, so the picture is a bit slow moving at times. On the positive side, the action concentrates on Chan himself, and we get to follow his every step through the investigation. Another fresh element in the plot, often reused in later pictures, is the time deadline.   Charlie has to race against the clock to save an innocent man. This adds to the suspense, which makes Chan's every question and every move important.

The opening credits are set against the backdrop of Big Ben and Parliament in the fog. Newspaper headlines proclaim Paul Gray will hang for the "Midnight Stable Murder." Pamela Gray, Paul's sister, is fighting desperately to save her brother. She speaks to the Home Secretary, Sir Lionel Bashford, who is unable to help. Kemp, an assistant of Sir Lionel, suggests she consult the famous detective Charlie Chan.

Pamela and her boyfriend, attorney Neil Howard, approach Chan at his hotel. Paul was convicted on circumstantial evidence for killing Captain Hamilton, a guest of Gray's employer Geoffrey Richmond. All appeals have been exhausted, and Gray is to be executed in three days. Pamela runs from the room and throws her engagement ring at Howard when she overhears him admit Gray could conceivably be guilty. Left alone, Charlie retrieves the ring and decides to help the young couple.

Geoffrey Richmond's main interest is fox hunting. Pamela visits him at his vast country estate where a party is in progress. Gray worked for Richmond as hunt secretary. When Chan later arrives, he is refused entrance by Richmond's butler. Charlie climbs in through the window of Pamela's room, and tells her that he spoke with her brother and believes he is innocent. Richmond pledges full co-operation with Chan's investigation, and arranges for him to speak with his guests who testified at Gray's trial. These include Bunny and Becky Fothergill, Lady Mary Bristol, Jerry Garton and Major Jardine. Chan learns that Hamilton and Gray were overheard quarreling in the study on the night of the murder, as they were both in love with the same girl. Two hours later, Jerry Garton and Major Jardine went to the stable to check on Garten's sick horse, and they-discovered Hamilton's body. He was stabbed with an ornamental knife from the wall of Richmond's study.

At the stable, Chan tries to reconstruct the murder with the help of Richmond and his guests. The horses become agitated while this is happening, particularly Lady Mary's horse Hellcat. Lake, the groom, is awakened and tries to calm the animal. Chan is suspicious because Hellcat was not alarmed during the murder. Lake is upset and frightened by Chan's questions, and claims the murder occurred on his night off.

Chan completes a thorough search of the grounds the next morning, and encounters Howard. He has been trying to reconcile with Pamela, but she refuses to see him. When Chan goes to Lake's room above the stable, he encounters Sergeant Thacker of the county police, who is investigating Lake's suicide. Observing the bullet wound in his head and the position of the gun in his hand, Chan proves Lake was murdered. In private he tells Pamela that Lake was paid hush money by Hamilton's real killer, who feared he would talk, so he silenced him permanently.

Major Jardine, now serving as hunt secretary, is busy with preparations for the next fox hunt. He tells Chan he used to be in the air force, like Hamilton. Pamela visits her brother in prison and tells him about Chan's progress, but

Gray is starting to despair.

That night, while Chan is examining the desk in the study, someone fires a dart at him with an air pistol. Thacker wants to launch a full search but Chan is certain the culprit has left. Policemen on the estate arrest Howard for trespassing. Charlie provides Howard with an alibi, saying he telephoned him to come and consult him.

The fox hunt starts early the following day. When Lady Mary hears that someone attempted to shoot Charlie with an airgun, she tries to find the detective. She saw something from her window involving the attack, and writes a note for Becky to deliver to Chan. She then joins the fox hunt. Meanwhile, Chan visits the Farnwell air force base to investigate the late Captain Hamilton. The commandant says he was a fine officer as well as a practical inventor. He was able to make useful improvements on many devices, particularly an air stabilizer. An officer friendly with Hamilton tells Chan he had been working on an aircraft motor silencer.

Receiving Lady Mary's note, Chan asks Howard to help him locate the fox hunt. He fears Lady Mary's life is in danger. Chan is too late, however, because the horsewoman was deliberately injured when pepper was thrown in Hellcat's eyes. The doctor affirms she will recover, but she will remain in a coma for a full day.

With only a few hours remaining before Gray's execution, Chan calls a conference. He believes the plans for Hamilton's latest invention were the actual motive for the crime, and the man who stole the plans is the killer. Chan sets a trap, claiming he knows where the plans are hidden, and fingerprints on the documents will expose the killer. Charlie meets with a suspect in the study, who tries to shoot Chan when his back is turned. The police are concealed in the room and seize the killer. Phillips the butler reveals himself to be an undercover agent for military intelligence, and he asserts the killer is using an alias. His real identity is Paul Franck, a foreign agent.

The film ends as the liberated Paul Gray toasts Chan as "the greatest detective in the world" at a dinner celebration. Charlie modestly replies that he is just lucky. He returns Pamela's engagement ring, which Neil Howard replaces on her finger. "Case now complete," Charlie says in the final fade out.

PERFORMANCES

Warner Oland carries most of this film on his able shoulders. He is resourceful, persistent and extraordinarily polite. His interview with the preoccupied Jardine, for example, is a masterpiece of timing. His byplay with various characters is quite entertaining, particularly when he refers to Hellcat as "Cat of Hell." He also shows Chan as human, capable of making errors. Pamela beseeches him to press Lake for explanations at once, but Chan wants to wait. After Lake's murder, he had to admit this error in judgment, a most poignant moment as the hour of Paul's execution draws near. There are fewer distractions between the character of Chan and the audience than in any other film, and Oland is masterful at making Charlie interesting and appealing.

Ray Milland (Howard) was featured in the first talking British film, *THE FLYING SCOTSMAN* (1929), but had been relegated to minor parts since his arrival in Hollywood. Milland was born Reginald Truscott-Jones in Wales, and he had an extraordinary screen career, playing as many villians as heroes. He was most exceptional as Satan in *ALIAS NICK BEAL* (1949), and he won an Academy Award for his harrowing portrait of an alcoholic in *THE LOST WEEKEND* (1945). This is one of his first major roles, and he is excellent as Neil Howard, the romantic lead. The reliable Drue Leyton is very compelling as heroine Pamela Gray. Her plea to Chan to take the case is very moving. She is also quite effective when imploring Charlie to question Lake at once, instead of waiting. She and Milland make a most interesting couple.

E. E. Clive, forever memorable as the pedantic and stodgy burgomeister in *THE BRIDE OF FRANKENSTEIN* (1935), here plays Detective Sergeant Thacker in a similar vein. He also seems to be hard of hearing and keeps calling Charlie "Mr. Chang." Thacker's method is to write every detail in his notebook, and soon he starts including Charlie's colorful sayings as well.

Murray Kinnell is exceptional as always, this time as Phillips the butler who is also an undercover agent. When reviewing the film, notice how Kinnell does subtle things to indicate this, and his initial belief that Chan is an enemy quickly changes when he learns his true identity.

Other performers, including George Bernard (Jardine), Mona Barrie (Lady Mary) and Walter Johnson (Garton) perform their parts with style and distinction. Douglas Walton is a bit too hammy as Pamela's brother, and his prison histrionics are overdone.

London-born Alan Mowbray was one of the busiest of all character actors. Usually cast as a British country gentleman (as in this film), he was versatile enough to play numerous roles ranging from George Washington in two films to Satan himself (although in a satiric vein quite unlike Milland) in *THE DEVIL WITH HITLER* (1942). He also once played Scotland Yard Inspector Lestrade opposite Reginald Owen as Sherlock Holmes in *A STUDY IN SCARLET* (1933). Mowbray was equally adept at playing sympathetic roles as well as scoundrels. Coincidentally, Mowbray was the father-in-law of another popular character actor often seen in Chan films, Douglass Dumbrille.

CHARLIE CHAN'S SAYINGS

⋄ Front seldom tell truth. Occupants of house always look in back yard. Every front has back.

⋄ Little things tell big story.

⋄ No time to expose lies, must expose truth.

⋄ Englishmen mind own business, not always Chinamen.

◇ Thoughts are like noble animal, unchecked, they run away causing painful smash-up.

◇ Murder not very good joke, quite unfunny.

◇ Case like inside of radio, many connections, not all related.

◇ When death enters window, no time for life to go by door.

◇ If you want wild bird to sing, do not put him in cage.

CHARLIE CHAN IN PANAMA (1940)

Rating: ✳✳✳✳

TWENTIETH CENTURY FOX. Written by John Larkin and Lester Ziffren; Photographed by Virgil Miller; Edited by Fred Allen; Musical direction by Samuel Kaylin; Produced by Edward Kauffman; Directed by Norman Foster. 67 minutes.

ANNOTATED CAST LIST

Sidney Toler....................Charlie Chan
Victor Sen Yung.............Jimmy Chan (Number two son)
Jean Rogers....................Kathi Lenesch (Nightclub singer)
Lionel Atwill.................Cliveden Compton (British novelist)
Mary Nash.....................Jennie Finch (Spinsterly school teacher)
Kane Richmond..............Richard Cabot (American engineer)
Chris-Pin Martin.............Montero (Sergeant who arrests Chan)
Lionel Royce..................Dr. Rudolph Grosser (Viennese scientist)
Jack LaRue....................Emil Manolo (Panamanian cabaret owner)
Edwin Stanley................Col. Webster (Governor of Canal Zone)
Don Douglas..................Captain Lewis (Intelligence officer)
Frank Puglia..................Achmed Halide (Tobacco merchant)
Addison Richards.............R.J. Godley (American secret agent)
Edward Keane.................Dr. Fredericks (Military doctor)
Ed Gargan......................Power plant employee
Helen Ericson.................Airplane stewardess
Lane Chandler.................Corporal at Manola's cabaret
Eddie Acuff....................Sailor at Manola's cabaret
Jimmy Aubrey................Drunk at Manola's cabaret

SYNOPSIS AND APPRAISAL

This is a fascinating "slice of history" film that works on many levels as Charlie Chan saves the American fleet a year before the attack on Pearl Harbor. It also foreshadows Chan's eventual move away from straight murder mysteries to plots involving the secret service during the war years. A colorful cast of characters, a tight plot, and a surprise conclusion elevate this film to rank among Toler's finest efforts.

The film opens in the Panama Canal Zone, where American guards are thwarting some espionage agents from taking illegal photographs. A group of tourists have left their ship and are flying across the Canal Zone to Panama City, including the following passengers: British author Cliveden Compton; a tourist named Godley; engineer Richard Cabot; Chicago grammar school teacher Jennie Finch; European nightclub singer Kathi Lenesch; scientist Rudolf Grosser; tobacco merchant Achmed Halide; and a flashy cabaret owner named Manolo.

Charlie Chan is working with the federal government as an undercover agent in Panama City, posing as a Panama Hat merchant named Fu Yuen. Godley shows up at his store, and gives him a password. He tells Charlie that there will be a sabotage attempt against the American fleet when it passes through the canal on the following day. The mastermind behind the scheme is a devious Nazi secret agent called Reiner, but Godley collapses before he can tell Chan about his tip on identifying Reiner. Since Godley was killed by a poisoned cigarette in his shop, Fu Yuen is arrested on a murder charge by Sergeant Montero.

Jimmy Chan, working as a steward on a ship, is arrested as a spy for taking an illegal photo while on his way to visit his father. In jail together, Charlie reminds his son that he is known as Fu Yuen. Captain Lewis, an intelligence officer familiar with Charlie's real identity, takes him to see the governor, where he reports on the Reiner sabotage plot. Chan is provided with a passenger list of Godley's flight, since that was the only time when the poisoned cigarettes could have been planted. Charlie concludes that Reiner is disguised as one of the passengers.

Jimmy is assigned by his father to investigate Dr. Grosser, a specialist in tropical diseases, while Charlie goes to Manola's cabaret to check on the other suspects. Jimmy overhears a curious conversation on the street between Compton and Halide the tobacconist. When Dr. Grosser leaves his lab, Halide follows him, and Jimmy slips into Grosser's lab where he has a skirmish with an affectionate monkey. He becomes alarmed when he discovers a cage of rats infected with bubonic plague.

At the cabaret, Compton sneaks into Kathi Lenesch's dressing room and rummages through her papers. Sergeant Montero is very surprised to see Fu Yuen free, and starts to question him. A commotion arises when Jennie Finch asks if Fu Yuen is a spy. Jimmy, who has just arrived, becomes concerned for his father's safety and blurts out that he is Charlie Chan. The crowd is startled when they learn his identity, and Charlie comforts his son, saying, "Perhaps it is better to let cat out of bag." Everyone now treats the detective as a major celebrity, and Montero is kidded for having arrested the world famous detective, Charlie Chan.

Returning to Dr. Grosser's lab, Jimmy shows his father what he discovered, but the infected rodents are now missing. Chan also finds Compton's business card in the lab.

Charlie then goes to Compton's hotel, where most of the suspects have also gathered in the cafe. Manolo seems to be blackmailing Kathi Lenesch. When Chan sneaks into Compton's room, he finds Jimmy already on the scene. Someone points a gun at Charlie from the balcony, but Jimmy knocks it away by throwing a humidor at the weapon. The assailant vanishes, and Charlie praises his son for his baseball skills, saying, "Aim already perfect!" The broken humidor contains Kathi Lenesch's identity card and a map of the cemetery. Moments later, Lenesch breaks into Compton's room, and is startled to run into Chan. She admits that she is actually Baroness von Czardas and is terribly frightened of being sent back to Europe because she has no passport. After Chan releases her, Jimmy finds Compton's body in the closet.

Going next door to Manola's room, Charlie calls military intelligence. When Jimmy gives Manolo a cigarette, Chan pretends they were Godley's cigarettes. The man panics, and Chan confronts the cabaret owner, saying only the police and the killer know about the poisoned cigarettes. Manolo knocks over his lamp and flees. A ballistics test proves that Manola's gun killed Compton.

The next day, Chan and Captain Lewis explore the cemetery using Compton's map. Jennie Finch approaches them, saying a man is trapped in one of the tombs. It turns out to be Jimmy, who trailed Halide to the spot before being knocked out. There is a secret chamber beneath the tomb, which contains a large quantity of liquid explosives as well as a make-up table loaded with many disguises. Some empty containers alert Chan that a huge bomb has been planted somewhere. When they try to leave, they find that they have been locked in the tomb.

Manolo, in disguise as a water cooler delivery man, places the nitroglycerin at the power control station for the canal. He sets a special timer on the device. It is night by the time he returns to the cemetery to drop off equipment in the secret hideout, but he unknowingly releases Captain Lewis, the Chans and Jennie Finch from the tomb. They try to capture the saboteur, but he is shot while trying to escape in the darkness. Jennie Finch asserts having seen the gunman who killed him. A close examination of Manolo's body reveals a pass to the power station, a clear indication of the intended target of the sabotage. The destruction of the power station would render the canal helpless, and trap the ships within the locks for an indefinite period.

The authorities are alerted to search the power station, but to no avail. Since the American fleet has already entered the canal, Chan orders that all passengers from the plane flight be brought to the site. He is gambling that Reiner will crack before the plant explodes. Halide accuses Dr. Grosser of being Reiner, who in turn charges Halide with stealing his plague-infested lab rats. The Egyptian admits stealing and destroying the rats which he fears is intended for germ warfare, and he explains that he was working with Compton, who was a British secret agent. He also tells Chan that he suspects that his cometary vault is being used for nefarious purposes. Finally, one of the suspects draws a gun, and tries to escape, but runs into the arms of military intelligence officers. Chan reveals that there was no real danger because the detonator had been located earlier. It was his only chance to expose the enemy agent. Chan also explains how cleverly Reiner had acted and how Manolo was killed.

The film concludes as Chan, the authorities and other cast members watch the American fleet passing safely through the canal on their way to Pearl Harbor.

"Intelligent defense of nation best guarantee for years of peace," intones Chan in the picture's final line, which foreshadows the Japanese attack to follow a year later. The soundtrack blares *Anchors aweigh* as the end credits appear on the screen.

PERFORMANCES

Sidney Toler gets a chance to play some variations on his usual Chan performance in this film. First, there is his undercover portrayal as Fu Yuen, who is quieter and far more humble than Charlie. Unfortunately, Jimmy gives away his disguise far too early in the plot to observe any additional subtleties in the Fu Yuen role. Second, there is a harder-edged Chan who forces a group of suspects at gunpoint to endure exposure to a possible massive explosion. It is a form of extreme psychological torture in which the innocent suffer as much as the guilty, since none of them knows the detonator has been deactivated. It is a cruel ploy, very atypical for Chan, and Toler makes it quite believable.

Victor Sen Yung also has some unusual moments that stress the bravery of Jimmy. He has to be held back by military police when he wants to join his father to face the risk of the power plant explosion. He is also quick enough to save his father's life when he spots a gun trained on him. His comic exploration of Dr. Grosser's chemical lab is also well done, particularly his encounter with the lab monkey.

Mary Nash steals the film with her multi-layered portrayal as Jennie Finch. It is a rich performance that can only be fully appreciated after several viewings. Lionel Atwill is splendid as Compton, although he appears far too briefly to be fully enjoyed. Jack LaRue (Manolo), Frank Puglia (Halide) and Lionel Royce (Grosser) are fascinating and colorful in their parts. Kane Richmond (Cabot), however, is rather bland and flat in his role, and Jean Rogers' song would not have been missed if cut. As for comic relief, Chris-Pin Martin is hilarious as the embarrassed police sergeant who arrests Chan. His interaction with Mary Nash is also very well done.

CHARLIE CHAN'S SAYINGS

  ◇ Thousand friends too few...one enemy one too many.

  ◇ Man without relatives is man without troubles.

  ◇ When prepared for worst, can hope for best.

  ◇ Young brain, like grass, need dew of sleep.

  ◇ Truth win more friendship than lies.

  ◇ Bad alibi, like dead fish, cannot stand test of time.

  ◇ No heart strong enough to hold bullet.

◇ Nerves make time crawl backward.

◇ Dividing line between folly and wisdom very faint.

◇ Patience lead to knowledge.

CHARLIE CHAN IN PARIS (1935)
Rating: *****

FOX. Written by Edward T. Lowe and Stuart Anthony; Story by Philip Mac-Donald; Edited by Alfred de Gaetano; Musical direction by Samuel Kaylin; Produced by John Stone; Directed by Lewis Seiler. 70 minutes.

ANNOTATED CAST LIST

Warner Oland.................. Charlie Chan
Keye Luke...................... Lee Chan (Number one son)
Henry Kolker.................. Paul Lamartine (Bank President)
Mary Brian.................... Yvette Lamartine (His daughter)
Thomas Beck.................. Victor Descartes (Bank Clerk)
Eric Rhodes................... Max Corday (Tipsy playboy and artist)
John Miljan................... Albert Dufresne (Yvette's old boyfriend)
Murray Kinnell...............Henri Latouche (Bank official)
Minor Watson................ Renard (Parisian police inspector)
Dorothy Appleby............Nardi (Apache dancer)
Ruth Peterson................ Renee Jacquard (Corday's girlfriend)
Perry Ivins................... Bedell (Lamartine's secretary)
John Qualen.................. Concierge
Henry Cording............... Gendarme
"?"............................. Marcel Xavier (Crippled beggar and killer)

SYNOPSIS AND APPRAISAL

This film was once considered lost, but film historian and producer Alex Gordon located a print at the Czech Film Archive, and the Museum of Modern Art in New York arranged a trade for the print, which was restored and made available on home video. This is a major Chan film, featuring the debut of Keye Luke as "Number one son" Lee Chan. The plot has many unusual aspects, as Charlie is seen working outside regular police jurisdiction, and winds up concealing and even destroying evidence. This picture was meant to be seen as the direct sequel to *CHARLIE CHAN IN LONDON* and there are numerous references to the events of that film.

The picture opens with scenes of Paris at night, and segues into Chan's arrival at *Bourget Airport*. His departure from the plane is observed by a crippled beggar wearing dark glasses and a thick moustache. The man, a war veteran named Marcel Xavier, approaches Chan for a handout. In the airline terminal, Charlie telephones Nardi, a famous nightclub dancer who is working as an undercover agent. She explains she has made a number of important discoveries, and they arrange to meet later. He then travels by taxi to visit his friend Victor Descartes, with whom he arranges an appointment the next morning at the Lamartine Bank.

Descartes is planning a night on the town, and he introduces Charlie to his fiancee Yvette Lamartine, daughter of the bank president. Max Corday, an artist with a fondness for drink, draws a quick sketch of Charlie. They escort Charlie to the *Cafe du Singe Bleu*, where Nardi is featured. As the group emerges from their taxi, Max Corday bumps into Marcel Xavier, and he gives the beggar a tip.

Nardi performs an acrobatic Apache dance, which concludes when her partner tosses her through a prop window. Hiding offstage, Xavier throws a knife at the dancer. She screams, and Chan rushes to her side. With her dying words, Nardi tells Charlie to search her suite. He breaks into her apartment, but is interrupted by the arrival of the police. He overhears Inspector Renard speak glowingly of him while he hides on the balcony. After they leave, Charlie finds Nardi's notebook hidden inside a cuckoo clock. Marcel Xavier attempts to kill Charlie by toppling a heavy stone pillar from the roof which narrowly misses the detective in the street below.

At his hotel, Charlie finds the door to his room unlocked. Lee emerges from the bathroom, his head covered with a towel. Charlie draws a gun, and Lee exclaims, "Hello Pop! What's the matter? Did I scare you?" They embrace warmly as Lee explains he completed his business trip to Rome, so they now can enjoy sightseeing together in Paris. Charlie explains that he is actually working on a case, and Lee is upset when he learns about the attempt on his father's life. Charlie agrees to let Lee work with him.

Next morning, as Chan arrives at the Lamartine Bank, Marcel Xavier is having an argument with bank official Henri Latouche, and he is ejected from the premises. Albert Dufresne, another employee who once romanced Yvette Lamartine, has kept her old letters to him. He now suggests that she visit his apartment if she wants them back. In his meeting with bank president Paul Lamartine, Chan explains that the bank's last bond offering contained forgeries. He was hired by banking clients in London to quietly investigate the fraud. Since publicity about the bonds would cause a bank panic, Chan is keeping his inquiry private, without informing the police. Lamartine is shocked by Chan's revelation, and promises his full cooperation in tracking down the forgeries. Charlie assigns Lee the task of trailing Dufresne, whose name appeared in Nardi's report.

That evening, Charlie dines with Inspector Renard. At his apartment, Dufresne is packing his bags. He argues on the phone about the forgeries with a criminal colleague who warns him not to flee. Yvette then pays him a visit. She is afraid that Dufresne will attempt to blackmail her, but he merely gives her the letters, saying he is not the villain she imagines him to be. Meanwhile, Marcel Xavier sneaks into Dufresne's apartment, and shoots him from an adjoining room. The killer tosses the gun into the room and slips away. Yvette panics when the concierge knocks at the door, and she picks up the gun and attempts to make an escape. A gendarme appears at the door and arrests her. In the street below, Lee has been noting all these comings and goings.

Renard is summoned to the murder scene, and asks Chan to accompany him. The inspector believes Yvette is guilty, and challenges her every statement. Behind the scenes, Chan motions for her to cooperate. He finds half of a broken bank seal on the floor in the next room, and discovers evidence that someone had climbed onto the balcony. Max Corday and his girlfriend show up at the apartment, asking to see Dufresne. He sobers up when he learns of his friend's murder. Meanwhile, Chan whispers a few questions to Yvette, who hands him the love letters she retrieved from Dufresne, and he promises to destroy them. Charlie then shows Renard the evidence that another party had broken into the apartment.

Posing as a chauffeur, Lee tells his father about his surveillance. He spotted Marcel Xavier leaving the building after the shots were fired. The cripple got into a taxi and later transferred over to a limousine. Lee was unable to follow the limousine, but he spotted the same car moments later back at Dufresne's apartment when Max Corday emerged with his girlfriend.

At Corday's apartment, Chan plays a clever game of cat and mouse with the artist about the identity of Marcel Xavier. Corday reminds him that Xavier had bumped into him on the street outside the *Cafe du Singe Bleu*, so hc couldn't be Xavier. After Chan leaves, Corday prepares to escape, but Charlie and his son are actually waiting for him outside his apartment. They capture the man, and Lee ties him up in his parlor. Chan finds some stolen bonds in Corday's luggage, as well as the other half of the broken bank seal. The detective accuses Corday of Dufresne's murder, and his unknown partner of the murder of Nardi, but Corday remains silent.

Charlie leaves Lee in charge of Corday, and goes to the bank where he obtains Xavier's address from Henri LaTouche. Victor Descartes, eager to clear Yvette, asks to assist Chan. They break into Xavier's dingy and oddly shaped underground flat. Against one wall they locate a secret passageway into the sewer. Charlie's remarks, "Many strange crimes are committed in the sewers of Paris." They locate a hidden chamber in the sewer which contains a printing press and engraving tools. This is where the Lamartine bank forgeries were created. Moments later, a figure arrives and a battle breaks out as Chan discovers the identity of Xavier.

Back at Corday's apartment, Lee interrupts a phone call alerting him that his father will be attacked at Xavier's flat. He contacts the police, and they storm Xavier's rooms. After locating the sewer passage, Renard finds Chan in control of the situation, as he hands over Corday's partner. He explains that Dufresne, Corday and Nardi's killer were partners in the bank fraud scheme. Marcel Xavier never existed, but was a character created by the forgers to give each other perfect alibis. Chan also tells Renard that Yvette went to Dufresne's apartment on his instructions, keeping secret her old letters. Renard feels that Charlie is being gallant, and congratulates him for solving the case.

PERFORMANCES

Warner Oland delivers a powerful performance enhanced by the presence of Keye Luke. The obvious warmth and affection between Charlie and Lee considerably broadens and enriches the character of Chan. The script provides him with many impressive moments, particularly when Nardi is killed. This is the only film where Charlie resorts to pidgin English after he is introduced to Max Corday. The artist asks him if he would like a "lil' dlinkey." Chan replies quite formally, then includes a mocking conclusion in pidgin English which puts Corday in his place. An ironic scene has Charlie hiding on Nardi's balcony. He eavesdrops on Renard, who is wondering what his old friend Charlie Chan is doing at the moment. Charlie's sneezing fit adds to the humor of the situation. The final shootout in the sewer is very suspenseful.

Keye Luke's debut as Lee Chan is most impressive, and sets up a wonderful new dynamic which is fully explored in future films. His youthful enthusiasm, genuine intelligence and filial love make Lee of incomparable importance to the series. The occasional generational and cultural clash between the Americanized Lee and his father is another important element added to the Chan formula.

There are some problems with some of the supporting characters who play Frenchmen as if they are Englishmen. This is particularly annoying with Eric Rhodes, whose Max Corday comes across as a dissipated English squire. He skirts in and out of drunkenness, which is exaggerated because his character is not really drunk but only pretending. His verbal sparring with Chan when the detective visits his apartment is excellent. The writers had some fun with references to French history in naming their characters. For instance, in July 1793, Charlotte Corday was the assassin of Jean Paul Marat, a revolutionary extremist who reportedly printed a newspaper while hiding out in the Parisian sewers.

Thomas Beck (Descartes), John Miljan (Dufresne) and Murray Kinnell (LaTouche) are adequate but not exceptional in their roles. The actresses are more impressive overall, particularly Mary Brian (Yvette) and Dorothy Appleby (Nardi). Brian is masterful in the scene where she is questioned by the police. Appleby is quite appealing, even if a stuntwoman replaces her during the more spectacular moments of her Apache dance, which remains the most entertaining of the many stage routines used in the series.

CHARLIE CHAN'S SAYINGS

◇ It is always good fortune to give alms upon entering a city.

◇ Young bird must learn to fly.

◇ Youth tonic for old blood.

◇ Mud turtle in pond more safe than man on horseback.

◇ Joy in heart more desirable than bullet.

◇ Kindness in heart better than gold in bank.

◇ Only foolish man waste words when argument is lost.

◇ Perfect case like perfect doughnut, have hole...Optimist only sees doughnut. Pessimist sees hole.

◇ Silence big sister to wisdom.

◇ Hasty conclusion like gunpowder, easy to explode.

◇ Very difficult to explain hole in doughnut, but hole always there.

◇ Eyes of kitten open only after nine days.

◇ Little keyhole big friend to stupid detective.

◇ Canary bird out of cage may fly far.

◇ Faith is best foundation for happy future.

◇ Grain of sand in eye may hide mountain.

CHARLIE CHAN IN RENO   (1939)
Rating: ****

TWENTIETH CENTURY FOX. Written by Francis Hyland, Albert Ray and Robert E. Kent; Photographed by Virgil Miller; Edited by Fred Allen; Musical direction by Samuel Kaylin; Produced by John Stone; Directed by Norman Foster. 70 minutes.

ANNOTATED CAST LIST

Sidney Toler...................Charlie Chan
Victor Sen Yung.............Jimmy Chan (Number two son)
Ricardo Cortez................Dr. Ainsley (Hotel physician)
Phyllis Brooks................Vivian Wells (Hotel social director)
Slim Summerville...........Tombstone Fletcher (Reno sheriff)
Pauline Moore................Mary Whitman (Woman charged with murder)
Kane Richmond..............Curtis Whitman (Her estranged husband)
Kay Linaker...................Mrs. Russell (Hotel owner)
Louise Henry.................Jeanne Bentley (Murdered socialite)
Morgan Conway............. George Bentley (Victim's husband)
Robert Lowery...............Wally Burke (Jeanne's boyfriend)
Eddie Collins..................Hotel driver
Charles D. Brown...........King (Reno chief of police)
Iris Wong......................Choy Wong (Mrs. Bentley's maid)
Hamilton MacFadden....... Sierra Hotel desk clerk

SYNOPSIS AND APPRAISAL

The second film of the Toler/Fox series clearly establishes a successful formula as every element clicks smoothly into place. The basic plot was adapted from a story by Philip Wylie called *DEATH MAKES A DECREE*, but it clearly blends seamlessly into the Chan milieu. The revenge elements of the story easily parallel the typical plot in Biggers' novels. The direction by Norman Foster is crisp and lively, making this picture a total delight.

The picture opens with a jazzy montage of the gambling casinos in Reno, Nevada. Mary Whitman arrives at the Sierra Hotel, where she meets Vivian Wells, the hotel's social director. Jeanne Bentley, who wants to marry Mary's estranged husband, taunts her rival in the hotel lounge, and also argues with Wally Burke, her old boyfriend. Mrs. Russell, owner of the Sierra, asks Bentley to vacate the hotel in the morning. Dr. Ainsley, the hotel physician, tries to calm the woman down, but she angrily storms off. Shortly after, Choy Wong, her maid, arrives to find Mrs. Bentley dead in her room with Mary Whitman standing over the body. Newspaper headlines reveal that Mary Whitman has been charged with the crime.

In Honolulu, Mary's estranged husband asks Chan to come at once to help his wife. The Reno Police chief welcomes Charlie with enthusiasm, but his presence annoys deadpan Sheriff Tombstone Fletcher. He and Charlie trade some clever quips. Jimmy drives from the University of Southern California to meet his father, but he gets held up and stripped of his clothes by car thieves just outside of Reno. While talking with Tombstone at the police station, Charlie is startled to see Jimmy half-naked in the line-up. He quickly vouches for him and gives him funds to buy a new wardrobe.

Mary is interviewed by Chan at police headquarters. She describes finding Mrs. Bentley's body after investigating a scream in the room next door. Mary didn't even recognize Bentley because she was wearing a beauty mask. She bent down to touch the body as the Chinese maid entered the room. Charlie argues for the release of Mary because Jeanne Bentley was stabbed to death, but no weapon was found on Mary or in Bentley's room. Tombstone disagrees, but Chan's logic convinces the Chief.

When questioning the owner and social director of the hotel, Chan learns that Jeanne Bentley was strongly disliked by many people. She was in the process of divorcing George Bentley, who has yet to be located despite the publicity of the murder. One of the hotel maids reports her passkey has been stolen. Chan explores the murder room, catching Dr. Ainsley in the act of searching it. He tells Chan he was looking for the money Mrs. Bentley won the night of her death. Tombstone prevents Wally Burke from leaving town. Previously strapped for funds, Burke now appears to have a great deal of money. Chan arranges to occupy the murder room during his hotel stay.

Jimmy looks through Jeanne Bentley's scrapbook, filled with her society news clippings. This intrigues Chan because no scissors were found in the room. The pages for the years 1935 and 1936 are missing from the scrapbook.

Charlie throws a party in the hotel lounge for the doctor, the owner, the social director and Wally Burke. Tombstone is flabbergasted by Chan's approach to the case, particularly when he sees him mixing drinks for the suspects. Everyone is startled when Curtis and Mary Whitman enter the lounge together. Under the detective's questioning, the suspects start to argue, and a fistfight breaks out between Burke and Ainsley. Tombstone gets knocked out while trying to break it up. Meanwhile, Jimmy discovers that Burke had been cabled $1,500, explaining his sudden wealth.

An intruder enters the hotel room, and is tackled by Jimmy, but it turns out to be Choy Wong who has been given permission to pack up Mrs. Bentley's belongings. Charlie questions her, and learns Mrs. Bentley went riding the day before her death. Her muddy boots indicate she spent a long time on foot. Jimmy and Choy Wong become acquainted and chat about the case.

An analysis of the mud at police headquarters detects wooden splinters, red clay and copper shavings. Chief King suggests she might have visited a nearby ghost town. Chan heads off to explore the site that night with the hotel driver. Tombstone Fletcher, following Charlie, also shows up. It is a very atmospheric sequence, featuring a brooding search through dilapidated buildings, with the howls of coyotes filling the background. At one point, Chan falls through the floorboards of a building. He eventually locates a car, and notices a light in one of the buildings. A man attacks him, and their battle in the dark is interrupted when Tombstone mistakenly tackles Charlie. The assailant escapes by car, and Chan explores his hideout, where he finds a mining engineer's kit with a bill of sale to George Bentley, the murdered woman's husband.

Back at the hotel, Jimmy catches Burke trying to sneak out of the hotel with a pair of scissors. Burke claims Mrs. Bentley borrowed them from him and never returned them. Suspecting they are the murder weapon, he believes Dr. Ainsley planted them in his room, and he was trying to dispose of them. The other suspects also claim finding scissors in their rooms, the result of a scheme by Jimmy and Choy Wong to smoke out the killer. Curtis Whitman also found scissors in Mary's room, but these were not planted by Choy Wong. In fact, this pair was the actual murder weapon. Tombstone heads off to see the District Attorney to demand the rearrest of Mary.

Chan questions Mary about a burn on her sleeve. Examining the floor of the room, Charlie finds an acid burn on the rug, which Jimmy believes is nitric acid, and when Dr. Ainsley is questioned about his bottle of nitric acid, he thinks a portion of his bottle is missing. Chan notices each of all of the doctor's medicine bottles have a gauze seal, but the nitric acid has a different style of gauze. The next day, Chief King reports George Bentley was apprehended, and that a report from Jeanne Bentley's bank reveals she had been making large payoffs to Dr. Ainsley. An examination of the newspaper files reveals that in 1935, Mrs. Bentley was married to Mrs. Russell's ex-husband, and that in 1936, Wayne Russell died while under the care of Dr. Ainsley. Jimmy reports Mrs. Russell was attacked and strangled, but not killed. Chan prevents Dr. Ainsley from treating her with an injection.

Jimmy discovers the gauze in Mrs. Russell's bathroom matches the gauze on the bottle of nitric acid. Charlie orders all suspects to dress in the clothes they wore on the night of the murder and gather at the crime scene. George Bentley, under arrest, is brought by Tombstone to the hotel. Chan sums up the evidence and possible motives of each suspect. George Bentley claims he was hired as a mining engineer to inspect the ghost town mine. He hid out at the town so it wouldn't interfere with his divorce proceedings. He jumped Chan because he thought he was a robber. The reason Jeanne visited him was that she desperately needed $5,000, but he had little money with him.

Chan accuses Dr. Ainsley of blackmailing Jeanne Bentley because she murdered Wayne Russell. Mrs. Russell admits she obtained the nitric acid to disfigure Jeanne Bentley, but did not carry out her attack when she found her wearing a beauty mask. They argued, and some acid spilled, but she left Jeanne unharmed. The suspects start accusing each other of the crime. Chan and Jimmy play a trick that reveals the killer, who is arrested and taken away, after eloquently explaining the motive for the crime. Dr. Ainsley is also arrested for blackmail and attempted murder, because the syringe he was planning to inject into Mrs. Russell contained poison. The film ends with Tombstone's frustration over the case, and Jimmy's budding romance with Choy Wong.

PERFORMANCES

Sidney Toler confidently makes the Chan role his own in his second performance. He not only handles the dramatic moments, but reveals a knack for humor more incisive than Oland's gentler style. His double take when Jimmy appears in the line-up is a great example. His friendly rivalry with Tombstone is also rich and quite amusing. At one point, after Tombstone is struck by a bottle, Charlie says, "Think head needs examination," with an obvious double meaning. The cocktail party scene is well organized, where Charlie plays an amiable host mixing the drinks, and gently probing with leading questions. Finally, the lengthy ghost town sequence includes some marvelous scenes of Toler, both in lamplight and in total darkness, that clearly help to establish him as a more active Chan.

This is Victor Sen Yung's best performance as Jimmy Chan. He seldom has so rich an opportunity as Jimmy in future films. His comic timing is deft, and he shows a vast improvement over his debut in the role in *CHARLIE CHAN IN HONOLULU*. His relationship with Toler never becomes as warm on screen as that between Oland and Keye Luke. On the surface, Chan is often quite biting in his criticisms of Jimmy, yet his fatherly affection still manifests itself in sometimes unexpected ways. Sen Yung's romance with Choy Wong is very well handled.

Slim Summerville's role as Tombstone, a witty, rustic lawman, may be the finest comic Chan sidekick in the entire series. Their rivalry and begrudging mutual respect is priceless and enjoyable to watch. His dry mutterings and his byplay with Chan are among the highlights of the film. One good exchange is when Charlie invites Tombstone to join him in his search of the murder scene. Tombstone says, "I've been through that room so much, I could search it with eyes shut." Charlie responds, "Will search then this time with eyes open." Tombstones exclamation "Horse feathers!" becomes another running gag in the film.

The performances of other cast members are equally strong and compelling. Series regulars Kane Richmond (Curtis Whitman), Pauline Moore (Mary Whitman), Kay Linaker (Mrs. Russell) and Robert Lowery (Wally Burke) have never been finer. Linaker in particular performs with an added sparkle to her polished reading. Ricardo Cortez (Ainsley), Louise Henry (Jeanne Bentley) and Iris Wong (Choy Wong) are also colorful and top-drawer in their parts.

Hamilton MacFadden, the director of *THE BLACK CAMEL* and other early Chan pictures has a wonderful cameo as the desk clerk. The only weak performance is by Eddie Collins as the loquacious hotel driver, but fortunately he becomes far more palatable after Chan threatens him with the possibility of being a witness in court.

CHARLIE CHAN'S SAYINGS

- ⋄ Man yet to be born who can tell what woman will or will not do.
- ⋄ Very difficult to believe ill of those we love.
- ⋄ Tombstones often engraved with words of wisdom.
- ⋄ Ancient ancestor once say, "Words cannot cook rice."
- ⋄ Charming company turn lonely sandwich into rich banquet.
- ⋄ If want wild bird to sing, do not put him in cage.
- ⋄ When searching for needle in haystack, haystack only sensible location.
- ⋄ Sometimes must strike innocent to trap guilty.
- ⋄ Praise in any language very sweet.
- ⋄ Sometimes tears from woman very happy sign.

CHARLIE CHAN IN RIO (1941)

Rating: *

TWENTIETH CENTURY FOX. Written by Samuel G. Engel and Lester Ziffren; Photographed by Joseph P. MacDonald; Edited by Alexander Troffey; Musical direction by Emil Newman with additional music and lyrics by Mack Gordon and Harry Warren; Produced by Sol M. Wurtzel; Directed by Harry Lachman. 60 minutes.

ANNOTATED CAST LIST

Sidney Toler...................Charlie Chan
Victor Sen Yung.............Jimmy Chan (Number two son)
Victor Jory.....................Alfredo Marana (Psychic)
Jacqueline Dalya..............Lola Deane (Nighclub entertainer)
Ted North......................Clark Denton (Wealthy bachelor)
Mary Beth Hughes...........Joan Reynolds (Lola's friend)
Richard Derr...................Ken Reynolds (Joan's husband)
Corbina Wright, Jr..........Grace Ellis (Lola's friend)
Hamilton MacFadden.......Bill Kellogg (Grace's escort)
Harold Huber..................Senor Souto (Rio police chief)
Kay Linaker...................Helen Ashby (Secretary of Lola Deane)
Truman Bradley...............Paul Wagner (Lola's ex-husband)
Leslie Dennison..............Rice (Butler of Lola Deane)
Iris Wong......................Lily Wong (Maid of Lola Deane)
Eugene Borden................Armando (Souto's aide)
Ann Codee....................Margo (Cook)

SYNOPSIS AND APPRAISAL

This film is a reworking of *THE BLACK CAMEL* grafted onto a South American setting. The plot is further padded with Latin dance numbers, popular at the time. The result is the one of the weaker films in the Toler/Fox series, highlighted by a few clever moments at the film's climax. The main weakness is that this picture just seems tossed off, compared to the brilliant film which inspired it.

The credits roll over a view of the world famous beach at Rio de Janeiro while a hot rumba number blares on the soundtrack. The film segues directly to the floor show at the Carioca Casino where Charlie and Jimmy are guests of Rio police chief Souto. Jimmy accompanies the music with vigorous shaking of his own maracas. Chan is in Brazil to arrest singer Lola Deane for murdering a man in Honolulu two years earlier.

Backstage at the club, Clark Denton has just proposed to Lola, who plans a supper party to celebrate. Many of her friends are in the audience, as she sings *They met in Rio*. Back in her dressing room, Lola receives a bouquet of flowers from Paul Wagner, her former husband. Lola stops on her way home to consult Marana, the famous mystic. He drugs her, and asks her about Manuel Cardosa, with whom she was madly in love. Cardosa refused to divorce his wife, so she killed him. When she awakes, Lola has no memory of her confession. Marana starts to speak about Cardosa when Clark Denton arrives to escort her home.

Lola impulsively persuades Denton to elope with her at once, and she instructs her staff to help her pack. Her cook, butler and maid discuss how Lola's marriage will affect them. Meanwhile, the entertainer's friends start to gather for her late night party, and they discuss her engagement.

Finally, Chan and Souto arrive, demanding to see Lola. Her maid, Lily Wong, finds her stabbed in the back, and Chan starts to investigate her murder. Jimmy discovers a number of clues on the floor near the body, including a crushed corsage, a platinum broach and a handkerchief monogrammed with the letter "W" and a broken wristwatch. The watch had stopped at 12:15, but the maid reports Lily arrived home at 12:30. Chan notes that the stem of the watch was in the time-setting position, so the murderer deliberately tried to mislead investigators about the time.

Souto, Jimmy and Charlie make numerous observations about the crime, particularly that the clues were arranged to deceive. Chan asks Helen Ashby, Lola's secretary, to open the wall safe, where her jewel box is found empty. As Souto inspects the other rooms, Charlie suddenly grills Lily, and declares her innocent. He then gives his tacit blessing to a romance between Lily and Jimmy, who seem attracted to each other.

Helen Ashby recounts to Chan about Lola's activities during her final hours, including her meeting with Marana and her elopement plans with Denton. The remaining guests are also questioned: Ken Reynolds; Clark Denton; Grace Ellis and Bill Kellogg. The police also send for Marana the psychic and Paul Wagner who sent Lola flowers at the nightclub.

The coroner reports that Lola was murdered while bending over, probably packing. Chan concludes the victim was unaware of any danger. Out in the garden, Lily teaches Jimmy the samba, when Joan, the drunken wife of Ken Reynolds, stumbles in. When she learns of Lola's death, she says, "Somebody beat me to it!" She then accuses Grace Ellis of the crime in front of everyone.

Joan has a gun that Chan determines was recently fired, and he pretends that Lola was killed by a gun. Charlie and Jimmy converse in Chinese, and Charlie instructs his son to pocket Joan's weapon.

Paul Wagner and Marana arrive. Wagner is upset at being pulled off his boat at two in the morning. He admits that he was Lola Deane's former husband and that he sneaked in to visit her earlier that evening. When he learned of her plans to remarry, Lola had Rice, her butler, escort him to the door.

Marana is then examined, and he plays Lola's confession on a phonograph record. He explains that she was drugged by a combination of an herb in her cigarette that interacts with caffeine from coffee. Chan reveals that Marana is really Manuel Cardosa's brother. The psychic explains he "compelled" Helen Ashby to suggest to Lola to consult him. Jimmy mocks the psychic's story, who offers to demonstrate the procedure on Jimmy. After smoking the herbal cigarette and drinking coffee, Jimmy slips into a trance. Charlie questions him and learns a number of Jimmy's recent deceptions, including how the car at home became dented.

Refreshments are served to everyone while Chan studies the crime scene. He discovers the end of the pin from the broach had snapped off, and perhaps the murderer's shoes picked it up. He and Souto examine the floor in the dining room and locate some pin scratches. Jimmy catches the butler rummaging through the crime scene, and nabs him after a fight. Rice confesses to stealing the jewels. He also claims he knows the identity of the killer. The lights are then snapped off, and the butler is shot. The murder weapon was the gun which was lifted from Jimmy's pocket.

Chan makes the guests resume their original seating arrangements in the dining room, which show that Helen Ashby's shoes have the incriminating broken pin. Charlie suggests that the secretary smoke one of Marana's herbal cigarettes with coffee, and submit to questioning.

After falling under the influence of the drug, Helen reveals no knowledge of the crimes. Other suspects offer to go through the same procedure with the drug when Charlie announces he will try it himself. This opportunity delights Jimmy, and Marana offers Charlie a fresh cigarette, but instead he uses the same one smoked by Helen. Unexpectedly, Chan's experiment leads directly to the solution to the murders. The picture ends as Charlie lets his son know about a message he received from Honolulu. Jimmy has received his draft notice for military service.

PERFORMANCES

Sidney Toler's work in this film has a nice range, from bemusement with Jimmy's interest in Iris, to irritation with his deceptions. Most of his aphorisms seem lame in this story, and he delivers each of them as throwaway lines, without any of his usual relish. The highlight of this picture is his extravagant mugging as he smokes Marana's cigarette. It is perhaps Toler's hammiest scene in the entire series, and a particularly treasured moment for every Chan fan.

Victor Sen Yung delivers a winning performance after his overdone scenes in the nightclub. His finest moments occur when he falls victim to Marana's cigarettes that act like a truth serum. He reveals he lied about damaging Charlie's car and the reason for his poor math grades. On the other hand, his genuine feelings for Lily are also revealed by the drug. In fact, Jimmy's relations with Lily (Iris Wong) makes for a very entertaining subplot. Their romance is nipped in the bud, however, when he learns about his draft notice. But he faces it with bravura, saying, "With me in it, it's in the bag. This war is..." "A cinch?" injects Charlie, completing Jimmy's thought.

Victor Jory underplays the role of the mystic, and he suffers in comparison to Bela Lugosi's rendition of the same part in *THE BLACK CAMEL*. Harold Huber (Souto) is superlative as the Brazilian police chief who works with Chan, but then Huber is always good except when he is cast as a Frenchman. Truman Bradley (Wagner) is also good in his too brief role as Lola Deane's husband. Hamilton MacFadden, the director of *THE BLACK CAMEL*, gives a textbook performance as one of the bystanders. It must have been a difficult film for him, knowing the excellence of his original picture with this tepid remake.

Except for Kay Linaker (Ashby) and Iris Wong, the actresses in the story give rather flat performances. Jacqueline Dalya is absolutely dreadful as Lola, and her warbling nightclub song provides one of the lowest points in the Toler/Fox series.

CHARLIE CHAN'S SAYINGS

◇ Interesting problem in chemistry...sweet wine often turn nice woman sour.

◇ Biggest mistakes in history made by people who didn't think.

◇ Pretty girl, like lap dog, sometimes go mad.

◇ Long experience teach, until murderer found, suspect everybody.

◇ (Spoken to Jimmy in Chinese and translated in subtitles) Good policy to have murderer consider detective dope.

◇ Slippery man sometimes slip in own oil.

◇ Experience teach, unless eyewitness present, every murder case is longshot.

◇ Prefer not to walk across before coming to bridge.

◇ To one who kill, life can suddenly become most precious.

◇ Fruits of labor sometimes very bitter.

CHARLIE CHAN IN SHANGHAI
(1935)
Rating: ✶✶✶✶✶

FOX. Written by Edward T. Lowe and Gerard Fairlie; Photographed by Barney McGill; Edited by Nick De Maggio; Musical direction by Samuel Kaylin; Produced by John Stone; Directed by James Tinling. 70 minutes.

ANNOTATED CAST LIST

Warner Oland..................Charlie Chan
Keye Luke...................... Lee Chan (Number one son)
David Torrence................Sir Stanley Woodland (Secret agent)
Irene Hervey...................Diana Woodland (His niece)
Jon Hall........................ Philip Nash (Secretary to Woodland)
Russell Hicks.................James Andrews (American secret agent)
Halliwell Hobbes............ Colonel Watkins (Chief of police)
Neil Fitzgerald................ Dakin (Police lieutenant)
Frederick Vogeding.......... Ivan Marloff (Opium smuggler)
Harry Strang...................Chauffeur (Marloff's henchman)
Max Wagner...................Taxi driver (Member of Marloff's gang)
Pat O'Malley..................Forrest Belden (Andrews' butler)

SYNOPSIS AND APPRAISAL

This is one of the most special of all Chan films, spotlighting many key elements that made the series so popular. It has a fresh and delightful sense of humor, and the mystery plot is brisk and intriguing. The characters are warm, engaging and believable. The sets, such as the house to which Chan is brought when he is kidnapped, are fascinating, and the main title music is sprightly and appropriately Oriental. It is a shame that Fox didn't use this melody as the official Chan theme. Oddly enough, it was only mid-way through the Monogram series that a recurring Chan theme was adopted.

The picture opens on a steamship where Chan is playing hopscotch with a group of children. As the steward helps him up, Charlie intones, "Sixty summers young...sixty winters old...brrrr!" He then entertains the children with a song.

As the ship docks in Shanghai, a threatening note is slipped into Charlie's pocket, advising him to stay on board. Once ashore, Charlie is surprised by Lee who was sent to Shanghai by his employer to look into the trade situation. They attend a banquet in his honor given by Sir Stanley Woodland, whose letter brought Charlie to Shanghai. Colonel Watkins, the police chief and an elderly Chinese businessman make speeches in praise of Charlie, and he gives a long reply in Chinese. When a reporter asks a companion for a translation, he is told Chan said his customary "Thank you so much!"

Sir Stanley whispers to Charlie about an important discovery. As the next speaker, Sir Stanley will present Chan with a ceremonial scroll. When he opens the antique box with the gift, Sir Stanley is shot by a trick gun concealed in the box, a deadly booby trap. Charlie and Watkins question Philip Nash, Sir Stanley's secretary, about when someone might have tampered with the box prior to the banquet. Charlie vows to find the killer.

Lee is concerned that his father may be the next target. In the middle of the night, a gunman shoots at Charlie while he lay in bed. Lee telephones for help, but then discovers his father created a dummy figure under the covers using pillows. Variations on this scene was repeated in later Chan films, but this version is the most effective.

The next morning, the hotel's phone operator is stunned when Chan calls for room service, and she immediately notifies Ivan Marloff that the detective is still alive. Charlie heads to Sir Stanley's residence, where he learns from his niece Diana that someone rummaged through Sir Stanley's files.

Lee chats on the phone with a girl he met while traveling to Shanghai until his father returns. A messenger arrives to bring Charlie to meet with Watkins. Chan calls police headquarters to verify the arrangement, but the devious operator connects him with Marloff instead. After his father leaves, Watkins himself calls Lee, and they realize that Chan is falling into an ambush. Lee takes a cab and tries to catch the limousine with his father. The taxi driver, however, is one of Marloff's men, and he knocks Lee out. Marloff confronts Chan after he is brought into an elegant house. Lee is dragged in a few moments later. Marloff threatens to kill them, but Chan bluffs that the police are surrounding the house. When Marloff's gang is distracted, Lee tackles their gunman, and they make a hasty escape into the busy street below.

Philip Nash visits the apartment of James Andrews, a friend of Sir Stanley who has just arrived in Shanghai. Watkins and Diana bring Andrews a sealed envelope from Sir Stanley which was found in his desk. The letter, however, is simply a welcome note, revealing nothing. Andrews leaves his other guests to consult in private with Chan as soon as he arrives. Andrews reveals that he is a secret agent, the American counterpart to Sir Stanley. They were investigating an opium smuggling ring operating out of Shanghai. Someone fires a shot at Chan from the doorway, dropping the gun in the room. Belden, Andrew's butler, implicates Nash, who had left the other guests apparently to spy on Andrews. Nash stole Sir Stanley's note to Andrews, which Chan then appropriates. Charlie demonstrates that an intruder could have fired the shot, but a fingerprint on the gun has a scar which is identical to the one on Nash's thumb. Watkins arrests Nash, to the distress of Diana who is in love with him.

Back at his hotel, Charlie shows Lee the note, which includes a secret message from Sir Stanley written in invisible ink that identifies Ivan Marloff as the operator of the smuggling ring. Chan is suspicious of Andrews, who made no effort to keep possession of the letter. He plans to check up on Andrews, who then arrives at Chan's door and asks for the return of the letter. Andrews reads the secret message, which appears upon application of heat.

Andrews and Chan investigate the house where Marloff had brought him. Chan finds a stamp pad that was burned in the fireplace. He also locates a paper with Nash's scared fingerprint. They surprise a mysterious beggar, who turns out to be Lee in disguise. At police headquarters, Nash escapes after conferring with Diana, and she slips him a gun.

Lee, working undercover, spots the taxi driver who works for Marloff, and tracks him to the *Versailles Cafe* on the waterfront. Andrews phones Chan after trapping an intruder in his apartment, one of Marloff's men. Charlie gives Lee a special assignment and meets Andrews, who has learned from his prisoner that Marloff's headquarters is at the *Versailles Cafe*. Andrews calls for police backup, and he and Charlie head to the cafe. As soon as they leave, Belden releases the prisoner, and they discuss the trap that is being arranged at the cafe.

Nash shows up at the *Versailles Cafe* and asks Marloff for his help in escaping from Shanghai. Marloff doesn't trust him and knocks him out. When Chan and Andrews enter the cafe, they follow one of Marloff's men into the basement. They uncover a huge shipment of opium hidden in wine bottles and also find a trapdoor leading to a hidden dock. Marloff's gang are waiting in ambush at this location. Just before Chan enters the trap, his flashlight fails, and he exclaims, "Insignificant offspring of searchlight seems to have internal trouble!"

A police motorboat then attacks the clandestine dock, and capture Marloff and his gang after a brief battle. Marloff's gang was responsible for the death of Sir Stanley. Nash is revealed as Chan's undercover agent. Andrews is surprised that his butler Belden is a member of the gang. Chan explains that the fingerprint of Nash was faked by Marloff, which is proven by evidence contained in the burned stamp pad.

Charlie then names the mastermind who gave Marloff his orders. Lee arrives with evidence to support Chan's accusation. In the closing lines of the picture, Charlie tells his son that there now is time for him to call his girlfriend. Lee replies, in imitation of his father, "Thank you so much."

PERFORMANCES

This is Warner Oland's warmest and perhaps richest portrayal of Chan. His first appearance in the film is unique, as Chan is seen playing hopscotch with a group of children. This is a rare glimpse of what Charlie's home life must be, as he delights in the joys of the children. He then sings a charming lullaby (in Oland's own voice, not dubbed) about the daughter of emperor Fu Manchu. This is the first of several "inside" jokes, as Oland played Dr. Fu Manchu, the villain named after the emperor, in three popular Paramount films in the early Thirties. This opening sums up the uniqueness of Chan, a family man who loves children. Oland stresses Chan's grace and intelligence throughout, and his reading shows Charlie as a complete person, not a one dimensional characterization.

The relationship of father and son has never been showcased better in any film. This is certainly Keye Luke's finest film as Lee Chan, particularly as he is a genuine helper throughout, not merely comic relief. When Chan and Lee are kidnapped, Lee quickly grasp's his father's intent to distract the gang members, and he acts like lightning when their attention wanders to save his father's life. In many films, Lee, or Jimmy adopt a disguise, but this film is the only one where the masquerade fools Charlie himself. Lee's illusion as a local beggar is perfect. There is also ample opportunity for Lee's devotion and concern for "Pop" to be beautifully conveyed. There are times where Charlie criticizes his son, but without the acid that Toler or Winters often added to their comments. Keye Luke has stated that he and Warner Oland had developed a genuine liking and respect for each other that spilled over into their onscreen relationship. An additional inside joke is when Lee draws a caricature of himself and his girlfriend, a clever opening for Luke to display his notable artistic ability. The subplot of Lee's tying up the phone while talking with his girlfriend even blends well into the story. This second screen appearance of Lee Chan displays the best representation of his character.

Jon Hall, billed in this film as Charles Locher, is brilliant as Philip Nash. Hall changed his name shortly after this film, partly in tribute to his uncle, the novelist James Norman Hall, who was co-author of the *MUTINY ON THE BOUNTY* trilogy with Charles Nordhoff. Hall became famous for his memorable series of light-hearted adventure films with Maria Montez in the Forties, and as television's *RAMAR OF THE JUNGLE* in the Fifties. Hall's cousin is Ben Chapman, a genuine Chan enthusiast, who played the original Gill-Man in *THE CREATURE FROM THE BLACK LAGOON* (1954).

Russell Hicks (Andrews) was a screen veteran who appeared in over two hundred films, usually playing an executive. He was Porthos in *THE THREE MUSKETEERS* (1939) and Robin Hood in *THE BANDITS OF SHER-WOOD FOREST* (1946). He was also a wonderful straight man for many comedians, such as Bud Abbott and Lou Costello, Stan Laurel and Oliver Hardy and the great W. C. Fields.

David Torrence, a fine character actor active in both the silent and talking era, plays Sir Stanley Woodward, the agent who summoned Chan. Another inside joke is a throwaway line at the banquet where we learn Chan and the police chief became friends in England at the time of the murder of Sir Lionel Bashford. In *CHARLIE CHAN IN LONDON*, Torrence played the role of Sir Lionel. Ironically, of course, Sir Stanley gets killed moments after this remark.

The other supporting performers, especially Irene Hervey (Diana), Halliwell Hobbes (Watkins) and Frederick Vogeding (Marloff) are striking and deliver solid readings. Harry Strang (Marloff's henchman) is another prolific actor who often gets overlooked. For example, He played Brayley in the landmark serial *MANHUNT OF MYSTERY ISLAND* (1945), who was the man who transformed himself into the villainous Captain Mephisto.

CHARLIE CHAN'S SAYINGS

⋄ Holiday mood like fickle girl, privilege to change mind.

⋄ Most anxious to renew acquaintance with land of honorable ancestors.

⋄ Idea of making speech bring goose pimples.

⋄ Old excuse, like ancient billy goat, has whiskers.

⋄ Two ears for every tongue.

⋄ Motive like end of string tied in many knots, end may be in sight but hard to unravel.

⋄ Only one enemy necessary to commit murder.

⋄ Talk cannot cook rice.

⋄ Silence best answer when uncertain.

⋄ Distance no hindrance to fond thoughts.

⋄ Dreams like good liars, distort facts.

⋄ Cold omelette like fish out of sea, does not improve with age.   If answer known, question seem unnecessary.

⋄ Hasty conclusion like hind leg of mule, kick backwards.

⋄ Beauty of poppy conceal sting of death.

⋄ Spider does not spin web for single fly.

⋄ Long journey always start with one short step.

⋄ Owner of face cannot always see nose.

⋄ Shot in dark sometime find eye of bull.

⋄ Soothing drink like summer shower, bring great relief.

⋄ Smart rats know when to leave ship.

⋄ Only foolish dog pursue flying bird.

⋄ Appearances sometimes deceiving, like wolf in lamb's clothing.

⋄ No one knows less about servants than the master.

⋄ (To the guilty man) Gave you plenty of rope, you make excellent noose for neck.

TEXT OF CHAN'S SONG

Long the journey, hard the way
But his heart was gay
For was he not a prince both strong and brave
Vowed the princess fair to save?
And he slew the dreadful dragon,
Even cut off his seven heads
And in his cave he found the princess
Bound to her lowly bed,
Then came they both back to the land
Of the mighty Emperor Fu Manchu
To claim his reward, the dainty hand
Of the lovely Ming Liu Fu.

CHARLIE CHAN IN THE SECRET SERVICE (1944)
Rating: *

MONOGRAM. Written by George Callahan; Photographed by Ira Morgan; Edited by Martin G. Cohn; Musical direction by Karl Hajos; Produced by Philip N. Krasne and James S. Burkett; Directed by Phil Rosen. 63 minutes.

ANNOTATED CAST LIST

Sidney Toler.................Charlie Chan
Marianne Quon..............Iris Chan (Number two daughter)
Benson Fong.................Tommy Chan (Number three son)
Mantan Moreland............Birmingham Brown (Winters chauffeur)
Lelah Tyler...................Mrs. Winters (Nervous dowager)
Arthur Loft...................Jones (Secret Service agent)
George Lewis................Paul Aranto (Handicapped guest)
Gwen Kenyon................Inez Aranto (Paul's sister)
Sarah Edwards...............Mrs. Harge (Melton's housekeeper)
Gene Roth....................Louis Philippe Vega (War refugee)
George Lessey...............David Blade (Political economist)
Muri Seroff...................Peter Laska (Aranto's servant)
Barry Bernard................George Melton (Murdered inventor)
Eddie Chandler..............Lewis (Secret Service agent)

SYNOPSIS AND APPRAISAL

This is the first Monogram Studios Chan effort, and it launches the series off with a real thud. All of the usual Monogram shortcomings, such as artificial-looking sets and cheesy recycled music, are immediately apparent. The plot is static and limited to one basic locale. The plot development is tedious. The whole picture just plods along until the conclusion. The only good point is that the Monogram series could only improve after this feeble and inadequate initial attempt.

Charlie Chan is settling into his new job as a troubleshooter for the Secret Service in Washington, D.C. George Melton, an inventor under government protection, is murdered and his plans for a new torpedo are stolen. Chan is assigned the case, and he suspects that Manleck, a master enemy agent, is involved. Melton had been giving a cocktail party when he was mysteriously killed in the main hallway of his home, and the Secret Service has detained all his guests. They include: David Blade, a political economist; Louis Vega, a war refugee working as an exporter; Mrs. Winters, a wealthy socialite; Paul Aranto, who is confined to a wheelchair; his sister Inez and his servant, Peter

Laska. Also on the scene are Mrs. Harge, the old-fashioned housekeeper, and Birmingham Brown, Mrs. Winters' chauffeur.

Iris and Tommy Chan, who are visiting their father in the nation's capital, later turn up at Melton's house to help their father. The missing plans are discovered in a bookcase in Melton's den, but Charlie quickly determines that they are forgeries. The criminal takes a shot at Chan, who then reluctantly allows Iris and Tommy to help.

Iris is assigned to watch Paul Aranto, and Tommy and Birmingham aid Chan in his survey through Melton's laboratory. Tommy notices a model bomb marked with an "X" on the side. The mysterious assassin attempts to strike again as the lab search continues, but Tommy saves his father by creating a chemical explosion that wards off the attack.

Charlie gathers all the suspects in the main hallway, where he demonstrates how Melton was electrocuted while turning on a light in the closet. A circuit activated by a switch in another room triggered the death trap. Birmingham helps in this demonstration. Chan then asks the suspects if they are familiar with the name Manleck. He reveals that Vega is actually Philippe Von Vegan, an electrical engineer. He devised the deadly trap that murdered Melton, and he also tried to kill Chan. As he accuses Vega, the engineer slumps over, shot by a noiseless spring gun.

Chan launches a rapid-fire interrogation of the other suspects and arranges to have another Secret Service agent threaten Inez Aranto. This alarms her brother Peter, who rises from his wheelchair and claims he was masquerading as an invalid to deceive his political enemies. The housekeeper turns over to Chan a key that she found on the piano. Charlie opens the wall safe, which is booby-trapped with a firearm. Chan boasts to everyone that the third attempt on his life has also failed, and he will arrest the killer within ten minutes.

He begins to grill Peter Laska, and makes an arrest. He then demonstrates that the spring gun that killed Vega was activated by a magnet. The detective releases all the suspects, but as they leave he unexpectedly stops one of them, and demonstrates how this person is smuggling out the Melton's secret torpedo plans. In reality, this individual is Manleck, the notorious spy, who masterminded the entire escapade and later killed Vega. Chan provides a sincere apology to Peter Laska and the other suspects for his atypical strong-arm tactics in solving the case. Birmingham Brown in particular is relieved that the nerve-wracking investigation has come to an end.

PERFORMANCES

Sidney Toler is rather acerbic in this particular film and is unusually abrupt while questioning the various individuals in the Melton Household. He is also rather hard on his son, Tommy, who in actuality provides little provocation for Charlie's acid comments. Charlie only seems relaxed while talking to the Secret Service agents, most of whom are old colleagues. One of them asks about Charlie's wife and seven children, and he is startled to learn Charlie has seven more. These brief friendly chats are Charlie's most human moments in the film, which seems to portray him as too hard-edged compared to the Chan from the Fox series.

Newcomer Benson Fong is both likable and believable in his debut as Tommy, Number three son and regular companion to his father in the early Monogram films. Fong provides an excellent balance to Mantan Moreland, and he sets off Moreland's style of humor quite well. He can be naturally funny in his own right, such as when he teases his father with jive expressions, saying he's "a hep cat of a younger generation. You're Confucius, and I'm Confucius, Jr." Charlie's reaction to this comment is a priceless double take. Overall, Fong seems more earnest and less obtrusive than Victor Sen Yung as Jimmy, and in some ways his take is closer to Keye Luke's traditional interpretation as Lee Chan.

Marianne Quon is also quite winning as Iris, Chan's Number two daughter. It is always fun to watch Charlie's attitude towards his daughters, who like his sons are eager assistants who try to help their illustrious father. *BLACK MA-GIC* later provides an even greater opportunity to watch the dynamics of a "Charlie and daughter" relationship.

This film introduces the brilliant comedian Mantan Moreland in the role of continuing character Birmingham Brown. Mantan served as a drawing card for black audiences, who frequented the Chan films and insured their profitability. It would take three films before Birmingham became Chan's regular employee and chauffeur, but from this picture on, Moreland would appear in all but two of the seventeen Monogram Chan films with both Sidney Toler and Roland Winters. Mantan did not have particularly strong material in *CHARLIE CHAN IN THE SECRET SERVICE*, but his exchanges with Tommy, Iris and Charlie still remain among the highlights of this film. The remaining players were rather flat, providing lifeless and perfunctory readings of their roles. Only Arthur Loft as Special Agent Jones and Gene Roth (sometimes billed as Stutenroth) as Vega, provided any memorable screen characters.

CHARLIE CHAN'S SAYINGS

- ◇ (To Agent Jones, commenting on his fourteen children) Everything grow rapidly in Hawaii.

- ◇ When alibi pushed at me, always suspect motive in woodpile.

- ◇ Detective without curiosity is like glass eye at keyhole...no good!

- ◇ Ninety-nine times out of a hundred, right or left handed person turn instinctively towards controlling side.

- ◇ Children go through life with same tact as tornado.

- ◇ (To Tommy, Iris And Birmingham) Always someone about to stick fly in ointment. This time I am unlucky man with three flies.

◇ (To Tommy) You are like business end of water spout, always running off at mouth.

◇ (To Tommy) You are very smart boy. Trouble with modern children, they do not smart in right place. (Tommy responds, "Did Confucius say that, Pop?") No, I say that.

◇ If man places self in way of finger of suspicion, must 1 not be surprised if he receive poke in the eye.

◇ Suspicion, like rain, fall on both just and unjust.

◇ Murderer always choose weapon he know best.

CHARLIE CHAN ON BROADWAY (1937)

Rating: ✻✻✻✻✻

TWENTIETH CENTURY FOX. Written by Charles Belden and Jerry Cady; Story by Art Arthur, Robert Ellis and Helen Logan; Photographed by Harry Jackson; Edited by Alfred De Gaetano; Musical direction by Samuel Kaylin; Produced by John Stone; Directed by Eugene Forde. 68 minutes.

ANNOTATED CAST LIST

Warner Oland..................Charlie Chan
Keye Luke.....................Lee Chan (Number one son)
Donald Woods.................Speed Patten (Ace reporter)
Joan Marshall.................Joan Wendell (News photographer)
J. Edward Bromberg.........Murdock (Editor of *Daily Bulletin*)
Douglas Fowley..............Johnny Burke (Nightclub owner)
Harold Huber..................Nelson (New York police inspector)
Louise Henry..................Billie Bronson (Gangland informant)
Joan Woodbury...............Marie Collins (Nightclub entertainer)
Leon Ames....................Buzz Moran (Crime boss)
Marc Lawrence................Thomas Mitchell (Gangster)
Tashia Mori...................Ling Tse (Vendor of photo supplies)
Charles Williams............Meeker (Burke's lawyer)
Eugene Borden................Louie (Burke's associate)
Lon Chaney, Jr...............Newsman in *Daily Bulletin* office
Creighton Hale...............Reporter
Jack Dougherty...............Policeman
James Flavin..................Policeman
Edwin Stanley................Lab technician

SYNOPSIS AND APPRAISAL

This entertaining film is sometimes overlooked by critics and fans, but it is an underrated gem containing a nifty mystery with a surprise conclusion. Chan solves the case while on a one day layover in Manhattan on his way back to the Hawaiian Islands, presumably from the Olympic Games in Berlin. Snappy dialogue, a whirlwind plot, crisp performances and the backdrop of a big city newsroom and nightclub make this an excellent entry, the last great Chan film of Warner Oland's career.

The credits are featured over scenes of Broadway and Times Square at night as viewed from the back of a speeding automobile, while *Give my Regards to Broadway* is played in a peppy orchestral arrangement. The film opens on an ocean liner as Charlie suffers from sea sickness. After a hearty lunch, Lee meets his father on deck and escorts him back to his cabin.

Another passenger, Thomas Mitchell, sneaks in and searches Billie Bronson's cabin while she is bathing. She shouts when she realizes a chair is jammed against the bathroom door. Her cries alert Charlie and Lee, who free her. After looking over her room, she asks Chan not to report the incident since nothing was stolen. When alone, she removes a small book hidden in her trunk's secret compartment. Later, she asks Lee for some aspirin, and hides the book in Chan's luggage.

Inspector Nelson leads a police delegation to greet Chan when his boat docks in New York. Reporter Speed Patton and photographer Joan Wendell are also on hand to meet Charlie. Joan snaps a photograph of the detective standing next to Billie Bronson. Nelson remarks that Bronson fled the city the previous year when the grand jury wanted to call her as a witness. Speed shares a cab with Bronson, who arranges to stay in the same hotel as Chan.

At the *Daily Bulletin*, Joan sells Murdock, the editor, her photo for a hundred dollars. Speed says Billie promised him a hot story that evening, but she calls Murdock and arranges a meeting with him instead. Billie then bribes a bellhop for a duplicate key to Chan's room.

Speed teasingly proposes to Joan, who asks him to take her to the *Hottentot Club* that evening. Chan heads to a police banquet in his honor, while Lee plans to sightsee. His money is stolen by a pickpocket, so Lee returns to his hotel only to catch Billie trying to enter his room. She says she is on the wrong floor, and that her room is one flight above. Becoming suspicious, Lee follows her, and she also heads to the *Hottentot Club*, where it is "candid camera night."

Buzz Moran is amazed to see Billie enter the club, and on the back stairway orders her to leave town in the morning. Denied entrance to the couples only club, Lee sneaks in through a window, where he encounters Ling Tse, a vendor selling photo supplies from a portable tray. She agrees to help him after learning he is Charlie Chan's son.

Nightclub owner Johnny Burke chats with Speed Patten and Joan at their table. When he returns to his office, he is startled to find Billie Bronson, his old girlfriend. She accuses him of jilting her for Marie Collins, a star dancer at the club. Billie draws a gun on Johnny. Marie then enters the office, and the scene fades out.

The police banquet is concluding when Nelson is called away on a murder case at the *Hottentot Club*, and he asks Chan to accompany him since Lee is being held as a suspect. Speed greets them as they arrive, and Nelson orders all pictures taken at the club confiscated. Billie Bronson was shot in Burke's office at the nightclub, and Speed discovered the body. Marie Collins, Johnny Burke and his sidekick Louie are the suspects, since Charlie cleared Lee who had been discovered peering through the office keyhole. Joan has a photograph of the victim, and claims she found the body before Speed. An examination of the picture reveals several changes, including a missing key from the victim's open purse. A napkin, now on Burke's desk, is mysteriously missing in Joan's picture. Louie switches off the light and both Burke and the napkin vanish. Nelson orders a dragnet for Burke.

With a magnifying glass, Chan and Lee discover the key in the photo is to their own hotel room. Nelson accompanies them back to their room, where they find the body of Thomas Mitchell, stabbed to death. Chan concludes that Mitchell was searching for an item planted in his own luggage by Billie. After shooting Billie, the murderer stole the key and caught Mitchell in the room with the mysterious hidden item. This article was important enough to provide motive for murder. Marie Collins admits Mitchell is her ex-husband. Chan finds a page from a diary on the floor.

They next proceed to Billie's room, where they discover Murdock. The editor claims he was planning to buy her diary, which is filled with secrets of the New York crime scene and its political connections. Since the open window would provide easy access to Chan's room, Murdock is also considered a suspect. Speed enters with a fresh copy of the *Daily Bulletin*, which includes his story of the Billie Bronson murder.

The next morning, Buzz Moran returns to his apartment and finds Johnny Burke hiding there. He throws Burke out, who then surrenders at police headquarters. He testifies that he and Marie talked with Billie in his office, and then left her alone. Chan suggests a paraffin test, which proves that Burke had not fired a gun in the past three days. The club owner is released, and returning to his office finds Lee and Ling Tse reconstructing the murder. After a fistfight, Lee is ejected out into the street.

Chan studies all the photos taken at the club. Back at the hotel, Lee nurses a black eye as his father gently chides him. Speed visits Charlie to warn him that his life may be in danger. After Nelson arrives, he tells Speed that Charlie is planning a showdown that night at the *Hottentot Club*. Speed insists that he should be included.

Using the candid snapshots, Chan weaves a possible motive for Marie Collins, Buzz Moran and Johnny Burke. The missing napkin, he concludes, was used by the killer to cover the gun, so there would be no fingerprints. When Joan came to the office, she interrupted the murderer, who hid while she took her photo. When she left, the killer placed the napkin back on Burke's desk without thinking. Speed then came to the office, discovered the body, and called his newspaper. Murdock is questioned about Billie's diary. The editor admits he just received an envelope containing a page from the diary. Inspector Nelson reads the entry which mentions most of the suspects by name, until one of them exclaims that the page is a forgery, written on the wrong type of paper.

"You are murderer," Chan replies softly, since only the police and the killer would know it is a forgery. The killer whips out a gun, but is jumped by Lee. The police drag the killer away, as Lee starts to nurse a second black eye. Nelson tries to persuade Charlie and Lee to remain in town for a week as his guest, but Charlie replies, "Perhaps better to return to Honolulu. Evidently, Broadway very hard on eyes."

PERFORMANCES

Some have criticized Warner Oland for not fitting in with the rapid pace of this film, but actually his calm, deliberate cadence provides a perfect contrast to the rhythm of the story. His battle with seasickness is amusing, but a puzzle since usually Charlie has quite reliable sea legs, particularly with so many Chan films set on ocean liners. His banter with Keye Luke is as charming as ever, particularly in an extended sequence when he uses deductive logic to track his missing collar button.

Keye Luke is also marvelous in this scene. He knows the solution, and watches with mirth as his father arrives at the inevitable conclusion that Lee himself appropriated the missing button. In this film, Keye Luke is almost permitted an equal status with Oland, particularly as Lee has a number of correct suspicions in the course of the story. His final leap upon the killer is also startling for the athletic vigor of his response.

Harold Huber is exceptionally good as the streetwise Inspector Nelson. He performs a clever rendition of a typical, fast-talking New Yorker, and his characterization never goes over the top like his French parodies in later films. He has two excellent running gags, one involving his cigarette borrowing, and the other his longing for a vacation so he can go fishing.

The other cast members are equally good, and their brisk ensemble repartee is essential for preserving the clever surprise of the killer's identity. Donald Woods (Speed) buoyantly plays a slicker version of the typical leading man. Born Ralph Zink in Manitoba, Canada, Woods appeared in over a hundred films, and he remained active in television and movies until 1969, making his final appearance with John Wayne in *TRUE GRIT*. Woods died in March, 1998.

Joan Marshall (Joan) is equally good as his rival and girlfriend. Louise Henry (Billie) is hard-edged as the jilted victim, and Douglas Fowley (Burke) is very convincing as the tough gangster. The murdered Thomas Mitchell is played by Marc Lawrence, making the first of three Chan film appearances. Lawrence, born Max Goldsmith, had an extraordinary long film career, usually playing gangsters. He was memorable in such classic films as *DILLINGER* (1945), *KEY LARGO* (1948) and *THE ASPHALT JUNGLE* (1950). He was also very memorable in the opening credits sequence of the James Bond thriller *MAN WITH THE GOLDEN GUN* (1974) who apologizes to the dummy of Al Capone after shooting it. More recently, Lawrence played Mafia Boss Carlo Gambino in *GOTTI* (1996).

J. Edward Bromberg (Murdock) plays a sinister and quiet editor. Joan Woodbury (Marie) even gets to do an extended Latin dance number in the nightclub sequence. Only the sharpest viewers will pick out Lon Chaney, Jr. in a brief bit at the news office. He quips, "You just think you can make it," as Joan passes his desk.

CHARLIE CHAN'S SAYINGS

⬧ Mention of food more painful than surgeon's knife without anesthetic (when one is seasick)...Good dose of land is only effective medicine...Only sight of dock can renew interest in life.

⬧ Etiquette ignored when lady in distress.

⬧ One cabin too small for two detectives.

⬧ Will feel like sparrow perched on limb with peacocks.

⬧ New York English too baffling for humble detective.

⬧ New York like mouth of great river. Many reefs in channel to wreck small sightseeing boat from Honolulu.

⬧ (To Lee, after his money is stolen by a pickpocket) Suggest you return to room and lock self in before dinner suit snatched from body.

⬧ Camera remember many things human eye forget.

⬧ Position of body sometimes gives solution of murder.

⬧ (Quoted by Joan Wendell) As Mr. Chan would say, "One picture worth ten thousand words."

⬧ Missing key may fit door to solution.

⬧ Mud of bewilderment now beginning to clear from pool of thought.

⬧ (To Lee) Have hit tack on cranium.

⬧ No poison more deadly than ink.

⬧ (To Lee) Regret slow progress of thought, but rejoice at final arrival.

⬧ Murder case like revolving door, when one side close, other side open.

⬧ (Quoted by Lee Chan) Pop says, "One woman's intuition better than ten scientists."

⬧ Puppy detective perhaps now realize snooping very dangerous business.

⬧ Triangle very ancient motive for murder.

⬧ To know forgery, one must know original.

CHARLIE CHAN'S MURDER CRUISE (1940)
Rating: ✳✳✳

TWENTIETH CENTURY FOX. Written by Robertson White and Lester Ziffren, adapted from the novel *CHARLIE CHAN CARRIES ON* by Earl Derr Biggers; Photographed by Virgil Miller; Edited by Harry Reynolds; Musical direction by Samuel Kaylin; Produced by John Stone; Directed by Eugene Forde. 75 minutes.

ANNOTATED CAST LIST

Sidney Toler....................Charlie Chan
Victor Sen Yung..............Jimmy Chan (Number two son)
Layne Tom, Jr.................Willie Chan (Number seven son)
Lionel Atwill..................Dr. Suderman (Tour leader)
Robert Lowery................Dick Kenyon (Nephew of murdered man)
Don Beddoe....................Frederick Ross (Fun-loving tourist)
Leo G. Carroll................Professor Gordon (Archaeologist)
Cora Witherspoon...........Susie Watson (Wealthy tourist)
Marjorie Weaver..............Paula Drake (Secretary to Susie Watson)
Charles Middleton...........Jeremiah Walters (Psychic on cruise)
Claire DuBrey.................Sarah Walters (His wife)
Leonard Mudie................Gerald Pendleton (Nervous tourist)
Kay Linaker...................Linda Pendelton (His wife)
James Burke...................Wilkie (Hotel house detective)
Richard Keene.................Buttons (Ship's steward)
Montague Shaw..............Inspector Duff (Scotland Yard detective)
Harry Strang...................Sailor (Guard of Pendleton's room)
Walter Miller...................Ship's officer who shoots at beggar
Wade Boteler..................Honolulu police chief
Harlan Briggs.................Coroner (Moderator at inquest in San Francisco)
Emmett Vogan...............Hotel manager
Cliff Clark.....................Lt. Wilson (Police detective)
John Dilson....................Police doctor

SYNOPSIS AND APPRAISAL

This remake of *CHARLIE CHAN CARRIES ON* is an average entry, but entertaining nonetheless, bolstered in part by a strong supporting cast. The storyline is rather complex, but the film's pace is quite rambling. It is quite interesting comparing this story to the plot synopsis for *ERAN TRECE,* which very closely duplicates the original Oland film. By this point in the Fox series, the shipboard setting was becoming somewhat hackneyed. In the original novel and film, Chan enters half-way through the story. This film includes him right from the start.

After an Oriental fanfare, the credits begin with Hawaiian music playing over a tropical setting complete with palm trees and ocean. At Honolulu police headquarters, Jimmy Chan and his younger brother Willie are at their father's desk searching his unopened mail for Willie's poor report card. Jimmy urges his brother to be honest, and he is proven correct when Charlie appears and already knows about Willie's low grades. But Willie's spanking for his attempted deceit is interrupted when Inspector Duff of Scotland Yard arrives at Charlie's door.

The inspector is traveling incognito aboard a ship, the *Southland*, on the trail of a murderer. His suspects are the ten passengers on a tour organized by Dr. Suderman. When the cruise sailed from New York, a judge was strangled during the first night out, after requesting a list of Suderman's party. Duff joined the tour in Liverpool, but has been unable to learn the identity of the strangler. He asks Chan to help set a trap that evening.

When Chan leaves his office to confer with the police chief, Duff is strangled through an open window by a bearded assailant. The chief has just received news about the murder of one of Suderman's party at the hotel. They return to Charlie's office to alert Duff, and are shocked to find his body. Charlie vows to "carry on" and asks the chief to be assigned to the case.

On his way to the hotel, Chan is approached in the street by a beggar with a scraggly beard who is seeking a handout. Professor Gordon tries to get rid of the panhandler, and introduces himself to the detective. The victim of the murder at the hotel turns out to be a wealthy manufacturer named Kenyon, who has been choked with a suitcase strap. In a meticulous sequence, Chan pieces together the crime step by step, making numerous deductions which he shares with Wilkie, the house detective.

Dr. Suderman is present, but he appears faint after learning about the strap. There are many clues at the crime scene, including a small pouch containing thirty dimes, which Chan identifies as the Biblical symbol of betrayal. The hotel attendant who discovered the body believes he ripped the coat pocket of the killer as he escaped. Chan thinks Kenyon was killed in the adjoining room, and dragged back to his own room. The tour member assigned to the murder room, a jittery man named Pendleton, immediately moves to another hotel.

Dr. Suderman brings Chan his suitcase strap, saying it is a duplicate of the one used to kill Kenyon. When another tour member, wealthy Susie Watson is frightened by a prowler, Chan takes the opportunity to question the remaining suspects on the tour: Dick Kenyon, lawyer and nephew of the slain man; Paula Drake, his sweetheart and Susie's secretary; Professor Gordon, an archaeologist; Fred Ross, a jovial traveler; and a dour pair of psychics, Mr. and Mrs. Jeremiah Walters. The house detective tackles an intruder, who turns out to be Jimmy. Chan reveals that Duff was also murdered earlier in the evening, and that he was after a killer among the tour passengers. Charlie finally orders everyone to return to the ship at once.

Chan joins the tour as their vessel sets off for San Francisco. Paula is upset that Kenyon was overheard arguing about her with his late uncle. The other passengers are unhappy, suspicious and nervous, particularly when the ship becomes shrouded in fog. Jimmy is discovered hiding in a lifeboat, and as Charlie refuses to acknowledge him, he is put to work as a steward. Charlie later gives him a special assignment to use this job to search for a jacket with a torn pocket.

Pendleton refuses to open his stateroom door, so Chan employs a ruse with Jimmy to gain entrance. The passenger is a nervous wreck, and confesses to Chan that he and Kenyon had agreed to switch rooms at the hotel in Honolulu. He found Kenyon dead in his bed, and dragged him back to his original room. Chan concludes that Pendleton was actually the intended victim. This is confirmed when a pouch with thirty dimes is pushed through the grate on his door. Pendleton explains that his wife received a similar bag five years ago, and an attempt was made on her life the following day. Pendleton claims he has no idea who would want to kill him. Chan posts a member of the crew as guard outside Pendleton's door.

Charlie then chats with Dick Kenyon and Professor Gordon while they play mahjong. He discusses Chinese law with Kenyon, and the Han dynasty with Gordon, who claims to be an expert on the subject. Jimmy finds the jacket with a torn pocket belonging to Jeremiah Walters, who chases him back to Charlie's cabin. The psychic claims the pocket got caught on a doorknob on the night of the Kenyon murder.

Dr. Suderman throws a party for all the guests, and asks Chan to judge the hobby horse contest. Meanwhile, the guard is knocked out by the bearded beggar, and Pendleton is strangled with leather shoelaces. Jimmy discovers his body and summons his father.

Chan determines that the murderer sent a telegram to Mrs. Pendleton in her husband's name, asking her to meet him in San Francisco. Prof. Gordon informs Chan that his leather shoelaces were stolen. Charlie is able to fix the exact time of the murder, which took place at the same moment as one of the hobby horse races. The bearded man knocks out Chan while he is developing the negatives of the race. After stealing the negatives, the beggar is spotted by Jimmy who chases him through the ship, with the crew and passengers joining the pursuit. The bearded man is mysteriously shot in the hold of the ship, and he is discovered to be Frederick Ross, wearing a mask with a beard. Chan believes he was shot by a confederate, and was one of two men who used the same disguise.

An inquest at the morgue is scheduled as soon as the ship docks in San Francisco. A telegram is received stating that Mrs. Pendleton was hurt in an airline accident. Chan's presence at the inquest is delayed, since he went to bring Linda Pendleton as a witness. Her eyes are covered with bandages, and she relates that she was once married to a jeweler named Jim Eberhart. When she discovered he was a smuggler and thief, she informed the police, and he swore vengeance.

Five years ago, Eberhart escaped from prison, and tried to kill her. He was re-captured, but was released from jail the past May, shortly before the Suderman cruise began.

Chan announces that Ross was not Jim Eberhart, but a wholesale merchant who served as a fence for stolen gems. It was Eberhart who killed the judge, Kenyon and Pendleton. Ross was being blackmailed by Eberhart into wearing the disguise on occasion and doing minor tasks, such as stealing the negatives. Eberhart then killed Ross when he was about to be caught. Since Linda Pendleton has been blinded, Chan asks her to identify the killer by his voice. At this point, Dr. Suderman turns off the lights and runs from the room, saying "I'm not Jim Eberhart!"

The remaining suspects are dismissed, and the exhausted Mrs. Pendleton rests in the next room. Jimmy notices the beggars' mask is missing from the evidence table, and moments later the disguised killer assaults Mrs. Pendleton. It is a trap, however, and the police apprehend the murderer, and his true identity is revealed. Linda Pendleton was never in an accident, only pretending in order to serve as bait.

Jimmy brings in Dr. Suderman at gunpoint, only to learn that Suderman was following his father's instructions when he fled the room. Charlie explains that he needed the trap so Eberhart could be caught in the act. He had no proof against him, and mere identification by Linda Pendleton would have been use-less. The coroner is relieved the case is over and his morgue can return to nor-mal and the film ends as Jimmy accidentally fires his gun, again disturbing the peace and quiet of the San Francisco Morgue.

PERFORMANCES

Sidney Toler struggles valiantly with this problematic script, and is quite good with the many explanations that are required to clarify the plot, both with hotel detective Wilkie and the coroner. He also sparkles in several other scenes, including a long talk at the rail of the ship with Paula Drake and a fascinating discourse over the mahjong table with Kenyon and Gordon. At the end of the film we learn this conversation provided Chan with some vital insight.

Victor Sen Yung copes rather well with his part, even if his role reprises Lee's activities in *CHARLIE CHAN AT THE RACE TRACK*. Jimmy's function as a steward who spies on the passengers is inconsistent, since he was introduced to some of them as Chan's son back at the hotel in Honolulu. One suspect, Jeremiah Walters, finally recognizes him, but it seems an oversight that Chan didn't consider this issue. Sen Yung's best moment comes early in the film, when he provides sound advice to his younger brother. This is the last Chan film featuring Layne Tom, Jr. (Willie), who was the only actor to play three different Chan offspring in the series.

The variety of suspects, however, is one of the strongest and most interest-ing in the entire series. Lionel Atwill (Dr. Suderman) is absolutely outstanding in his role as a red herring. Charles Middleton, Ming the Merciless from the three *FLASH GORDON* serials, is also memorable as Jeremiah Walters, the stuffy and puritanical mystic, and Claire DuBrey matches him perfectly as his wife. Leo G. Carroll (Gordon) brings his usual suave charm as the archaeologist. Leonard Mudie (Pendleton) and Robert Lowery (Kenyon) are also ideal in their performances. Marjorie Weaver (Paula Drake) and Kay Linaker (Linda Pendleton) provide crisp and interesting presentation in their roles, but Cora Witherspoon (Susie Watson) is a little wearing as the feather-headed employer of Paula. Montague Shaw has a wonderful cameo as Inspector Duff. His scene in Chan's office is rather special and his genuine appeal makes his murder a very moving scene.

CHARLIE CHAN'S SAYINGS

- ◇ Like cotton wool, filial devotion softens weight of parental crown.

- ◇ Sometimes quickest way to brain of young sprout is by impression on other end.

- ◇ Better ten times a victim than let one man go hungry. (Response to criticism that he may be the victim of fraud by giving money to a beggar).

- ◇ Truth, like oil, will in time rise to surface.

- ◇ To speak without thinking is to shoot without aiming.

- ◇ Life has been risked for jewels far less valuable than friendship.

- ◇ Hours are happiest when hands are busiest.

- ◇ Man can more safely hunt for gold if world think he digs ditch.

- ◇ In China, mahjong very simple; in America, very complex, like modern life.

- ◇ When Chinese emperor have eight suspects of murder, he solve problem very simply: Chop off eight heads, always sure of getting one criminal...Not always easy to reduce suspects to one.

- ◇ Elusive offspring, like privacy, sometimes hard to find.

- ◇ Judge always honorable position.

- ◇ Young man's explanation, like skin of sensitive woman, very thin.

- ◇ One cloud does not make storm, nor one falsehood a criminal.

- ◇ Unfortunate profession make detective suspect innocent with guilty. Not so with lovers.

- ◇ Dead men need no protection.

⋄ Better a father lose his son than a detective his memory.

⋄ In darkness, sometimes difficult to distinguish hawk from vulture.

⋄ After wedding bells, prefer no phone bells.

CHARLIE CHAN'S SECRET (1936)
Rating: *****

TWENTIETH CENTURY FOX. Written by Robert Ellis, Helen Logan and Joseph Hoffman; Photographed by Rudolf Mate; Edited by Nick De Maggio; Musical direction by Samuel Kaylin; Produced by John Stone; Directed by Gordon Wiles. 72 minutes.

ANNOTATED CAST LIST

Warner Oland...................Charlie Chan
Jerry Miley.....................Allen Colby (Wealthy missing heir)
Henrietta Crosman...........Henrietta Lowell (Colby's aunt)
Rosina Lawrence.............Alice Lowell (Her daughter)
Astrid Allwyn.................Janice Gage (Her second daughter)
Edward Trevnor..............Fred Gage (Janice's husband)
Charles Quigley..............Dick Williams (Newsman engaged to Alice)
Herbert Mundin...............Baxter (Lowell family butler)
Jonathan Hale.................Warren T. Phelps (Lowell family lawyer)
Egon Brecher..................Ulrich (Caretaker of Colby House)
A. Edmund Carewe..........Professor Alfred Bowan (Spiritualist)
Gloria Ray.....................Carlotta Bowan (Psychic medium)
Ivan Miller.....................Morton (Homicide detective)
William N. Bailey...........Harris (Morton's assistant)
James T. Mack...............Detective (Fingerprint expert)
Landers Stevens..............Coroner
Francis Ford...................Captain of recovery ship

SYNOPSIS AND APPRAISAL

This was the first Chan film made after the merger of Fox Studios with the Twentieth Century Company managed by Darryl F. Zanuck. Significant production values were lavished on this picture including elaborate sets and a very effective musical soundtrack. The camera work is particularly noteworthy, and the stylish rendering of the seance sequences are both creepy and elegant. The script itself is top-notch, and the intriguing mystery has a very clever denouement. The acting is on a high level, a tribute to director Gordon Wiles. The weakest point is the comic relief by Herbert Mundin as the cowardly butler, which is sometimes overdone. It is a shame that Keye Luke was not included in this film, but Chan makes two noticeable references to his son Lee in the course of the story. This is the most gothic and beautifully photographed of all Chan films, and the production is a real landmark of flair and polish.

The film starts as a newspaper headline proclaims the sinking of the S. S.

Nestor in a storm off the waters of Hawaii. Charlie Chan is engaged by his friend Henrietta Lowell to locate her nephew, Allen Colby, reportedly a passenger on the ship. He accompanies a rescue ship with deep sea divers to the site of the mishap, and divers find Colby's briefcase in the wreckage, but not his body. All the other bodies in the sinking were located. Since Colby's actual fate is undetermined, Chan cables Henrietta Lowell about his intention to come to San Francisco to continue pursuing the case, since it was possible that Colby was rescued by another vessel.

Members of the Lowell family are deeply concerned about Allen Colby's fate. He was left a fortune by his father, but since he was missing for seven years, the Lowells have inherited his fortune. The wealth of the Lowell family itself is now almost diminished. Their family lawyer, Warren Phelps, explains that they will have to account for all the funds if Colby returns. The gracious Henrietta has expended a lot of her financial resources on psychic research. Her children, Alice and Janice, are relying on the Colby inheritance for their future. Alice is engaged to newspaper reporter Dick Williams, and Janice is married to Fred Gage. Professor Alfred Bowan and his wife, the medium Carlotta, are dependent on the Lowell money for their livelihood. Henrietta desires to consult her dead brother in a seance with the Bowans to be held at Colby House that evening.

Meanwhile, Allen Colby himself arrives at Colby House, which is unlived in but maintained by the Lowells. He rings the bell for Ulrich, the caretaker. After receiving no response, he climbs over the wall surrounding the estate and enters the grounds. The house is a large, eccentric structure, resembling a Tudor English cottage gone mad. A mysterious gloved hand pushes forward the time on the large antique clock in the living room. When Colby enters the room, he notices the incorrect time and tries to adjust it, but he is struck in the back by a thrown knife. A few minutes later, Dick Williams is seen in the room as Alice Lowell enters, bringing an arrangement of flowers as decor for that evening's seance.

Charlie Chan is escorted by Baxter, the Lowell family butler, to Colby House where the family is gathered for the seance. Henrietta seems genuinely concerned about Allen's welfare, but the others, including lawyer Phelps, seem interested only with the financial implications. Charlie reports that Allen had enlisted in the French Foreign Legion, and had been held prisoner for seven years by the Riffs, a hostile Berber tribe in Morocco. On his way home, Allen was aboard the *Nestor* when it sank, but could have been rescued by another ship. that did not have a wireless radio.

Professor Bowan begins the seance in an attempt to determine if Allen is really dead. Everyone gathers around a large table, and all lights are turned off except for a dim lamp in the center of the table. The medium Carlotta goes into a trance and reports that Allen Colby indeed is dead. The seance is interrupted when Allen appears from behind a secret panel, his face glowing with a mysterious light. His body collapses a moment later, and Chan discovers he has been dead for hours from a knife wound in his back.

The police are called, but their inquiry fails to uncover any new facts. Under questioning, Bowan and Carlotta claim total ignorance of the presence of Colby's body behind the panel. Inspector Morton points out that each member of the Lowell family, as well as the lawyer and the psychics, would have a financial motive for wanting Colby out of the way. One of the suspects intercepted a message from Allen announcing his rescue and arrival home, and this individual used this knowledge to ambush him. Professor Bowan, Alice Lowell and Dick Williams freely admit they visited Colby House earlier in the day, but Ulrich the caretaker was unaware of any visitors. At one time, Colby was engaged to Ulrich's daughter, who later committed suicide after Allen left home.

Morton releases the suspects, and the family returns to the Lowell Mansion. Charlie requests to spend the night at Colby House, and Henrietta assigns Baxter to remain with him. Chan wipes Allen's face with a handkerchief while his corpse is carried out. When asked about this by the fingerprint expert, Charlie replies, "As son Lee would say, play hunch."

As he settles into his quarters prepared by Baxter, Chan learns that Colby House is riddled with secret passages and hidden rooms. He tests the handkerchief with some chemicals, and identifies the presence of quinine. When this substance is exposed to ultraviolet light, it provides a faint luster that would account for the glow on Allen's face in the dark.

Baxter is very nervous about remaining in the house. Henrietta returns to see if she can assist Charlie. They discover an ultraviolet lamp hidden above the the fireplace, as well as a speaker which accounted for the music heard during the seance. Henrietta now believes the seances led by Bowan were faked. A gunman shoots at them from the secret passage while they are discussing their new discoveries. Moments later, Fred Gage arrives to escort Henrietta back to the Lowell mansion. Chan tells Gage that he believes the gunman was aiming at Henrietta, and he sends him to the police to arrange for a twenty-four hour guard for the woman.

The next morning, Charlie visits the caretaker and asks him why he was unaware of Colby's arrival. He notices Ulrich is interested in ham radio, but Ulrich denies that the radio distracted him. After exploring one of the secret passages in the house, he finds one of them that exits just outside Ulrich's cottage on the grounds.

Chan next pays a visit to Bowan's apartment. The professor is not there, and Carlotta tells him that she knows nothing about the ultraviolet lamp. She openly admits to the music set-up, which she says is used to enhance the mood for the seance. Carlotta demonstrates for Chan the broadcasting equipment. They can transmit music to any remote location with a receiver and speaker. While she is explaining, Bowan quietly returns and deliberately turns on the equipment which stuns Charlie. Carlotta is outraged by this and tells her husband that she will report him to the police.

Bowan flees, and when Inspector Morton arrives, he arrests Carlotta. Charlie is still dazed from the electrical shock, and Morton taunts him, saying, "You let the murderer of Allen Colby slip right through your fingers!"

At the Lowell mansion, Henrietta instructs Phelps to cut the Bowans out of her will. Phelps is also to be removed as administrator of the Colby Foundation for Psychic Research. Phelps agrees to prepare a new will, and Henrietta demands a complete inventory of all her financial accounts. Ulrich enters and angrily resigns as caretaker of Colby House. In private, Charlie tells Henrietta his secret plan to solve the case.

That evening, Henrietta sits with her back to the window as she and Baxter consult the Ouija board. Chan and the police watch this daily routine from the garden. As the nearby bell tower chimes nine o'clock, a bullet shatters the window. Morton and Charlie rush in, and announce to the shocked family that Mrs. Lowell was killed. Alice breaks down in tears, and Phelps denounces Chan for his ineffectiveness.

Plotting the trajectory of the bullet, Chan determines the shot came from the bell tower. Dick Williams and Chan explore the tower, where they uncover an elaborate set up with a high-powered rifle that is triggered by the clapper of one of the bells. Charlie reloads the weapon, and sets up a demonstration of the murder technique, placing a vase in the position of the late Henrietta Lowell by the Ouija board. The experiment almost goes wrong when Baxter unexpectedly enters the room as the rifle from the bell tower is fired. Morton is notified that Bowan has been captured. The professor admits nothing, and Morton agrees with Charlie's plan to restage the seance at Colby House.

The suspects gather that night for Charlie's staged event. Ulrich has to be dragged in by the police. In rather poetic language, Chan reviews the possible motives for the crime by each suspect. He then announces that he is going to summon Henrietta's spirit to reveal the identity of the murderer. In a very atmospheric sequence, the ghost of Henrietta appears in the same passageway where Allen Colby was found. The specter intones, "I have come back to tell you the truth."

A figure grabs an ornamental knife from the wall and throws it at Henrietta, but it strikes a mirror instead. Chan declares, "Very foolish mistake!" as he reveals Henrietta, alive and well. He explains that he, Morton and Baxter arranged for a dummy to be seated in front of the Ouija table. Charlie smeared the handle of the ornamental knife with graphite, and the killer is revealed when Chan spots the suspect with dirty hands. The culprit draws a gun but is overcome when he is distracted by Baxter. Henrietta and Charlie decide to drop charges against the Bowans since they participated in his trap to catch the murderer. The film ends as both Inspector Morton and Henrietta congratulate Charlie on the success of his secret plan.

PERFORMANCES

This is one of Warner Oland's most magnificent performances, a grand solo effort that combines all the finest elements of a great Chan film. He is sincerely embarrassed when he is stunned by Bowan, and Inspector Morton berates him. His humility and determination are both on display after he recovers from this setback with his most clever ruse in the entire series. It is amusing to note how Charlie gently plays with the butler's fears. As they approach Colby House, he tells him, "Mysterious shadows of night cling to old house like moss on tombstone." Oland delivers this line most effectively, so the audience is aware that his tongue is in his cheek, but the butler does not. It is a magical moment that contributes to this film being Oland's finest single outing as Chan. This film is a genuine artistic triumph for him.

Herbert Mundin (Baxter) may be the weakest link in the cast, but even his performance isn't bad. His quivering eyebrows become annoying after they are highlighted for the third time. Mundin has a few superb moments, particularly his ecstatic facial expression when he is asked to escort Mrs. Lowell home, and he can leave the spooky Colby House. His whining yell when the gunman shoots at Chan is bizarre and quite funny as well.

The other cast members are outstanding, delivering a wonderful ensemble performance that would be hard to top. Henrietta Crosman (Henrietta Lowell) is impeccable as the dowager, and Egon Brecher (Ulrich) is ideal as the grumpy red herring. Even the bit players such as James T. Mack as the fingerprint expert and Landers Stevens as the coroner, are top notch. It is amazing how they bring these minor parts to life with just a few lines.

This was among the last performances of the gifted character actor Arthur Edmund Carewe (Bowan), who had health problems and committed suicide not long after the release of this film. Carewe (sometimes billed as Carew) was most famous for his unforgettable appearance as "the Persian" who aided the hero in finding the underground lair of Erik in the original *PHANTOM OF THE OPERA* (1925). He was also memorable in Paul Leni's *CAT AND THE CANARY* (1927) and *DOCTOR X* (1932).

CHARLIE CHAN'S SAYINGS

◇ Mysterious shadows of night cling to old house like moss on tombstone.

◇ Greetings at the end of journey like refreshing rain after long drought.

◇ Chinese people interested in all things psychic.

◇ Best place for skeleton is in family closet.

◇ Most fortunate gift to be able to cross bridge to dwelling place of honorable ancestors before arriving.

◇ If strength were all, tiger would not fear scorpion.

◇ Fingerprints very valuable if detective can catch owner of fingers.

◇ Boy scout knife, like ladies' hat pin, have many uses.

◇ Necessity mother of invention, but sometimes step-mother of deception.

◇ When pilot unreliable, ship cannot keep true course.

◇ Role of dead man require very little acting.

◇ Finding web of spider does not prove which spider spin web.

◇ Punch in ribs more desirable than shot in back.

◇ Strange house have more than one skeleton in closet.

◇ So sorry. Like child who play with matches, get burned.

◇ Live and learn.

◇ Wheel of fate has many spokes.

◇ When weaving nets, all threads counted.

◇ Unknown danger like summer lightning, strike when least expected.

◇ Hasty deduction like ancient egg, look good from outside.

◇ With proper lever, baby's fingers can move mountains.

Marian Nixon and Alexander Kirkland look concerned, as a surprisingly menacing Warner Oland looks on.

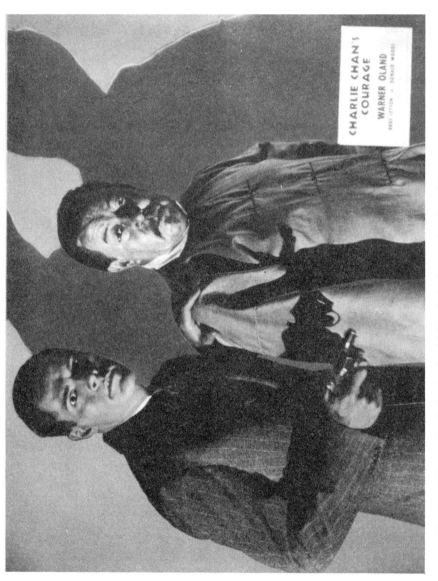

Donald Woods and Warner Oland, disguised as Ah Kim in the last missing Chan film.

Warner Oland reads a warning note not to leave the ship.

Boris Karloff, as Gravelle, is slowly won over by the gentle persuasion of Warner Oland.

Warner Oland and Keye Luke examine the evidence. Note the wedding ring on Chan's finger.

Warner Oland, Joan Marshall and Keye Luke observe the hijinks at THE HOTTENTOT CLUB.

Sidney Toler and Sen Yung question Douglass Dumbrille about the Borgia Ring.

Lelah Tyler and Sidney Toler in the first Monogram Chan film.

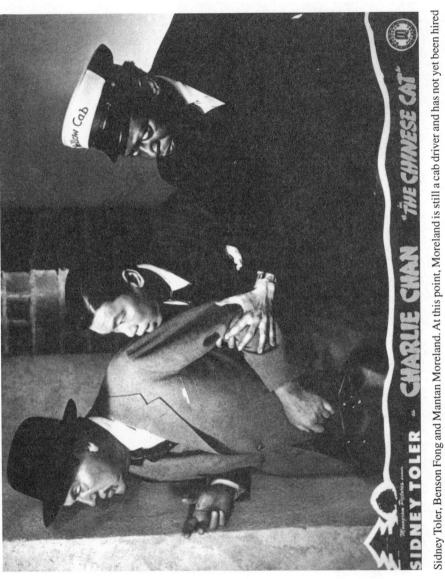

Sidney Toler, Benson Fong and Mantan Moreland. At this point, Moreland is still a cab driver and has not yet been hired by Chan as his regular chauffeur.

Robert E. Homans, Sidney Toler and Charles Jordan in a key scene in the police lab from *THE SCARLET CLUE*.

Roland Winters deliberately walks into a trap set by Douglas Fowley, Howard Negley and Carol Forman.

Mantan Moreland, Sen Yung and Roland Winters explore the Golden Eye Mine.

The spectacular dance number by Martha Roth is highlighted in this publicity card for *EL MONSTRUO EN LA SOMBRA*.

Chan, here called "Chan Li Po," oversees events in the Mexican Chan film.

Manuel Arbo may have starred as Chan in *ERAN TRECE*, but even the poster for the film used Warner Oland instead.

THE CHINESE CAT (1944) Alternate title: *CHARLIE CHAN IN THE CHINESE CAT*

Rating: **

MONOGRAM. Written by George Callahan; Photographed by Ira Morgan; Edited by Fred Allen; Music by Alexander Laszlo; Produced by Philip N. Krasne and James S. Burkett; Directed by Phil Rosen. 65 minutes.

ANNOTATED CAST LIST

Sidney Toler	Charlie Chan
Benson Fong	Tommy Chan (Number three son)
Mantan Moreland	Birmingham Brown (Taxi cab driver)
Sam Flint	Thomas P. Manning (Murdered man)
Joan Woodbury	Leah Manning (Stepdaughter of victim)
Ian Keith	Dr. Paul Retnik (Crime novelist)
Weldon Heyburn	Harvey Dennis (Police detective)
Cy Kendall	Webster Deacon (Manning's partner)
Anthony Warde	Catlen (Ringleader of gang)
Dewey Robinson	Salos (Catlen's associate)
John Davidson	Karl Karzos (Gem smuggler)
John Davidson	Kurt Karzos (Karl's twin brother)
Betty Blythe	Mrs. Manning (Widow of victim)
I. Stanford Jolley	Gannett (Hood who trails Chan)
Jack Norton	Hotel clerk (Front desk attendant)
Luke Chan	Wu Sing (Chinese artist)
George Chandler	Taxi cab dispatcher

SYNOPSIS AND APPRAISAL

This second film in the Toler/Monogram series is an improvement on every level over it's weak predecessor, *CHARLIE CHAN IN THE SECRET SERVICE*. Even so, most of the success of the film is due to entertaining action sequences, not a strong mystery plot. The criminal gang at the heart of the story is unconvincing, seeming more like villains from a comic serial than a straight mystery. The murder sequences, however, are masterfully staged and photographed.

The story opens with Thomas Manning sitting in his den, working on a chess problem. Someone enters, locks the door and shoots him. Before he dies, Manning knocks all the pieces off the chessboard but one, a black bishop. Other members of the family hear the shot, and break down the door, just as the mysterious killer is seen leaving through a secret wall panel.

Newspaper headlines show that Mrs. Manning is considered the prime suspect in the murder, but months later, the case against her is dropped due to lack of evidence.

Birmingham Brown, now employed as a cab driver, is recognized by his passenger, Charlie Chan. Birmingham forgets to collect his fare after dropping the detective off at his hotel. Leah Manning confides in Tommy Chan, telling him about her stepfather's murder. When Charlie arrives, he feels bound by Tommy's promise to the young lady that he would help. Leah is troubled because a recent novel about the case asserts her mother is the killer.

Chan's activities have aroused the interest of a criminal gang run by some oddball hoods named Catlen, Salos and the twins, Karl and Kurt Karzos. Their headquarters is located in an amusement pier funhouse that is closed.

Charlie obtains and reads the scandalous book that upset Leah Manning. When Birmingham returns to collect his fare, Chan receives a phone call from Kurt Karzos who has information on the Manning case. Birmingham drives Charlie and Tommy to their rendezvous with Karzos in an abandoned building, where they find Kurt's strangled body.

Detective Dennis shows up, and asks to work with Chan. Dennis identifies the dead man as a dealer in stolen gems. They also uncover a number of small art objects hidden in loaves of bread.

The next day Charlie visits Dr. Paul Retnik, the noted author of *MURDER BY MADAME*, the novel which accuses Mrs. Manning of being a murderess. Retnik is an arrogant man who foolishly challenges Chan to discover a more likely solution. Both men agree the loser will mail a check to the fund for Chinese war relief.

Charlie, Tommy and Dennis next investigate the scene of the murder, paying close attention to the secret panel which leads to Mrs. Manning's room. Manning's den is filled with Oriental art. Chan is particularly intrigued by a spot on Manning's desk where a heavy object had once been positioned.

Webster Deacon, Manning's old business associate, doesn't want Chan to reopen the case. Chan also learns that the Manning marriage was not a happy one. Salos places a bomb in Birmingham's cab. While driving Chan to his next destination, Birmingham says he hears two meters ticking in the cab. Chan instructs him to pull over. They abandon the vehicle which explodes offscreen moments later.

Chan hires a rental car which Birmingham agrees to drive. Chan visits Wu Sing, a Chinese artisan and craftsman, whose work Chan noticed in Manning's den. Wu Sing is famous for creating statues with hidden compartments, and Chan determines that one of Wu Sing's cat statues had stood on Manning's desk. Chan sends Tommy and Birmingham to track down the firm that purchased Wu Sing's art, while he concentrates on solving the clue of the bishop on the chessboard.

Webster Deacon, owner of the firm that bought Wu Sing's art, is questioned by Chan. Deacon leaves to get a ledger, but instead flees by car. Chan tracks him to the amusement pier where the criminal gang is located, but when he finds him, Deacon is dead.

Later, Charlie, Tommy and Birmingham are the victims of a poison gas attack, when deadly fumes are pumped into their hotel room. As Chan disconnects the device, Dr. Retnik arrives to check on Chan's progress. Tommy believes the author's appearance is more than a coincidence.

Back at the Manning house, the maid tells Charlie that two strange men were inquiring about the same cat statue. Mrs. Manning retrieves the large statue which she had removed to a closet. Chan discovers a famous stolen diamond in the hidden compartment of the Chinese cat. "Case almost finished," Chan announces as he leaves, "Know now who killed your husband, Mrs. Manning."

The gang receives a report from the hood trailing Chan. They are told he is approaching their pier headquarters again, so they plan to ambush him. The gangsters capture Charlie and his son, and they demand that he hand over the diamond to them. Chan refuses, and they start to torture Tommy.

Birmingham blunders onto the scene, and Charlie alerts him to run. The crooks, thinking Birmingham has the diamond, chase after him through the abandoned funhouse. An extended sequence follows in which the injured Tommy is hidden by his father. Then Chan and Birmingham play cat-and-mouse with the gang. Chan is about to be shot, but Tommy recovers and sprays the gunman with a fire extinguisher. Dennis and the police arrive just as Chan gets the upper hand in his battle with the crooks. He shows where he hid the diamond, right in the pocket of the gang leader himself.

After explaining that Manning was the original thief of the diamond, Chan describes how he betrayed the rest of the gang. The elusive clue of the bishop is then explained. In conclusion, Charlie leaves a message for Dr. Retnik to write a new book and send his check to the Chinese relief fund.

PERFORMANCES

Sidney Toler delivers a rather uneven performance in this picture, largely due to several absurd plot points. He is genuinely moving in the scene where Tommy is being tortured, but he looks foolish in the subsequent sequences where he and Birmingham take turns conking the criminals on the head as if this were a Three Stooges comedy. The writers also have him deliver endless harsh criticisms of Tommy with very little provocation, even after Tommy saves his life.

Benson Fong portrays Tommy as a truly noble soul, helpful and generous to others, and undeserving of his father's barbed comments, which all roll off him with no effect. He notices with genuine gratitude the two occasions when Charlie praises him to others. The scene in which Fong is tortured is one of the most striking in the entire series. His conduct rings very true in this pivotal scene, and this makes much of the hollow humor that follows seem even more artificial.

Mantan Moreland is at his weakest when wandering alone through the funhouse pretending to be frightened. In contrast, he is excellent interacting with others, particularly the maid, the taxi cab dispatcher, Tommy and Charlie himself. He is also funny in the scenes where his sees the murdered man's twin and confuses him with the victim.

The veteran actor Ian Keith is splendid as the obnoxious writer Paul Retnik. He manages to ooze arrogance with a dash of charm to make his character the most colorful in the overall dull cast. It is fun to watch the sparks fly between him and Charlie, and one could hardly criticize the philanthropic dimension of their friendly rivalry. John Davidson is interesting in his brief appearances as the Karzos twins. I. Stanford Jolley and Anthony Warde, two top notch character actors, are completely wasted in their roles.

CHARLIE CHAN'S SAYINGS

◇ Any detective will tell you, all mystery novels most horrible.

◇ Authors sometimes take strange liberties.

◇ (To Tommy) Your assistance about as welcome as water in a leaking ship.

◇ (To Tommy) You talk like rooster who thinks sun come up just to hear him crow.

◇ Bull in china shop is gentle creature, compared to detective who make pass at man wearing glasses. (This may be the most impenetrable and obscure Chan saying of all. He says it to Detective Dennis who is being taunted by the bespectacled author Paul Retnik.)

◇ Peculiar trait in Chan family...children all think Pop pretty good.

◇ Expert is merely man who make quick decision and is sometimes right.

◇ (To Tommy) Fear you are weak limb, to which no family tree may point with pride.

◇ Fear of future is wrong for young people in love. You should get married and raise large family. Once you have large family, all other troubles mean nothing,

◇ Dog cannot chase three rabbits at the same time.

◇ (To Tommy, who just walked into the gangster's trap) Like puppy who come to smell subway third rail, you will receive complete information in few moments.

◇ (To Tommy) You are like turtle. After everything all over, you stick your head out and find truth right under your very nose.

THE CHINESE RING (1947)
Rating: **

MONOGRAM. Written by W. Scott Darling; Photographed by William Sickner; Edited by Richard Heerman; Musical direction by Edward J. Kay; Produced by James S. Burkett; Directed by William Beaudine. 68 minutes.

ANNOTATED CAST LIST

Roland Winters...............Charlie Chan
Victor Sen Yung.............Tommy (Jimmy) Chan (Number two son)
Mantan Moreland............Birmingham Brown (Chan chauffeur)
Warren Douglas..............Bill Davidson (Homicide detective)
Louise Currie.................Peggy Cartwright (Reporter)
Philip Ahn.....................Kong (Captain of *Shanghai Maid*)
Thayer Roberts...............Captain James Kelso (Arms dealer)
Jean Wong.....................Mei Ling (Chinese princess)
Chabing........................Lilly Mae Wong (Mei Ling's maid)
Byron Foulger.................Armstrong (Bank manager)
Charmine Harker.............Kelso's secretary
Thornton Edwards............Palace Hotel clerk
Lee Tung Foo.................Armstrong's butler
Spencer Chan.................Chinese police officer
Kenneth Chuck...............Mute Chinese boy

SYNOPSIS AND APPRAISAL

This is the first film in the Roland Winters/Monogram series, incorporating a number of background changes. Chan has now left the Secret Service and is semi-retired and residing in San Francisco. There are no longer any references to his wife and family in Honolulu, and his second son Jimmy has adopted the name of third son Tommy. No reasons are provided for these changes, so fans must provide their own assumptions for them, such as the deaths of Mrs. Chan and his third son Tommy (perhaps during military service) with second son Jimmy assuming his brother's name in his honor.

This film is not bad on its own merits, once the viewer adjusts to Winters in the role. It takes awhile to make this adjustment. The screenplay was written by W. Scott Darling, who occasionally went back to the original Biggers' novels for some of his sayings. Darling also borrowed liberally from some of his earlier screenplays. This production is basically a retelling of *MR. WONG IN CHINATOWN* (1939). The picture has an indisputable harder edge than the Toler films, evident in the brutal death of a young Chinese boy and a beautiful Princess in the course of the story. It is obvious that Monogram put more effort into this picture than the last three Sidney Toler films, and up to a modest point, they succeeded in breathing new life to the series with slightly higher production values, including a very good musical score.

The picture opens with Princess Mei Ling appearing on Chan's doorstep, asking to see the great detective. Birmingham shows her into the den, and she gives him a ring to show to Chan as identification. Mei Ling is then shot with a poison dart and manages to scribble "Captain K." on a paper before expiring.

Tommy finds the body, and Sergeant Davidson is quickly summoned. While Chan is demonstrating his theory that an air rifle was used to kill her, reporter Peggy Cartwright, who is also Davidson's sweetheart, enters the den through an open window. She identifies the corpse, having seen Mei Ling on her arrival from China two weeks earlier. Davidson handcuffs Peggy to a chair and asks Tommy to watch over her while he and Charlie start their investigation.

Chan decides to interview Captain Kong of the *Shanghai Maid*, the ship on which Mei Ling was a passenger. The captain reports that Mei Ling came to America merely to sightsee. After the detectives leave, Kong confronts Captain James Kelso of the Kelso Aviation Company and accuses him of murdering the princess. Mei Ling had actually hired the ship in order to smuggle airplanes into China, and Kelso had just received $250,000 from her as payment for the fighter planes. Kelso in turn blames Kong for her untimely death.

Meanwhile, Peggy escapes from Tommy and snoops around Mei Ling's apartment. She hides when a masked man breaks in, but he is interrupted by the arrival of Chan and Davidson. They question the maid, who tells them that Mei Ling had no visitors except for a mute Chinese boy who lives in the building. The boy is not deaf, but speaks a Chinese dialect unfamiliar to Charlie, so he uses hand gestures to communicate with the boy. The youngster observed the intruder, and was able to provide Chan some information about him.

The next day Tommy discovers through the Tong that Mei Ling came to America to buy arms for her brother's army in China. Chan goes to the bank where Mei Ling purchased travelers checks, and learns that she was carrying over a million dollars. He is particularly interested in a large check cashed by Captain James Kelso. When Chan returns to Mei Ling's apartment, he discovers the body of the maid, dead from a gunshot wound, and he sarcastically shows it to the policeman guarding the rooms. "You are right, maid not go out!"

Charlie searches the roof to determine the position used by the shooter when he killed the maid. He discovers small footprints, and he and Sergeant Davidson find an air rifle in the mute boy's room. The police believe the missing boy is the killer, but Chan is dubious about their interpretation of the evidence.

The detective interrogates Kelso, who is a close friend of Mei Ling's brother. Kelso is unaware of what happened to the remainder of Mei Ling's money, but he was expecting a second payment from her. Davidson visits Chan and teases Birmingham, saying he may be the next victim because "he knows too much!" He tells Charlie that the Kelso Aviation Company is a fraud. Armstrong, the bank manager, is questioned again concerning the missing funds and the possibility of forgery. Kong and Kelso later show up, and demand Armstrong tell them what happened to the money. On their insistence, Armstrong calls Chan (telephone number MAjor-4782), and requests him to return.

Kelso abducts Chan at gunpoint, planning to take him to the *Shanghai Maid*. Birmingham follows the car, and the police are alerted. Davidson grills Captain Kong, who is evasive, while Birmingham locates the car at the dock, and unties Chan and Armstrong. When Peggy spots Kelso on the boat, a struggle ensues, and the police take over the ship.

Chan then reveals the actual murderer who killed Mei Ling, her maid and the missing Chinese boy. Tommy, Birmingham, Davidson and Peggy all claim their share of the credit for solving the crime. "You know, very funny thing, it seems Charlie Chan never find out everything," observes the detective wryly. The film ends with a close-up of Charlie adjusting his hat, an unusual close that somehow seems very appropriate.

PERFORMANCES

It takes some time to adapt to Roland Winters as Charlie Chan, but if one doesn't dwell on the obvious comparisons with Oland and Toler, there is much to admire in his reading. He delivers many lines with dry humor and zest. He can be sarcastic with a number of targets, including some suspects, the police, Tommy, Birmingham and as well as himself. He is overly courteous, but there always seems to be more going on behind his impassive exterior.

Victor Sen Yung is adequate as Tommy, but one can imagine the actor's own bafflement at the name change. He is energetic and actively helpful, but he is definitely on the sidelines in this plot. Mantan Moreland is better utilized in the storyline, even rescuing Chan at one point. He has more screen time than Sen Yung, and his comic interludes are largely effective.

Philip Ahn, a wonderful actor of Korean descent, previously played Chan's son-in-law in *CHARLIE CHAN IN HONOLULU*. Here he is masterful as the evasive but polite Captain Kong. Thayer Roberts is far less effective as Captain Kelso. Byron Foulger (Armstrong), a splendid character actor who usually plays mild-mannered clerks, is exceptional. Louise Currie (Peggy) plays the feisty reporter with enough charm to overcome the cliched elements of her part. Warren Douglas, on the other hand, just doesn't seem to come across as Sergeant Davidson. His part is very well written, and offers far more range than usual for Chan's police companion, but the young actor simply does nothing with it.

The most impressive roles are those played by the Oriental members of the cast, especially Jean Wong (Mei Ling), Chabing (Lilly Mae) and Lee Tong Foo (Armstrong's butler). It would have been better if the script could have provided them greater screen time.

CHARLIE CHAN'S SAYINGS

⋄ Death, my son, is the reckoning of heaven...in this case most complicated reckoning.

⋄ Strange events permit themselves the luxury of occurring in strange places.

⋄ Chinese chimpanzee not interfere with monkey business of big baboon.

⋄ Many questions arise. To all, in good time, we get answers.

⋄ Many times in the past it has happened, Charlie Chan hoarsely barking up incorrect tree.

⋄ (Referring to barking dogs) How loud it thunder, how little it rain.

⋄ Sometimes think successful detective one upon whom luck shows smiling countenance.

⋄ Man who ride on tiger cannot dismount.

⋄ Confucius say, "Luck happy chain of foolish circumstance."

⋄ Woman not made for heavy thinking, but should always decorate scene like blossom of plum.

⋄ Man who ride on merry-go-round all the time, sooner or later must catch brass ring.

DANGEROUS MONEY (1946)
Rating: *

MONOGRAM. Written by Miriam Kissinger; Photographed by William Sickner; Edited by William Austin; Musical direction by Edward J. Kay; Produced by James S. Burkett; Directed by Terry Morse. 66 minutes.

ANNOTATED CAST LIST

Sidney Toler....................Charlie Chan
Victor Sen Yung..............Jimmy Chan (Number two son)
Willie Best.....................Chattanooga Brown (Chan's assistant)
Gloria Warren.................Rona Simmons (Brace's girlfriend)
Joe Allen, Jr....................George Brace (Ship's purser)
Joseph Crehan................ Captain of the *Newcastle*
Selmer Jackson...............Ship's doctor
Rick Vallin....................Tao Erickson (South seas Trader)
Amira Moustafa..............Laura Erickson (Tao's wife)
John Harmon.................Freddie Kirk (Knife-throwing showman)
Dick Elliott....................P. T. Burke (Cotton shirt salesman)
Emmett Vogan............... Dr. Martin (Founder of sea life museum in Samoa)
Elaine Lange..................Cynthia Martin (Martin's wife)
Bruce Edwards.................Harold Mayfair (Martin's assistant)
Tristram Coffin...............Scott Pearson (U. S. Treasury agent)
Leslie Dennison..............Dr. Whipple (Missionary)
Dudley Dickerson............Big Ben (Ship's kitchen help)
Rito Punay....................Pete (Steward who deserts ship)
Alan Douglas.................Joseph Murdock (Underworld henchman)

SYNOPSIS AND APPRAISAL

This picture is one of the weaker entries in the late Toler/Monogram series, due largely to a rambling script by Miriam Kissinger. Her writing for Chan is weak in characterization, and her screenplay is rather muddled. The entire story is static and rather disjointed, and the denouement leaves a number of loose threads.

The picture opens on a foggy night aboard the *Newcastle* heading towards a number of South Sea ports, including Samoa. Chan is approached on deck by Scott Pearson. He reveals that he is actually a U.S. Treasury agent in disguise, tracking a counterfeiting ring. He believes his identity has been discovered, and attempts have been made on his life. As he is reporting this, an object comes crashing down, and Pearson is saved when Chan pulls him out of the way. Charlie suggests that they move inside, where a show is being presented for the passengers.

A knife-throwing act is in progress. A few minutes later, Pearson is killed by a knife in the back, and Chan takes charge of the investigation. The Captain reveals that Pearson had confided in him. Chan proceeds to question a number of the passengers who attended the show. They include Rona Simmons, a tourist; P.T. Burke, a loudmouthed salesman who markets cotton shirts in Samoa; Tao Erickson and his wife Laura, traders on a buying trip; Dr. Whipple and his wife, missionaries; Dr. Martin and his wife, Cynthia; and Harold Mayfair, Martin's assistant.

Dr. Martin is an ichthyologist who had founded a science museum in Samoa before the war. He is now returning to operate it. Charlie also queries the ship's doctor, the ship's purser and Freddie Kirk, the man who performed the knife-throwing act. Kirk was talking on-stage when the murder was committed, but Mrs. Erickson was in her cabin, and the Whipples had just left the room.

Chan examines Pearson's papers with the Captain of the *Newcastle*, and uncovers two clues. The treasury agent suspected a man called Lane was involved in the scheme, and that Samoa was their headquarters. Tommy Chan and Chattanooga Brown start their own investigation, trying to get fingerprints from all the suspects. Since there were no prints on the murder weapon, this effort seems rather pointless.

Charlie observes that the ship's purser is very fond of Rona Simmons, but he also believes that they are hiding something. However, they refuse to confide in him. Charlie sets a trap for the killer using a dummy of himself as a target. The dummy soon has a knife thrown at it, but Chan makes no effort to catch the attacker. Instead, he merely determines that the knife was not thrown by human hands.

Meanwhile, Burke conspires with Freddie Kirk to blackmail Rona Simmons. He has learned that the purser has smuggled Rona onto the *Newcastle* with false papers. Burke uses a native steward called Pete in his strategy, and he confronts Rona, who accedes to his demands. Pete deserts the ship after being threatened by Burke. Charlie cables Tommy, Number three son, to research Miss Simmons, and he discovers that at the outbreak of the war her father was entrusted with some valuable art objects which are now missing.

After landing at Samoa, Burke receives a valuable necklace from Rona for his silence. Chan and the Captain apprehend Burke, who then confesses to the blackmail scheme. He offers to tell what he knows about the murder, when he is killed by a hurled knife.

Chattanooga and Jimmy are trailing Big Ben, one of the kitchen help from the ship, who has a big bankroll. They suspect it is counterfeit and snatch it from him, but it turns out instead to be a "Kansas City bankroll" containing only one genuine bill and the rest paper cut-up to the size of money. They then stumble into Dr. Martin's museum, where they uncover a huge hidden cache of counterfeit money.

Charlie returns the necklace to Rona, and she and the purser tell Charlie that she is trying to salvage her father's reputation by recovering the objects he had hidden while fleeing from the Japanese. She has no money to undertake this mission, and Freddie Kirk had arranged her trip. Chan and the Captain follow Kirk, who is murdered while sneaking towards the museum. Jimmy and Chattanooga arrive and tell Chan about their discovery.

When Chan and his party search the museum, they locate the missing art treasures in addition to the "hot" money. The Ericksons arrive at the museum, holding the Martins at gunpoint. Mayfair turns out also to be working with them. Tao Erickson says that "Lane" was worried when he noticed that Mayfair was getting cold feet.

A battle follows when "Lane" and the killer show up at the museum. They are overcome, and Chan reveals that both Lane and the killer were operating in disguise. The killer was using a mechanical device that launched knives with deadly accuracy. Dr. Martin and his wife were innocent dupes. Besides capturing the counterfeiting ring, Chan has recovered the missing treasures, and secured the future for Rona Simmons and her sweetheart, Brace the purser. The wrap-up of the film is unduly hasty leaving a number of dangling issues still unclear, such as how the art treasures and counterfeiting cases overlapped.

PERFORMANCES

Sidney Toler, his real age becoming apparent, is somewhat drab and tired-looking in this film. He is also handicapped by a weak script that did not serve the character of Chan very well. Charlie really should have cleared up this meager mystery much sooner. Toler did get to perform a smooth waltz with Mrs. Erickson, however, and his byplay with Jimmy is more playful and gentle than usual. One other interesting aspect of the plot was Charlie's wire to Number three son Tommy to research some information that he wanted to have checked. In the later Monogram series, the other offspring are seldom mentioned during the course of a story.

Victor Sen Young is acceptable as Jimmy, but for most of this picture his character is merely involved in side plots. He shows the most zest while communicating with Chattanooga on a walkie-talkie.

Willie Best is sometimes criticized for his performance as Birmingham's cousin, Chattanooga Brown. Here, he acquits himself rather well, and provides the film with some needed energy in this rather anemic production. His interaction with Dudley Dickerson, another fine black actor, is particularly interesting and amusing.

Tristram Coffin (Pearson) is very good in his brief appearance as the threatened treasury agent. Emmett Vogan excels as the befuddled bookworm, Dr. Martin. Dick Elliott (Burke) is properly annoying as the "know-it-all" salesman, and John Harmon is fine as the shifty vaudevillan, Freddie Kirk. But most of the other performers are bland and lifeless, including the two young lovers played by Gloria Warren (Rona) and Joe Allen, Jr. (George Brace).

Alan Douglas is quite effective as Joseph Murdock, who spends most of the plot disguised as a female character. His impersonation is good and appropriate to the story. It is an effective surprise at the film's end. Unfortunately, his part is overshadowed by the incredibly large number of guilty characters. As Chan concludes, the brig on the *Newcastle* is going to be very crowded when the ship resumes its voyage

CHARLIE CHAN'S SAYINGS

◇ Problem seldom wait for clearing weather.

◇ Good wife's place should be at mate's elbow in time of trouble.

◇ Tiger going away from village is never feared.

◇ Guilty mind sometimes worse than ancient boot of torture.

◇ Hasty man could also drink tea with fork.

◇ In phraseology of Euclid, X over Y equals proposition still unsolved.

◇ Each country's dance is most beautiful in that particular country.

◇ Kangaroo reaches destination also by leaps and bounds.

◇ Good hunter never break twig under foot.

DARK ALIBI (1946)

Rating: ✳✳✳✳

MONOGRAM. Written by George Callahan; Photographed by William Sickner; Edited by Ace Herman; Musical direction by Edward J. Kay; Produced by James S. Burkett; Directed by Phil Karlson. 61 minutes.

ANNOTATED CAST LIST

Sidney Toler....................Charlie Chan
Benson Fong...................Tommy Chan (Number three son)
Mantan Moreland............ Birmingham Brown (Chan's chauffeur)
Ben Carter......................Ben Brown (Prison trustee and Birmingham's brother)
Edward Earle...................Thomas Harley (Man framed for murder)
Teala Loring...................June Harley (His daughter)
George Holmes...............Hugh Kenzie (Jail guard who helps June)
John Eldredge.................. Anthony Morgan (Public defender)
Joyce Compton...............Emily Evans (Showgirl tenant at hotel)
Anthony Warde...............Jimmy Slade (Prison trustee)
Janet Shaw.....................Miss Petrie (Secret wife of Slade)
Russell Hicks..................Cameron (Prison warden)
Ray Walker....................Danvers (Salesman of bank alarm systems)
Milton Parsons...............Johnson (Bookkeeper for Carey Warehouse)
Edna Holland..................Mrs. Foss (Hotel operator)
William Ruhl.................. Thompson (Fingerprint lab technician)
Tim Ryan......................Foggy (Convict)
Meyer Grace...................Punchy (Convict)
Frank Marlowe............... Barker (Fingerprint officer at prison)
George Eldredge............. Police detective who arrests Harley

SYNOPSIS AND APPRAISAL

This is the best entry in the Toler/Monogram series, and the last good film starring Sidney Toler. It is an excellent blend of atmosphere, mystery, humor, eccentric characters and snappy writing. Even the usual Monogram shabbiness works to the film's advantage. The seedy rooming house, for example, is a very apt use of a typical Monogram set. Director Phil Karlson knows precisely how to present a low-budget Chan drama, and writer George Callahan provides a well-tailored script for the characters.

This film also is the first one to employ standard theme music for Chan. The main title music for the four films that preceded *DARK ALIBI* was similar but unmemorable. The comparable elements included opening gongs and a stately fanfare. But the main title theme (which first occurred in *THE JADE MASK*) was elegant but rather slow and tiresome. The reworked Chan theme after the gong and fanfare was sprightly and very catchy, and probably many members of the audience hummed along. Monogram retained with theme for the main title for the remaining nine films in the series. The theme also became used on occasion during regular soundtrack.

The story of the picture centers on Thomas Harley, an elderly resident of the Foss Family Hotel, a bona fide flea trap. The man is arrested for a bank robbery and the murder of a security guard. Harley claims he was accidentally locked in a warehouse at the time of the crime, but he is convicted because he is a former convict and his fingerprints were located at the scene of the crime.

Charlie is visiting his old friend Anthony Morgan, the local public defender, when June Harley appears to ask Morgan if there is any chance that her father's execution might be delayed. Morgan tells her the chances are slim, and she asks if a private detective might be able to help. Chan overhears this exchange, and writes down the name of a detective who can help her. After he leaves, she shows the paper to Morgan. The name written on the paper is "Charlie Chan."

There are only two days remaining until Harley's execution, and Chan believes Harley's only chance is to uncover the real killer. June and her boyfriend, prison guard Hugh Kenzie, tell Chan all about the background of the case. Chan then goes to the Foss Family Hotel to interview the other residents. These suspects include: Mrs. Foss, the nosy owner of the hotel; Miss Petrie, a secretary for a local charity; Emily Evans, a former showgirl; Mr. Danvers, a brash salesman who markets bank security systems as well as tear gas; and Mr. Johnson, a mysterious bookkeeper who works for the Carey warehouse where Harley claims he was at the time of the crime.

Birmingham drives Tommy and Charlie over to the prison to speak with Harley himself. "Is this the shortest way to prison?" Birmingham asks. "No," replies Charlie, "Shortest way is to commit crime." A sniper takes a shot at the car as continues of its way.

At the jail, Charlie recognizes Slade, a prison trustee working under officer Barker who manages the fingerprint file. Another convict turns out to be Birmingham's brother Ben, and they begin a clever wordplay routine where each man anticipates the other man's thoughts. Later, Tommy and Birmingham cause a commotion by tailing two convicts and getting locked in a cell with them.

Meanwhile, Charlie interviews Harley and becomes convinced of his innocence. He now believes that the fingerprint evidence was forged. Chan and the public defender enlist the aid of Thompson, a lab expert, to explore ways that fingerprints can be forged. The main difficulty is the presence of skin oil, which allows the fingerprints to register. Chan also identifies two other similar cases where ex-convicts who denied ever being at the crime scene were convicted on fingerprint evidence. He suspects that the fingerprint file at the prison may be the source of these forgeries.

Charlie learns that Miss Petrie is in fact the wife of the convict Slade. Miss Petrie vanishes from the hotel as Charlie prepares to question her. Chan then investigates the Carey warehouse where stage props are stored. He, Tommy and

Birmingham are almost hit by a truck when they arrive at the warehouse. There Charlie confronts Johnson, the bookkeeper. Moments later, Miss Petrie is killed outside the warehouse, hit by the same truck that threatened Charlie. Back at the state prison, Charlie and the warden discover that someone has been tampering with the prison fingerprint file. Slade overhears this, and tries to escape. He is killed in a shootout by his own defective gun. The lab technician then discovers that fingerprints can be forged by a method of coating fingerprint stencils with animal oil.

Chan seeks to question Johnson again, but the man has disappeared. He returns to the warehouse where he discovers Johnson's body and the equipment used to forge fingerprints. Tommy pursues a shadowy figure in the warehouse, and traps him using the warehouse truck. The man turns out to be Danvers, the loud-mouthed salesman.

Danvers' confession is used by Chan to save Harley from execution. Charlie explains the details of the case to the prison warden, and then announces that the mastermind of the entire robbery and murder scheme has yet to be uncovered. He identifies the killer in dramatic fashion, and the culprit is taken into custody. As he leaves the prison, Charlie stops to chat with Birmingham and Ben. To Tommy's amazement, he enters into their cryptic wordgame with complete relish. "Pop, I don't get it," Tommy exclaims. "I never get that kind of talk. How do you do it?" Charlie replies, "You are familiar with pidgin English? Same difference." The film ends with a close-up of the confused Tommy, as bewildered as ever.

PERFORMANCES

Sidney Toler delivers his last top-notch performance as Chan in this film. Poor health and increasing age limited the effectiveness of his remaining films. Here, Toler is marvelous, both in his serious and reflective moments such as consoling June Harley and her father, or in his comic highlights, particularly in the film's closing moments. His timing and sense of irony are without peer in these scenes. There is one Toler slip-up, however. When he first questions Miss Petrie, he mistakenly calls her "Miss Baker" instead.

This is the last of Benson Fong's six Chan film appearances. He always presented Tommy as likable and straightforward. He always interacted well with Mantan Moreland, and always avoided the cocky aspects that sometimes marred the performance of Victor Sen Yung. This is one of Mantan Moreland's best films as well, due largely to his superb routines with his old vaudeville partner, Ben Carter. In fact, Moreland and Carter receive co-billing in the opening credits, stressing their background as a well known team. The routine they use in this film is one that they had honed to perfection, and it rivals the best bits of Abbott and Costello. The topper, of course, is when Toler joins in too. In some films, Moreland's antics are a distraction to the overall plot, but here he adds immeasurably to the film's success. One of his best comments is when Charlie and Tommy rush off to investigate. "Why do you always have to hurry to a murder. Why can't you just ooze on down to one?"

Most of the other players are good as well. Character actor Anthony Warde is excellent as Slade. Chan film veteran Russell Hicks makes a convincing warden, and John Eldredge is likable and sincere as the public defender. Joyce Compton, a wonderful actress, is exquisite in her bit as Emily Evans. Tim Ryan (Foggy), Ray Walker (Danvers) and Edna Holland (Foss) truly excel in their parts, but top honors belong to Milton Parsons (Johnson) who practically steals the show as the creepy, slithery bookkeeper.

CHARLIE CHAN'S SAYINGS

◇ Government work keep me hopping like dissatisfied flea from dog to dog.

◇ Ancient proverb say, "One small wind can raise much dust."

◇ (To Tommy and Birmingham) Wear out brains instead of seat of pants.

◇ Do not think of future. It comes too soon.

◇ He is like tooth which has been pulled. Tooth is missing but gap remains. From gap, we may deduce why tooth is gone.

◇ Ugliest trade sometimes have moment of joy. Even grave digger know some people for whom he would do his work with extreme pleasure.

◇ Earthquake may shatter the rock, but sand upon which rock stood still right there in same old place.

◇ What is my reputation compared to someone's life?

◇ Never believe nightmare no matter how real it may seem.

◇ At moment, I am like man trying to set clock by guess. And as time does not stand still, perhaps better not stand still myself.

◇ (To the chattering Tommy and Birmingham) First time I hear cuckoos outside of clock.

◇ Skeleton in closets speak loudest to police.

◇ No experiment is failure until last experiment is success.

◇ (To Tommy and Birmingham) You two sit down so often, you get concussion of brain.

◇ Everything now in lap of gods. Very soon I give very hardy shake. Perhaps clue fall off of laps.

DEAD MEN TELL (1941)

Rating: ✶✶✶✶✶

TWENTIETH CENTURY FOX. Written by John Larkin; Photographed by
Charles Clarke; Edited by Harry Leonard; Musical direction by Emil Newman;
Produced by Walter Morosco and Ralph Dietrich; Directed by Harry Lachman.
60 minutes.

ANNOTATED CAST LIST

Sidney Toler....................Charlie Chan
Victor Sen Yung.............Jimmy Chan (Number two son)
Sheila Ryan...................Kate Ransome (Typist)
Robert Weldon................Steve Daniels (Press agent)
Don Douglas..................Jed Thomason (Rare coin dealer)
Paul McGrath.................Charles Thursday (Actor in disguise)
Kay Aldridge..................Laura Thursday (Newlywed bride)
George Reeves................Bill Lydig (Newspaper reporter)
Truman Bradley..............Captain Kane (Captain of *Suva Star*)
Ethel Griffes..................Patience Nodbury (Owner of pirate map)
Lenita Lane....................Anne Bonney (Psychiatrist)
Milton Parsons...............Gene LaFarge (Dr. Bonney's patient)

SYNOPSIS AND APPRAISAL

This is the last "great" Chan film, a masterful blending of mystery, creepy
mood and exceptional camerawork. It is well written, tautly directed and features
an outstanding ensemble of characters. Elements of the supernatural are quite
successfully woven into the storyline to intensify the suspense. *DEAD MEN
TELL* is a masterful example of the highly entertaining product that the studio
factory system can produce on a streamline budget.

A treasure map appears as backdrop for the opening credits. The *Suva Star*
advertises a cruise to seek out a buried treasure worth sixty million dollars.
Captain Kane, master of the ship, talks with press agent Steve Daniels about
Patience Nodbury's desire to cancel the trip. Daniels organized the cruise for the
dowager after she discovered an old pirate map. Miss Nodbury now wants to
back out because she thinks a thief has signed on for the voyage. Kane wishes
to continue with the endeavor, however, and is determined to set sail at dawn.

Charlie Chan comes on board the schooner searching for Jimmy, a possible
stowaway. At first, the vessel seems deserted, but then Charlie locates Patience
Nodbury, who tells the detective about attempts to steal her treasure map. For
protection, she divided the document into four pieces, keeping one and secretly
sending out the other three fragments to members of the expedition. Patience
plans to delay the cruise until she learns who broke into her hotel room. Her
grandfather, Blackhook the pirate, originally drew the map, and she tells Chan of

the legend of Blackhook, whose ghost appears whenever a Nodbury dies and escorts them to the underworld.

After Chan leaves, Patience closely studies her map fragment. The sound of the footfalls of a man with a pegleg is heard slowly walking on the ship. The figure of a pirate with a hook in place of his hand approaches Patience's stateroom. He scratches at her door with his hook and enters her chamber. The old lady collapses in fright as Blackhook approaches her, and the pirate removes the map from her hands.

Steve Daniels helps Chan search the ship for Jimmy. They encounter Bill Lydig, a well-known news reporter from St. Louis, relaxing in one cabin. Chan remarks that he heard Bill Lydig had died recently, and the journalist awkwardly replies that it was his brother Phil Lydig who had died. Jed Thomassson, a rare coin dealer, comes aboard, claiming he had received a message from Daniels to come to the *Suva Star* at once, but Daniels left no message.

Another passenger, Kate Ransome, arrives unnoticed and screams after hearing a moan coming from a locked chest. Chan opens it, releasing Jimmy Chan, who is bound and gagged. Jimmy says he was attacked, and that he overheard someone walking with a pegleg.

Patience Nodbury is found dead in her stateroom, and Chan concludes that she was deliberately frightened to death by someone posing as the pirate ghost. His deduction is confirmed by traces of theatrical make-up in the cabin and the empty envelope that contained the map.

Two other passengers are located in their cabin, Charles and Laura Thursday, who had just been married three hours earlier. Chan recognizes the man as a film actor named Charles Parkes, who admits to using a pseudonym for privacy. Chan continues to search the ship, and discovers a talking parrot who screeches, "Murder! Murder!"

Charlie sends Jimmy ashore to call the police, but he gets sidetracked following some footprints made by a man with a pegleg. Bill Lydig slips off the ship with him. At one point, he seems on the verge of striking Jimmy with a club, but relents when Jimmy wanders towards a cafe. There Jimmy spots a harmless, peglegged sailor having a drink. Captain Kane is also at the bar, and Jimmy tells him about the murder. Two other passengers, Dr. Anne Bonney and her patient Gene La Farge, are in the cafe. Jimmy becomes suspicious of them, and the barkeeper tosses the inquisitive lad out the back door which opens directly over the water.

La Farge admits he had discovered Miss Nodbury's body, but, suffering from an anxiety neurosis, he attempted but was unable to summon help. He also saw Lydig's attempt to hit Jimmy. Dr. Bonney and La Farge, like the other passengers, had received a phony message to come to the ship that evening.

Chan asks all the passengers about the other portions of the treasure map. Two of them, Laura Thursday and Jed Thomasson, hand over their portions to Charlie. Meanwhile, Jimmy, searching for a change of clothes in Daniels' cabin, finds the costume of Blackhook and puts it on. He approaches the other passengers gathered in a large compartment. His appearance frightens them, but fails to elicit any reactions that might indicate guilt. Jimmy quickly announces that he is behind the disguise.

Charlie questions the Oriental cook, whose ocarina music was heard by Jimmy at the time of the murder. Jimmy finds the third map fragment in Daniels' coat. He turns it over to his father, who is astounded to discover that his own pockets have been picked, and that the map fragments he was holding have been stolen. It is a rare moment of genuine humiliation for Chan.

Meanwhile, Bill Lydig is unmasked as an escaped convict posing as a journalist when his photo is discovered in a magazine by Kate Ransome. He overpowers Kate and places her in Captain Kane's replica of an iron maiden. Lydig then escapes after assaulting La Farge, who cries out in alarm. Chan and the remaining guests investigate, locating Kate, who explains about Lydig.

While searching the ship's hold, Chan notices something odd about the diving bell. Jimmy opens the hatch and discovers Lydig's body, dead from suffocation. Jimmy exclaims, "Why was he killed?" Entering the stairway, La Farge responds eerily, "Dead men tell no tales."

Charlie goes ashore, leaving Jimmy in charge. The detective locates Captain Kane in his loft office on the dock, attracted by the call of his parrot repeating, "You die as you left me to die." Chan tells him about Lydig's death, noting the remark of his parrot. The captain relates to Chan how his former partner once marooned him to die on a deserted island while they were seeking Blackhook's treasure. The captain was eventually rescued, but changed his name in order to bait a trap for the man who tried to kill him. He remained absent from his ship so not to alert his enemy who is one of the passengers. Charlie presses, but Kane refuses to identify the villain. An intruder is heard hiding in the loft, and as Chan turns to look, Kane slips out the side door. Chan discovers Charles Parkes and his new bride embracing in a chair at the rear of the loft.

The police arrive and collect all the passengers who were about to leave the ship after thwarting Jimmy. Steve Daniels is accused by Jimmy as his prime suspect, and the press agent is arrested. The remaining passengers are released from custody, while Charlie explains to his son that he is allowing this in order to catch the real killer. As long as he has the last piece of the treasure map, the murderer will be after it. He gives Jimmy a police whistle to summon help when needed.

La Farge meets and walks with Charlie on the fog enshrouded dock, asking about the final map fragment. Jimmy is startled by the figure of Blackhook, who backs him off the dock and into the water. He tries to blow the whistle, but it is waterlogged. Chan and La Farge then face the pirate who removes his disguise when Chan announces his real identity. He admits killing Lydig to obtain the two map fragments that were stolen from Charlie. When the murderer attempts to kill the pair, Captain Kane seizes him, boasting that he now has his revenge. The captain decides to turn the criminal over to Chan, who promises to maroon him "in a death cell at San Quentin."

Chan picks up Jimmy, who is drying off before a stove in the cafe. As they leave, Jimmy goes through the wrong door again and splashes back into the harbor. Charlie cries out, "Honolulu directly west!" This weak closing, however, is the only disappointment in this fast-moving, atmospheric production.

PERFORMANCES

This film is an excellent vehicle for Sidney Toler, who is dragged into the case seeking a treasure-mad Jimmy. His encounter with Patience Nodbury is one of Toler's most gentle and finely played moments. His encounters with Captain Kane (and his parrot) are quite rich and very well handled. Another of Toler's best moments is his embarrassment when he realizes that two map fragments were lifted from his inside pocket. When his son hands him the map segment he found in Daniels' coat, Charlie beams "Now only one piece missing." Then moments later, he exclaims, "Contradiction please, still three pieces missing!" His son is equally amazed, saying "You had your pocket picked on this ship?" To which Charlie replies, "Have not been on any other ship!" It is a priceless moment for the audience to see that even the great Charlie Chan can get hoodwinked on occasion.

Unfortunately, Jimmy, as played by Victor Sen Yung, has slipped back into the juvenile, and his portrayal seems more like a twelve year old than a college student. His scenes in the cafe, while not bad, are the low points of this excellent film.

Ethel Griffes, as the dowager Patience Nodbury, literally steals the film with just one powerful sequence. The scene where she encounters Blackhook is magnificent and truly frightening, equal to the best shock scene from any horror film of the Forties.

Truman Bradley, a superlative announcer and host of *SUSPENSE* on radio and *SCIENCE FICTION THEATER* on television, is equally effective as the mysterious and vengeful Captain Kane. He appeared in many films (including *CHARLIE CHAN IN RIO*), but his extraordinary reading here may be the highlight of his film career. Other cast members work well together, delivering a truly outstanding ensemble performance. George Reeves, future Superman on television, is very sinister as Bill Lydig. The scene where he plans to club Jimmy, and then realizes isn't necessary, is subtly played with excellent timing. It is Sen Yung's best scene as well.

Sheila Ryan (Kate Ransome), Kay Aldridge (Laura Thursday) and Lenita Lane (Bonney) bring depth and interest to their roles, disproving the myth that the women suspects in the Chan films are colorless characters. The male suspects, Robert Weldon (Daniels), Don Douglas (Thomasson) and Paul McGrath (Parkes/Thursday) round out one of the finest groups of suspects in the entire series.

Special merit must be given to Milton Parsons (LaFarge), a remarkable character actor who has appeared in many Chan films, but never more effectively than in this one. There is a throwaway scene in which he is walking a plank on deck as therapy for his nervousness. When Jimmy says he can do the same thing blindfold, Parsons puts one on him and tricks him into walking onto a plank leading overboard. His later apology to Jimmy for this practical joke is hilarious while still seeming perfectly logical. No better example can be given of a character actor enriching the mood of an entire film.

CHARLIE CHAN'S SAYINGS

◇ Desire for ocean adventure is ailment very much like hives, give itch to many boys.

◇ Man has learned much who has learned how to die.

◇ Method sometimes hid in madness of practical joke.

◇ Swallow much, but digest little.

◇ Trouble, like first love, teach many lessons.

DOCKS OF NEW ORLEANS (1948)

Rating: ✱✱✱

MONOGRAM. Written by W. Scott Darling; Photographed by William Sickner; Edited by Ace Herman; Musical direction by Edward J. Kay; Produced by James S. Burkett; Directed by Derwin Abrahams. 64 minutes.

ANNOTATED CAST LIST

Roland Winters...............Charlie Chan
Victor Sen Yung.............Tommy (Jimmy) Chan (Number two son)
Mantan Moreland...........Birmingham Brown (Chan chauffeur)
Virginia Dale..................Rene Blanchette (Owner's niece)
John Gallaudet................Peter McNally (Police captain)
Howard Negley...............Andre Pareaux (Gang ringleader)
Carol Forman.................Nita Aguire (Phony countess)
Douglas Fowley..............Grock (Pareaux's henchman)
Harry Hayden.................Oscar Swendstrom (Scientist)
Dian Fauntelle................Mrs. Swendstrom (Radio show host)
Stanley Andrews............Theodore Von Scherbe (Chemical exporter)
Emmett Vogan...............Henri Castanaro (Chemical exporter)
Boyd Irwin....................Simon LaFontanne (Owner of firm)
Rory Mallison................Thompson (Office manager of firm)
George J. Lewis.............Dansinger (Police detective)
Ferris Taylor.................. Dr. Doobie (Police psychiatrist)
Haywood Jones..............Mobile (Garage attendant)
Fred Miller....................Overweight armed guard

SYNOPSIS AND APPRAISAL

This is the finest film of the Roland Winters series, despite its reliance on *MR. WONG, DETECTIVE* (1938) for much of its plot. Screenwriter Scott Darling greatly refined Wong script and loaded his screenplay with an abundance of Chan sayings gleaned from the original novels. The criminal's identity becomes obvious when all rival suspects are liquidated, but the plot is so brisk and entertaining that this isn't a serious drawback. There is no explanation about Chan's presence in New Orleans, and he seems to own a home there as well. Charlie now seems to have a collection of homes now in various cities.

The film opens in New Orleans, where members of a gang headed by Andre Pareaux are plotting to disrupt chemical shipments by the LaFontanne Chemical works. Simon LaFontanne, the head of the company, on the recommendation of Charlie Mitchell, consults Chan with his suspicions that someone is plotting against him. He also reports that a woman named Aguire recently approached him using a forged introduction.

As the businessman leaves, Tommy and Birmingham discover LaFontanne's chauffeur has been knocked out and replaced by a phony who quickly drives off with the car. Chan tells LaFontanne that he will take the case.

The next day, LaFontanne meets with Von Scherbe and Castanaro, two exporters with whom he made a business deal to ship chemicals to South America. They want him to sign a document to cover their agreement in case one of them dies, which LaFontanne reluctantly signs. After they leave, Oscar Swendstrom, a scientist who believes he was swindled when the company purchased his chemical formula, threatens LaFontanne in front of Thompson, the office manager and Rene, Simon's niece and secretary. She summons the police, but expresses sympathy for the troubled scientist. When Captain McNally arrives, Simon is found slumped over his desk in his office. When Chan arrives for his appointment moments later, the police asks his help.

Chan is curious why the radio, which is turned on, produces no sound. Rene says her uncle always listened to music when he was alone, and that the set had just been repaired. Captain McNally finds a broken radio tube, which Chan wishes to examine.

The police arrest Swendstrom, assuming he provoked LaFontanne's heart attack, but the coroner reports that poison gas was the cause of death. Charlie proposes that the broken radio tube contained the deadly gas. Von Scherbe and Castanaro are questioned, and they report that the radio was playing when they left the office.

In another part of town, Pareaux is yelling at his two associates, Nita Aguire and a thug named Grock, who was the phony chauffeur. The gang continues to scheme to obtain Swendstrom's chemical formula.

Tommy and Birmingham are checking all garages, looking for the LaFontanne car which was driven off by the phony chauffeur. Birmingham engages in banter with one garage attendant while Tommy locates and steals the car. They are quickly stopped by the police, but Captain McNally is very impressed with their discovery and accomplishment. A search of the auto reveals some cigarette ash with coquinna bark, which suggests to Charlie that someone favoring Mexican cigarettes had ridden in the car.

Back at home, Tommy and Birmingham relax by playing some jazz on the violin and piano. Charlie, analyzing radio tubes, is startled when one of them pops when Tommy plays a high note on the violin. Charlie asks Tommy to continue playing, and a second tube explodes in his hand. He considers this to be a significant development, although he is noncommittal when Tommy asks about it.

Chan next visits Henri Castanaro, who is interrupted by two visitors, who are actually Pareaux and Aguire in the guise of a countess and her cousin. Chan becomes suspicious and pretends to recognize the countess. He then borrows a cigarette from Pareaux, which he notes contains coquinna bark. Thompson and Rene Blanchette also appear with some documents requiring Castanaro's signature. His butler also hands him a letter which turns out to be a letter from Swendstrom warning Castanaro of great danger. He locks himself in his den, calling the police. When they arrive, sirens blaring, Castanaro is found dead in the locked chamber, murdered in the same manner as LaFontanne.

The police grill Swendstrom concerning his letter, but he remains silent. They learn Swendstrom's wife, a noted radio broadcaster, smuggled this letter out of jail for him. Meanwhile, Pareaux and his associates argue about the death of Castanaro at their hideout. Each one thinks the other may have been responsible for the crime, or else "somebody else must be sitting in on this game!" They decide they need to dispose of Chan at once.

Swendstrom finally tells the police that Von Scherbe is the murderer, but by the time they get to his office, he also has been eliminated by gas. Chan observes that Von Scherbe's radio is turned on, but not working. He asks McNally to come to his home with the remaining suspects for a meeting that evening.

Birmingham and Tommy are overpowered by Grock, Aguire and Pareaux at Chan's house. The three gangsters then lie in wait for Charlie. He knowingly enters this trap, and is defiant when they try to question him about the case. He reels off his critique of their scheme step by step, while Birmingham and his son revive. Rene Blanchette arrives at Chan's door, and the criminals seize her as well.

Charlie claims to have a sample of Swendstrom's poison gas formula sealed in a radio tube, and breaks the tube using a high-pitched recording. His vivid description of the effects of the gas frightens the criminals, who are then easily subdued by Tommy and Birmingham. McNally and the police appear, and Chan explains how he fooled the crooks by simply using the power of suggestion, since the tube contained nothing. The police take the criminals into custody, and Chan announces the identity of the murderer and the method of the killings. With the case closed, Chan, Tommy and Birmingham prepare to return to San Francisco.

PERFORMANCES

This film represents the best Roland Winters has to offer in the role of Chan, and with a strong script, he can be quite enjoyable. If he is not in the same league with Oland or Toler, he is still can be credible and stimulating in the part, far superior to J. Carol Naish and others who attempted the role on radio. Winters is unable to convey the lovableness of Charlie or his warmth as a family man, but he is strong enough to be convincing in the part and be entertaining as well. His other main drawback is his halting manner of speech and syntax, some of which is a reflection of the Chan from the novels. Winters is magnificent in this film in the long scene where he is held hostage by the criminals. His word portrait of the effects of the poison gas is spellbinding, and represents one of Winters' finest moments in the role.

Victor Sen Yung and Mantan Moreland deliver worthy supporting roles, and their byplay is never obtrusive of the main storyline. Moreland even gets to perform a few moments of his vaudeville routine with Haywood Jones, the garage attendant, and this material comes across terrifically well.

All the other actors deliver colorful, interesting performances, especially Carol Forman (Aguire), Howard Negley (Pareaux), Emmett Vogan (Castanaro) and Boyd Irwin (LaFontanne). The ensemble work is snappy, particularly in the long, involved sequence culminating in Castanaro's murder. Harry Hayden has the most difficult role as Swendstrom, and while not fully convincing, he gives the role enough flair to be successful. John Gallaudet is also very pleasant as Captain McNally, and while not particularly memorable like Tim Ryan as Mike Ruark, he fills the part with distinction. Only Virginia Dale (Rene) seems too unsubstantial among the supporting players.

CHARLIE CHAN'S SAYINGS

- ◇ He who takes whatever gods send with smile, has learned life's hardest lesson. I personally find it difficult to achieve that smile.

- ◇ (To Tommy) Please be sorry out of my sight because while in it, vision blurs and find self-control leaving me.

- ◇ Sometimes most essential clue very difficult to find.

- ◇ If matter not solved, it is will of fate, but feel inclined to give fate small tussle.

- ◇ Death one appointment we must all keep, and for which no time is set.

- ◇ Man would have to be dead whole year to be killed with this gun. Same have not been fired for many moons.

- ◇ (In response to McNally, saying something "looks" bad). Looks sometimes are frightful liar.

- ◇ Patience very lovely virtue...your race, I perceive, does not regard patience with great favor.

- ◇ Patience...must harvest rice before you can boil it.

- ◇ Even melon grown in shade will ripen in the end.

- ◇ The ignorant always loud in argument.

- ◇ All cards should repose on table when personal liberty at stake. You know, Chinese very funny people. Say "go," mean "go!"

- ◇ Can fallen fruit return to branch?

- ◇ He who squanders today talking about yesterday's triumphs have nothing to boast of tomorrow.

- ◇ Must gather at leisure what may use in haste.

⬦ It is fool in hurry who drink tea with fork.

⬦ He who go in hills after tiger must pay price.

⬦ Ship with too many pilots sometimes have difficulty reaching port.

⬦ After dinner is over, who cares about spoon?

⬦ Where ever one is not, that is where heart is.

ERAN TRECE (1931) Spanish language version of the lost film *CHARLIE CHAN CARRIES ON*

Rating: ✳✳✳

FOX. Written by Philip Klein, Barry Conners, Peggy Lent and Helen Barnhart; Spanish dialogue written by José López Rubio; Photographed by L. B. Abbott under the name Sidney Wagner; Directed by David Howard. 79 minutes.

ANNOTATED CAST LIST

Manuel Arbó	Charlie Chan
Rafael Calvo	Duff (Scotland Yard Inspector)
Ana María Custodio	Elen Potter (Member of Lofton tour)
Juan Torena	Dick Kennaway (Nielsen's companion)
Antonio Vidal	Paul Nielsen (Sickly tourist)
Julio Villarreal	Dr. Lofton (Tour group leader)
Raúl Roulien	Max Minchin (Reformed racketeer)
Blanca de Castejón	Peggy Minchin (His wife)
Miguel Ligero	Frank Benbow (Photography buff)
Amelia Santee	Mrs. Benbow (His wife)
Carmen Rodriguez	Mrs. Rockwell (Matronly tourist)
José Nieto	Captain Roland Kin (Evasive tourist)
Carlos Díaz de Mendoza	Walter Decker (Nervous tourist)
Lia Torá	Sybil Conway (His wife)
Martín Garralaga	John Ross (Fun-loving tourist)
Ralph Navarro	Gardiner (Duff's assistant)

SYNOPSIS AND APPRAISAL

ERAN TRECE (*"There were thirteen"*) was filmed simultaneously with Warner Oland's very first Chan film, *CHARLIE CHAN CARRIES ON*. Since the Oland picture is missing and considered lost, the Spanish language version offers a unique insight into the first traditional Chan film. The working method of *ERAN TRECE* was fascinating and closely followed the English language production, shooting the same scenes on the same day. The pictures were also based on the same script, but the Spanish version runs three minutes longer than the English counterpart due to some skits and songs added to the shipboard party sequence. The Spanish cast and crew took over the sets at night, using the same props and the same camera set-ups. Both pictures shared establishing shots and the same musical tracking as well. This procedure was not unique, being quite similar to the Spanish language version of *DRACULA* filmed at Universal in 1931. Manuel Arbó played an asylum orderly in this film. Alternate language versions were also made of many films during this period. A number of Laurel and Hardy films, including *PARDON US* (1931), were simultaneous done in several languages. Laurel and Hardy reprised their roles, learning the lines phonetically, with the different cast employed for each language. One unusual bit of casting from this era was Boris Karloff in the tough convict role for the French language version of *PARDON US*.

This technique proved too costly and difficult, and eventually foreign markets were serviced with dubbed and subtitled versions. *ERAN TRECE* provides a close approximation of the Warner Oland version, which makes it especially valuable for Chan fans. There are numerous name changes, however, in the Spanish version. Mark Cowan becomes Dick Cowan. Pamela Potter evolves into Elen (Helen) Potter. Sadie Minchin becomes Peggy Minchin. Elmer Benbow is transformed into Frank Benbow. Mrs. Luce becomes Mrs. Rockwell. The most radical change has Patrick Tait transformed into Paul Nielsen. Both films remain faithful to Earl Derr Biggers' novel, and Chan only appears in the final half of the story. A later picture, *CHARLIE CHAN'S MURDER CRUISE* (1940), used the same plot, but it was extensively revised.

As this film opens, Oland rather than Arbo makes the initial appearance as Charlie Chan. At Scotland Yard Headquarters in London, Inspector Duff receives a letter and photograph from his friend Charlie, and the picture displayed is a pose of Warner Oland as Chan standing in line with his wife and eleven children. Duff's police associate exclaims "Caramba!" when Duff shows him the photo.

Moments later, Duff is assigned to undertake an investigation of a murder at the *Broome Hotel* on a floor occupied by individuals on an around-the-world tour led by Dr. Lofton. A member of this group, Louis Potter, was strangled in his bed. (Potter is called Hugh Morris Drake in the English version and the Biggers' novel.)

Dr. Lofton is very protective of the other members of his party. After evidence suggests that one of them committed the crime, Duff questions them all, including: John Ross, a lumber exporter from Tacoma, Washington; Max Minchin, a reformed gangster from Chicago and his wife Peggy; Frank Benbow and his wife, photography buffs; an affluent widow Mrs. Rockwell; Captain Roland Kin, a slick ladies' man; Paul Nielsen, a frail criminal lawyer; Dick Kennaway, his traveling companion; the nervous Walter Decker; and Elen Potter, the granddaughter of the victim. The inspector obtains several clues, but not enough evidence to detain any individual, and the tour is allowed to continue.

Later, a hotel employee reveals some suspicious actions he observed by Walter Decker on the night of the murder, and Duff heads to Nice to question him. By the time he arrives, Decker is dead, his murder staged as a suicide. Mrs. Rockwell tells Duff that Decker was in fear of his life, and that he wrote a letter to be delivered to his wife, Sylvia Conway, an entertainer staying in San Remo.

Inspector Duff goes to Sylvia Conway's hotel in San Remo, where the woman claims that a murderer is masquerading as a member of the Lofton group. This man's real name is Jim Maynard (Jim Everhard in the novel), a criminal with whom she was once involved. Maynard killed Decker and now plans to kill her. Decker's letter confirms that Maynard is a member of the Lofton tour and that Louis Potter was murdered by accident after he and Decker had switched hotel rooms. Duff plans to bring Sylvia to Nice to expose the criminal, but she is shot as they ride in an open-cage elevator. Duff is horrified, and he is now unable to penetrate Jim Maynard's disguise.

The world tour continues. Duff tells Elen Potter about these events, and entrusts her safety to Dick Kennaway. The Lofton group then tours Egypt, India and Japan. While in Yokohama, Dick and Elen overhear a man on the street who points out Jim Maynard among the Lofton tourists. They confront try to confront the man who runs away. The pair are later fired upon while they cable Duff with the news. The inspector plans to meet the tour when they travel to Honolulu, and he goes directly there to consult with Charlie Chan.

Arbó's first appearance as Chan occurs in his home where he is dressed in a traditional flowing Chinese robe. Warner Oland must have looked just as impressive in his opening scene. Duff telephones Charlie, and when they meet he explains the difficult case that he is trying to crack. When Chan leaves Duff alone in his office at headquarters, an assailant shoots the Englishman from an outside window. The wounded inspector briefly revives and asks his friend Chan "to carry on."

Charlie and the chief of police are outraged by this outrageous attack in Charlie's office. Chan demands the assignment, takes Duff's briefcase with the files on the case, and rushes to join the tour as their ship leaves Honolulu. His wife and his son named John see him off at the dock.

Chan tells the members of Lofton's tour about the assault on Duff. He also proclaims his intent to uncover the killer. Nielsen challenges the detective's authority to question them. The other tourists, however, are more co-operative.

Someone tries to shoot at Chan from a window while he is in his cabin, but Charlie spots the gun and is able to wrestle it out of the hand of the felon who then escapes unseen. After pursuing several clues, Chan hatches a scheme to force Jim Maynard's hand. He writes a letter to each male suspect threatening them with arrest upon arrival in San Francisco. He slips the letters under the stateroom doors of these individuals while the Lofton group is gathering for a farewell party.

Nielsen, superstitious because there are thirteen guests at the table, asks Chan to join them as he enters the dining hall. Charlie tells everyone about the presence of Jim Maynard, who is a member of their tour. His speech dampens their festive mood. Back in their cabins, each suspect reacts differently as they read Chan's letter.

Charlie asks Dick Kennaway to help him arrange a dummy figure of himself in his cabin. They position the figure in front of the window, and wait on deck for the killer to strike. Moments later, a shot rings out, and the assassin is captured. The other tour members appear after hearing the gunfire, and Chan reveals which member of their group is actually Jim Maynard.

The film ends as Charlie prepares a cable to Inspector Duff who is recovering from his wounds. He described the denouement of the case, and he also tells him that "Miss Potter and Mr. Kennaway have decided that two shall be one. Perhaps more later!"

PERFORMANCES

Manuel Arbó is quite credible as Chan, but seems lacking the natural charm that the role requires. Also, the slightest action renders him totally breathless. He is best in his one-on-one conversations with the suspects. He is splendid in the scene after Duff is shot. He is also quite good in the party sequence. Many of the Chan sayings in the film are reused in later films. The picture's closing line, for instance, is reprised at the conclusion of *CHARLIE CHAN AT THE CIRCUS*. His finest moment is his very first scene in the film where he is dressed in traditional Oriental garments, seemingly like a mandarin out of the heyday of Chinese history. On the whole, Arbó performs the role in a straight-forward manner, lacking any real embellishments.

Most of the comic relief in the picture is provided by Raúl Roulien (Max Minchin), a very popular Latin performer, and he is showcased in an extended vaudeville scene with the perky Blanca de Castejón (Peggy Minchin) in the ship-board party sequence. Julio Villarreal is excellent as the eccentric Dr. Lofton. He plays the red herring with vigor as he rolls his eyes behind his pince-nez. Martín Garralaga is good as Ross, and oddly enough he appeared seventeen years later in the next to the last Monogram/Chan film, *THE FEATHERED SERPENT*. Garralaga became a fixture on American television, appearing on many programs from *ZORRO* to *MY LITTLE MARGIE*.

The other performers are adequate, although probably not as effective as their counterparts in the Warner Oland version which included Marguerite Churchill, George Brent, Jason Robards, William Holden and the superb C. Henry Gordon as the killer. One should note that the William Holden listed was a fine American character actor who died in 1932. He is unrelated to the famous actor who won the Academy Award for best actor in *STALAG 17* (1953) and starred in countless other films such as *SUNSET BOULEVARD* (1950) and *THE WILD BUNCH* (1969), and whose actual name was William Beedle.

It is very fortunate that *ERAN TRECE* has recently surfaced and has become easily available on video. It is a genuinely good film and provides new light on the initial Warner Oland film that launched the traditional Chan series.

CHARLIE CHAN'S SAYINGS

(Whenever possible, I used the original formulations from the English language script or the original Biggers novel.)

◇ (Note from Charlie Chan to Inspector Duff written on the back of his family photo) Nunca el zorro ve el final de su cola. ("The fox can never see the end of his tail.") The original note in the English version read "Each man thinks his own cuckoos better than the next man's nightingales."

◇ (Quoted by Inspector Duff) Only a very clever man can shoot off a cannon quietly.

◇ Only a very brave mouse will make its nest in cat's ear.

◇ Too late to dig well after house is on fire.

◇ Honolulu, paradise of the Pacific...tonight history repeat self, serpent appear in paradise.

◇ All mischief begins with the opening of one's mouth.

◇ Man seldom scratches where does not itch.

◇ Man should never hurry except to catch flea.

◇ He who feeds the chicken deserves the egg.

◇ A big head is only a good place for a big headache.

◇ Advice after mistake is like medicine after the funeral.

◇ Ancient proverbs must not be taken too literally.

◇ A good wife is the best household furniture.

THE FEATHERED SERPENT (1948)
Rating: **(*)

MONOGRAM. Written by Oliver Drake; Photographed by William Sickner; Edited by Ace Herman; Musical direction by Edward J. Kay; Produced by James S. Burkett; Directed by William Beaudine. 68 minutes.

ANNOTATED CAST LIST

Roland Winters...............Charlie Chan
Keye Luke.....................Lee Chan (number one son)
Victor Sen Yung.............Tommy (Jimmy) Chan (Number two son)
Mantan Moreland............ Birmingham Brown (Chan chauffeur)
Nils Asther.................... Paul Evans (Expedition leader)
Robert Livingston...........John Stanley (Expedition leader)
Leslie Dennison..............Henry Farnsworth (Missing archaeologist)
Carol Forman.................Sonya Cabot (Farnsworth's fiancee)
Beverly Jons..................Joan Farnsworth (Sister of lost man)
Martin Garralaga............. Pedro Francisco Lopez (Guitar singer)
George J. Lewis..............Juan Gonzalez (Police Captain)
Jay Silverheels................Diego (Assassin with blowgun)
Milton Ross...................Professor Scott (Elder archaeologist)
Charles Stevens.............. Dr. Castelaro (Mexican doctor)
Juan Duvan....................Manuel (Expedition guide)
Frank Leyva...................Jose (Expedition driver)
Erville Alderson..............Filippe (Expedition driver)

SYNOPSIS AND APPRAISAL

This is an incredibly silly film with numerous outlandish elements, including influences from a George Zucco horror film, *THE FLYING SERPENT* (1946) about the Aztec winged serpent Quetzalcoatl and hidden treasure. The film, although ridiculous, is tremendously entertaining (accounting for the bonus star in the rating). Another major bonus is the return of Keye Luke as Number one son, Lee Chan. The byplay and interaction among the three Chans makes this film unique, the only time Keye Luke and Victor Sen Yung appear together as brothers. The screwball plot unmasks the villain early in the story, making this a rare film in which Chan has no startling revelations at the conclusion.

After the credits, the picture opens in the village of San Pablo in Mexico, where a special expedition is gathering to seek the lost Aztec Temple of the Sun. Professors John Stanley and Paul Evans are leading the expedition. The other members are Sonya Cabot and Joan Farnsworth, the fiancee and sister of Professor Farnsworth who disappeared with Professor Scott the previous spring while searching for the same temple. Pedro, a strolling guitar serenader, asks the group for a job as cook.

Charlie Chan and his two sons, Lee and Tommy, are on vacation, motoring through Mexico in a car driven by Birmingham Brown. They stop to help a man lying unconscious by the side of the road. As he is given water, he mutters that he must get to San Pablo. They rush him to the town where the members of the expedition identify him as Professor Scott.

Chan deduces that the professor was recently held prisoner and forced to work very hard. The archaeologist revives and announces that Farnsworth has discovered an Aztec temple filled with treasure. They were then captured and tortured to uncover all the gold. While Scott becomes more coherent, the light is turned off, and a figure appears at the window. The professor is killed, stabbed in the back with with an ancient Aztec sacrificial knife. Charlie concludes that the crime was done by someone in the room. This accusation upsets the entire company, and Chan agrees to accompany the expedition.

Later that night Charlie confers with the police chief in his office. A man in a sombrero watches through the window and prepares to attack Chan using a blowgun. He is prevented by Lee. After a struggle, the attacker escapes and Lee thinks he could have been an Indian. Captain Gonzalez finds a pack of poisoned darts on the ground near the scene of the struggle.

The expedition sets off at dawn, including a Mexican guide named Manuel, two drivers called Jose and Filippe, and Pedro the singing guitarist as cook. That night, Birmingham has a witty conversation with Pedro about his hot chili. After everyone retires to their tents, Chan tells Lee, Tommy and Birmingham that he expects an attack to occur, and for everyone to keep alert. Birmingham spots Manuel sneaking out of camp, and Charlie and Lee follow him. They notice Stanley also slips out into the jungle.

Sneaking through a secret passage, Stanley enters an underground chamber where members of his gang are pressuring Professor Farnsworth to translate the Aztec writing that reveals the entrance to the tomb of Quannek. When Stanley threatens to harm his sister and fiancee, Farnsworth agrees to do his bidding. Manuel tells Stanley that they have been followed by Lee and his father, and the archaeologist sends Diego to kill them. Just as this cutthroat is about to strike, he is shot and killed by Pedro, who explains that he and his companions Jose and Filippe are members of the Mexican secret police. Lee recognizes Diego as the Indian with a blowgun, and they now discover he is actually wearing makeup, proving the Indians are not involved in the case.

Chan questions Stanley when he returns to camp, who claims he was merely tailing Manuel. A hurled knife whizzes by them and hits the tree behind the two men. They wonder which one of them was meant to be the target. Stanley then awakens Pedro to ask him about Manuel. Joan screams, and Sonya is found dead outside her tent with Paul Evans standing over her body. When Evans says someone stole his knife and used it to kill Sonya, Chan orders him brought back to San Pablo.

Next day, Stanley warns everyone that unfriendly Indians may be in the area.

The expedition splits into two groups, and Chan compliments Pedro for throwing the knife into the tree the previous night as a diversion which allowed the agent to slip unnoticed back into his tent. Stanley leaves his group to meet with Manuel, who tells him that Farnsworth has located the covert entrance to Quannek's tomb, and it is filled with treasure. He also tells Stanley that he found Diego's body. Stanley arrogantly boasts he will frighten Joan Farnsworth into canceling the expedition. Meanwhile, Birmingham accidentally finds the secret entrance to the Aztec Temple when he sits on a rock, and two thugs grab him.

Stanley drops his charade and takes Joan and Filippe prisoner. He takes them into the temple, where Joan embraces her brother. Filippe draws a gun, but is shot by Manuel.

Lee and Tommy tell Charlie about Birmingham's mysterious disappearance and the inscription they found portraying a feathered serpent. Chan sends Pedro for reinforcements, while Lee locates the secret temple entrance, and they sneak in. Birmingham, put to work by Stanley, accidentally gives away Chan's presence, and a fight breaks out. Even Charlie gets involved, knocking the gun out of Stanley's hand. After a terrific struggle, Lee and Tommy outfight and overcome the villains, who are then apprehended.

Back in San Pablo, Chan clears up the loose ends of the case, but there are no surprise revelations since Stanley is clearly the ringleader. Chan points out that Sonya was his accomplice, and actually stabbed Professor Scott. Stanley murdered her because she was getting jealous over his desire for Joan. The film closes as the Chans plan to resume their vacation, but Captain Gonzalez alerts them that the police in Mexico City are stumped by a recent murder case.

PERFORMANCES

Roland Winters has a grand time as Chan in this picture, despite the madcap scenario. The script provides him with marvelous opportunities to shine. The fact that the storyline itself is weak, with very poor development, goes by almost unnoticed because of the rich tapestry of familiar characters. Also in this film, a number of typical Chan sayings are delivered not by Charlie but by his sons, who are quite familiar with his vast reservoir of witticisms.

Keye Luke returns to the role of Lee Chan after a ten year absence, and brings a special magic to the role. He works very well with Roland Winters, and their interaction is delightful. Luke presents a more mature Lee, who even resembles his father at times when guiding his younger brother. There are a few inside jokes as well. Keye Luke himself was originally an artist, and when he left the series, Sen Yung mentioned that Lee went to "the New York Art School." Now, in this film, when Charlie asks Lee to copy a map, he remarks, "Here's where that old art school training comes in handy!"

This is the last of Victor Sen Yung's eighteen Chan film appearances. The byplay between Victor Sen Yung and Lee is also fascinating and marvelous. Unfortunately, the script keeps having him sing and play *La Cucuaracha* in an atrocious fashion. Incidentally, this film indirectly confirms that Tommy is not the same Tommy performed by Benson Fong, because in *THE RED DRAGON*, Tommy spoke fluent Spanish. Sen Yung's Tommy (actually Jimmy with a name change) can only speak fractured Spanish.

Mantan Moreland, instead of being edged out by Lee, blends in quite well. He still is more frequently paired with Tommy, but there are many charming scenes of him with both brothers. His long conversation with Pedro in camp is his main highlight, particularly when he remarks in amazement that he is already speaking Spanish! When Birmingham is taken prisoner by Stanley's men, he gives them a difficult time with his endless complaining. His reactions in the temple when he first sees Stanley and later sees Chan are also priceless. The actor who plays Pedro, Martin Garralaga, is a Chan veteran who previously appeared in the Spanish version of the first Chan feature with Fox Studios.

The supporting cast, except for Beverly Jons (Joan) and George J. Lewis (Captain Gonzalez), overact shamelessly, but with the bizarre plot this over-the-top approach is the correct one to take. Jay Silverheels, the fine American Indian actor best remembered as the Lone Ranger's ally Tonto, is cast as an American bandit masquerading as a Mexican Indian. This gives a clear idea of the wild construction of the story.

CHARLIE CHAN'S SAYINGS

- ◇ Man who improve house before building solid foundation apt to run into very much trouble.

- ◇ (Spoken by Lee Chan) Confucius reminds us...that only children and fools open their mouths when they have nothing to say.

- ◇ Sometimes human tissue tell more than human lips.

- ◇ Very difficult to estimate depth of well by size of bucket.

- ◇ Guilty conscience always first to speak up.

- ◇ Hunch not sufficient evidence to convince jury of guilt.

- ◇ (Spoken by Tommy Chan) Confucius say, "He who live in fear, lives longest."

- ◇ (Spoken by Lee Chan) Confucius reminds us, that he who fights and runs away...(Completed by Birmingham Brown)...will live to fight another day.

THE GOLDEN EYE (1948)
Rating: ✳✳✳

MONOGRAM. Written by W. Scott Darling; Photographed by William Sickner; Edited by Ace Herman; Musical direction by Edward J. Kay; Produced by James S. Burkett; Directed by William Beaudine. 68 minutes.

ANNOTATED CAST LIST

Roland Winters...............Charlie Chan
Victor Sen Yung.............Tommy (Jimmy) Chan (Number two son)
Mantan Moreland............ Birmingham Brown (Chan chauffeur)
Tim Ryan......................Mike Ruark (Police Lieutenant)
Wanda McKay................ Evelyn Manning (Daughter of mine owner)
Bruce Kellogg.................Talbot Bartlett (Geologist and assayer)
Evelyn Brent.................. Sister Teresa (Missionary nun and nurse)
Ralph Dunn................... Jim Driscoll (Manager of Golden Eye mine)
Lois Austin....................Margaret Driscoll (Wife of manager)
Forrest Taylor.................Manning (Owner of Golden Eye mine)
Lee "Lasses" White..........Pete (Prospector)
Edmund Cobb.................Bert (Miner and gang member)
Tom Tyler...................... Gang member
Lee Tung Foo................Wong (Curio shop owner)
Bill Walker................... Dr. Groves (Manning's doctor)
Barbara Jean Wong.......... Bystander in Chinatown
Richard Loo.................. Bystander in Chinatown

SYNOPSIS AND APPRAISAL

This offbeat and charming film is entertaining and comes close to being a Charlie Chan Western. The screenplay has a number of surreal elements that will delight some viewers but confuse others. Some elements from Biggers' *THE CHINESE PARROT* are adapted to this story. The mystery element is slight, and the guilty party is obvious. But the picture has a strong and lively sense of fun that allows it to stand out as unique in the series.

The opening is particularly moody and creates a powerful ambience. An old prospector named Manning has Charlie summoned at night to an old curio shop in Chinatown. An attempt is made on Manning's life, ánd Chan agrees to go to Arizona to help protect him. He plans to go undercover to the Lazy Y Dude Ranch which is near Manning's tract of land and mine. Evelyn Manning, the prospector's daughter, tells Chan that she also feels threatened by their unknown adversary.

Tommy and Birmingham go overboard in cowboy attire for this venture.

They are surprised to find Mike Ruark of the San Francisco police also at the ranch in the guise of a drunken tourist named Vince O'Brien. He is working on a case for the government, and in private he and Charlie compare notes. Ruark discloses that Manning just had a serious fall at his mine, which is known as the Golden Eye. Ruark is investigating the recent unusual productivity at the nearly dormant mine, which suggests a camouflage for smuggling. Chan arrives at the Manning ranch, claiming to be a curio dealer with a valuable jade piece that was ordered by Manning. He meets Jim and Margaret Driscoll, the manager of the mine and his wife. Talbot Bartlett, the local assayer, is also present. Evelyn takes the incognito detective to see her father, who is unconscious and wrapped in bandages. The doctor tells Chan about his injuries, and Driscoll arranges for a nun, Sister Teresa from the missionary school, to act as nurse.

Bartlett is waiting for Charlie in his room at the ranch. Since he was a high school classmate of Lee Chan, Number one son, Bartlett recognized Charlie and guessed that he was working on a case. He too is puzzled by the sudden volume of gold produced at the mine.

The next day, Evelyn visits Bartlett and tells him the nursing nun is "a weird character." When Charlie arrives, she finds out that Bartlett knows Chan's real identity. She reports her father remains in a coma, and that she knows nothing about any recent productivity at the mine. Pete, a grizzled prospector who stole some ore from the Golden Eye Mine, learns from Bartlett's assay that it is practically worthless. The prospector agrees to let Charlie use his entrance to the mine from a trap door in his shack.

That night, Birmingham, Tommy and his father reach the location of the shack, but Pete is missing. They enter the trap door in his shack and carry out an intensive search of the Golden Eye Mine, discovering the prospector's body. When they get back to the dude ranch, they discover their rooms have been searched. Chan is uncertain if his masquerade has been penetrated or if thieves were after his fictitious jade. Ruark and Chan plan to search the mine together in the near future.

Evelyn calls and leaves a message with Birmingham that she needs to see Chan at once, while Ruark receives a report that Driscoll has a criminal record. At Manning's ranch, Evelyn tells Charlie she thought she overheard her father speaking, but Sister Teresa insists he is still in a coma. Charlie deduces the nun as an impostor due to her incorrect footwear and scant medical knowledge, but he doesn't allow his suspicions to show.

Ruark decides to sneak into the Golden Eye Mine by himself, and observes some Mexicans unloading boxes from a truck near an entrance to the mine. He is knocked out by one of the miners, who discovers Ruark's police badge. Another gang loads the boxes onto another truck, and then head into the mine to kill Ruark. A gunfight ensues when the police lieutenant revives, and he is rescued by Chan. Sister Teresa appears in the mine and tells the gang members they have to hold out until a second shipment is delivered the next day.

Back at the dude ranch, Chan and Ruark discuss the clever smuggling scheme. Charlie thinks a prominent man has to be the mastermind, and Ruark believes it must be Driscoll. The Mexican authorities are notified about the smuggling, and Ruark also appraises the local police and enlists their support. Tommy and Birmingham search the mine again with Charlie. Birmingham finds the body of Manning, which has disappeared by the time he fetches Chan to the site. A loaded mining car is pushed after them, which they easily avoid.

Chan visits Evelyn at the ranch house, and is astonished when she says her father is resting in bed unconscious. Sister Teresa is called to the telephone, and Charlie uncovers Manning's bandages, revealing Mrs. Driscoll in disguise. Ruark arrests both her and the nun, as Charlie informs Evelyn about her father's death. Driscoll sneaks in and pulls a gun on Ruark, but Tommy snatches his weapon. As Driscoll tries to escape, he is shot outside by Bartlett.

Ruark is about to wrap things up, when Charlie announces the identity of the mastermind. Tommy disarms the culprit, and holds him prisoner. At this point, the most bizarre ending in the entire series occurs. The action freezes, and Birmingham Brown steps out of the scene and directly approaches the camera, speaking about the amazing abilities and strategies of Charlie Chan. This is completely unexpected, a surreal satire of the theatrical device used in numerous plays, such as Eugene O'Neil's *STRANGE INTERLUDE* and Thornton Wilder's *OUR TOWN*. As a one-time gag, this parody is quite successful, and brings this eccentric film to an unconventional finish.

PERFORMANCES

Roland Winters is fabulous, almost hammy, in this picture. The script portrayal has Charlie responding too slow. Chan almost allows Manning to be killed since he takes no action after spotting the phony nun. His investigating method seems haphazard at times, and it is odd that he seems unconcerned about Evelyn being alone and unprotected in a house filled with desperate criminals. Despite the absurdities of the plot, Winters is particularly diverting as Chan in this episode.

Victor Sen Yung is playful as Tommy, and his character alternates between mimicking a cowboy and seriously helping his father. His actions in the denouement of the film are quite decisive, acting cleverly both to disarm Driscoll and later to capture the mastermind.

Mantan Moreland has two very effective scenes, first when packing to go to the dude ranch, and second when discovering Manning's dead body. However it is his wild conclusion where he is most memorable when he steps out of the scene. His face practically fills the entire screen as he declares, "Ain't that something, ain't that something! Good gracious-a-me! That's Mr. Chan all over. When you think it is, it ain't, and when you think it ain't, that's just when it is!" He then launches into an infectious giggle. Also note Victor Sen Yung's reaction over Mantan's shoulder. He is supposed to remain frozen, but he keeps glancing over to Mantan while trying not to laugh.

Tim Ryan is good as usual as Mike Ruark, but his drunk routine is laid on just a little too thick and goes on just a bit too long. Forrest Taylor is excellent as Manning, but he really only appears in the opening scene. His interaction with Lee Tung Foo as Wong makes the opening first rate. Many other excellent vignettes grace the film. Lee "Lasses" White (Pete) is perfect as the old prospector, and Edmund Cobb, veteran of countless Republic Westerns and serials, stands out as one of the gang members. Evelyn Brent is quite good as the phony Sister Teresa, and Wanda McKay (Evelyn) as the heroine is more charming than usual.

CHARLIE CHAN'S SAYINGS

- ◇ People who listen at keyholes rarely hear good about themselves.

- ◇ Small things sometimes tell very large story.

- ◇ Desert present many mysteries.

- ◇ Willingness to speak not necessarily mean willingness to act.

- ◇ Little knowledge sometimes very dangerous possession.

- ◇ Bear should not toy with tiger.

THE JADE MASK (1945)
Rating: **

MONOGRAM. Written by George Callahan; Photographed by Harry Neumann; Edited by John C. Fuller; Music by Dave Torbett; Produced by James S. Burkett; Directed by Phil Rosen. 66 minutes.

ANNOTATED CAST LIST

Sidney Toler..................Charlie Chan
Edwin Luke..................Edward Chan (Number four son)
Mantan Moreland............ Birmingham Brown (Chan chauffeur)
Frank Reicher................Harper (Murdered scientist)
Hardie Albright..............Walter Meeker (Lab assistant)
Edith Evanson................Louise Harper (Harper's sister)
Cyril Delevanti..............Roth (Harper's butler and confidante)
Janet Warren..................Jean Kent (Harper's niece)
Alan Bridge..................Mack (Sheriff assisted by Chan)
Dorothy Granger............ Stella Graham (Puppeteer employed by Harper)
Lester Dorr..................Michael Strong (Mute chauffeur)
Joe Whitehead................Dr. Samuel R. Peabody (Coroner)
Ralph Lewis..................Jim Kimball (Motorcycle cop)
Jack Ingram..................Lloyd Archer (Stepson of victim)
Henry Hall..................Inspector Godfrey (Friend of Chan)
Danny Desmond..............Hotel bellboy

SYNOPSIS AND APPRAISAL

This picture is an unconventional and grotesque bizarre concoction, mixing elements of *CHARLIE CHAN IN THE SECRET SERVICE* (1944) with traditional Monogram thrillers such as *THE CORPSE VANISHES* (1942) and *VOODOO MAN* (1944). In some ways it is the Chan entry most typical and representational of the Monogram Studio product. The picture reeks of cheapness. Even the sound effects seem cut-rate, such as the swinging iron gate which sounds like someone rubbing a plastic-covered chair. Yet the film also has a baffling aura which many Monogram films have that make them entertaining despite their chintzy and seedy atmosphere.

The dreary music score by Dave Torbett is similar to those used in the Monogram horror films. The opening title music is distinctive, an attempt to create a standard theme music for Chan. The Oriental melody is almost stately, and it would be recycled as the title music for the next three Chan films. It wasn't until *DARK ALIBI* that this melody is refined with added charm and a more sprightly tempo. This final version became the standard Chan theme for the remainder of the series.

The film's title makes little sense, since there isn't any reference to jade in the entire film. Something like *THE MYSTERIOUS GAS CHAMBER* would have been a more accurate and intriguing title. Almost all the action takes place in one locale, the fog-bound and remote Harper estate. The plot has some atmospheric and memorable moments with clever twists, but at least one of the guilty characters is quite obvious early in the film.

The picture opens one dark night at the home of Dr. Harper, a crabby and suspicious scientist who is working on a secret gas formula that can harden wood to the strength and durability of metal. The scientist conceals his formula in a hidden chamber that can only be opened by a special word code spoken by Harper himself. His butler, Roth, is the only other person who knows this code.

Roth is performing his nightly chores when someone shoots at him from the main gate. A motorcycle patrolman comes to the house, but he is ambushed and replaced by an impostor. Moments later, Dr. Harper is murdered in his gas chamber laboratory by a poisoned dart.

Chan is returning to Washington when he is called by Inspector Godfrey, who tells him about the murder at the Harper estate. The Secret Service wants Charlie to handle the case since Dr. Harper was working on a formula vital to the national interest. On his current trip, Charlie is accompanied by Edward, his fourth son who is a studious bookworm. Chan leaves Edward and Birmingham at the hotel to travels out to the scene of the crime.

Sheriff Mack is in charge of the case, and he openly welcomes Chan's help. Roth explains that he heard Harper's voice on the intercom saying he was being murdered. He rushed to the laboratory, but Harper had vanished. Sheriff Mack searched the entire estate, but found nothing. The sheriff and Chan interrogate the employees of the missing scientist. They include: Louise Harper, his sister and housekeeper; Jean Kent, his niece and housemaid; Walter Meeker, his lab assistant; Michael Strong, his mute chauffeur; Roth, his butler; and Stella Graham, an experienced puppeteer. Another of Dr. Harper's experiments was the development of a toy robot.

Everyone had a strong personal dislike of Harper, who had a very unpleasant personality. Some of these suspects claim they noticed a policeman sneaking around the house at the time of the attack. Birmingham and Edward are forced to leave the premises, because Chan had already checked out of the hotel. They have no choice but to proceed to the Harper house, where Edward wishes to help his father crack the case.

Charlie finally discovers Dr. Harper's body on the stage in the puppet room, an unusual chamber adorned with plaster masks on the wall, including likenesses of each occupant of the house. Birmingham is startled when he watches Stella Graham carrying all four of the heavy Chan suitcases at once. Roth explains that Stella once performed as a strong woman as well as a ventriloquist.

The next day, Mack and Chan learn that Officer Kimball is missing. Jean Kent admits to Chan that she and Kimball were having a romance. She had planned to let him in, but Roth answered the door and refused him entrance. When Roth is questioned, he claims to have figured out the identity of the killer, but asks for five minutes in order to gather some important evidence.

The butler heads upstairs, but he is seen by Edward wandering in a downstairs corridor. Roth them collapses, killed by a dart. Mack and Chan conclude that Roth was killed upstairs, knocking over a vase of flowers as he fell. Water from the vase had soaked his shoes. In the same room, a dictaphone machine is still on. When activated, Harper's voice comes through the speaker gasping, "Murder...Here! Here!" A puzzled Sheriff Mack tries to figure out how it might be possible for Roth to appear to be walking in a downstairs corridor after he was already dead. Lloyd Archer, Harper's stepson, then arrives and insists the gas formula belongs to him.

A poisoned dart is shot at Chan while he is tracking Roth's wet footprints. Due to the layout and dimensions of the rooms, Chan deduces that there is a hidden room in the house. Later he hears an alarm, and Louise Harper tells him that someone is trapped in the hidden chamber. She claims it can only be opened by a word code in Harper's own voice. Edward gets the dictaphone, and Chan plays it until the hidden chamber opens, triggered by the right phrase. Jean Kent is inside, unconscious due to the gas that filled the chamber. When she recovers, she explains the secret panel was open and she simply went in and got trapped.

Edward gets a note from Michael, the mute chauffeur, saying he noticed something that would reveal the identity of the murderer. Michael is killed while carrying one of the plaster masks, which breaks after he collapses. Later Chan discovers all of the other masks are missing, but he locates an ear fragment from the broken mask.

While searching the house, Edward and Birmingham find the body of Kimball, the missing policeman. Chan gathers the suspects and announces his findings. The darts were fired from an air gun concealed in a ventriloquist's dummy. Chan uses Edward to demonstrate how the murdered Roth was able to walk, because he was animated like a puppet. Then Chan explains that Harper's dictaphone said "Murder... Ear! Ear!" rather than "Here! Here!" because Harper recognized the killer because of his distinctive ear.

It is the same plaster ear that Chan took from the broken mask. With this clue, Chan accuses a pair of suspects, and reveals that one of them is in disguise. This killer posed first as the policeman. He slew Harper, then killed and took the place of another member of the household. Chan rips the mask off the suspect's face. It turns out the guilty pair are husband and wife, and Mack takes them into custody. Chan officially takes charge of the secret gas formula on behalf of the government.

PERFORMANCES

Sidney Toler is commendable in the fourth entry in the Monogram series, but he generously shares the spotlight with Alan Bridge who practically steals the film as Sheriff Mack. Chan and Mack trade scintillating comments and observations throughout the film, and Mack clearly is one of the most successful companion investigators in the entire Chan series. Mack is laconic, witty and self-depreciating. At one point he observes, "Seems to me when folks asked me to run for sheriff, I missed a fine chance to keep quiet." Another time, he remarks to the coroner, "It's wonderful what doctors know. It's what they don't know that will kill you." Chan obviously enjoys Mack's company, and their relationship is without doubt the highlight of the film.

Edwin Luke, Keye Luke's younger brother, makes his only appearance in the series as Edward, Chan's fourth son. At first, Luke make a refreshing contrast to the other sons in the series. He is a bespectacled intellectual, calmer and more formal than his brothers. He also has a trace of arrogance. Edward dislikes being called "Eddie," and he and Moreland have some amusing exchanges where Moreland calls him "Eddie, I'm sorry, I mean Edward!" Edwin Luke provides a fresh alternative in his role, but he also lacks Keye Luke's charisma or the charm of Victor Sen Yung and Benson Fong. The character of Edward might have become tiring if used in more than one film. Like his brothers, Edward desires to assist his father, but his clear thinking on scientific principles becomes muddled when applied to criminal detection. Edwin Luke make very few screen appearances after this film, most notably in *THE KING AND I* (1956), and he always comported himself very well.

Mantan Moreland is wonderful in many scenes with Luke, but the writers did not provide him with very strong material in this picture. He is at his best in the early scene at the hotel. The film ends with a ridiculous conclusion, in which Birmingham outruns the sheriff's car while fleeing the Harper estate. This outlandish and cheap gag undermines the character of Birmingham, and no doubt Moreland must have raised some objections to the misuse of his character in such a manner.

Several other members of the cast deserve credit for their fine performances, particularly Hardie Albright (Meeker), Jack Ingram (Archer) and Cyril Delevanti (Roth). All the actresses, on the other hand, deliver lifeless and bland performances. In the case of Dorothy Granger (Stella), this is disappointing since her character could have been colorful.

CHARLIE CHAN'S SAYINGS

⋄ My personality always count in end. (Joking as he sits on an over packed suitcase.)

⋄ No barber shaves so close but another barber finds some work. (To which Mack replies, "That is a cutting remark!")

⋄ (To Edward) Every time you open your mouth, you put in more feet than centipede.

⋄ To get information from him is like putting empty bucket into empty well.

⋄ Things misplaced sometimes furnish very good clues.

⋄ Murder know no law of relativity.

⋄ (To Edward) My boy, if silence is golden, you are bankrupt.

⋄ Like fingerprints, no ears are exactly alike.

MR. MOTO'S GAMBLE (1938)
Revised version of *CHARLIE CHAN AT THE RINGSIDE*
Rating: ****

TWENTIETH CENTURY FOX. Written by Charles Belden and Jerry Cady; Photographed by Lucien Andriot; Edited by Nick De Maggio; Musical direction by Samuel Kaylin; Produced by Sol M. Wurtzel and John Stone; Directed by James Tinling.   71 minutes.

ANNOTATED CAST LIST

[Warner Oland.................Charlie Chan] Replaced in film by:
Peter Lorre.....................Kentaro Moto (Japanese secret agent)

Keye Luke.....................Lee Chan (Number one son of Charlie Chan)
Dick Baldwin.................Bill Steele (Boxer accused of murder)
Cliff Clark.....................Tom McGuire (Steele's manager)
Lynn Bari......................Penny Kendall (Fashion news reporter)
Maxie Rosenbloom.........Horace Wellington (Lee Chan's pal)
Harold Huber.................Lt. Riggs (Head of the Homicide squad)
John Hamilton................Philip Benton (President of boxing syndicate)
Jayne Regan...................Linda Benton (His daughter)
Russ Clark.....................Frankie Stanton (Murdered fighter)
George E. Stone.............Jerry Connors (Stanton's manager)
Ward Bond.....................Biff Moran (World heavyweight boxing champ)
Douglas Fowley..............Nick Crowder (Moran's manager)
Lon Chaney, Jr................Joey (Crowder's sidekick)
Bernard Nedell.................Clipper McCoy (Notorious gambler)
Charles D. Brown............Scotty (Editor of *Daily Chronicle*)
Charles Williams............ Gabby Marden (Sports news reporter)
Jack Stoney....................Kid Grant (Moran's sparring partner)
Pierre Watkin.................District Attorney
Edward Earle..................Boxing arena physician
George Chandler.............Rambunctious fight fan

BACKGROUND, SYNOPSIS AND ANALYSIS

This motion picture began production as *CHARLIE CHAN AT THE RINGSIDE* and filming commenced on January 10, 1938. One week later, the project was suspended after it became apparent that Warner Oland would be unable to continue. It is well known that Oland had a drinking problem, but it never interfered with his ability to continue his work. Some believe he actually gave a better performance when he was drinking, although he had some difficulty remembering his lines. During the making of *CHARLIE CHAN AT THE RINGSIDE*, Oland was beset by many personal problems, including a divorce suit by his wife Edith. Oland was unwell, both mentally and physically, and he left the set. At the time some thought it was a money dispute. The actor was hospitalized a few weeks later. By the time he was released in March 1938, his health was greatly improved, and he reportedly signed a three picture deal for future Chan films.

Oland then took off on vacation to Sweden, where he developed bronchial pneumonia. He and his wife were planning a reconciliation, and Edith rushed to Europe when she learned of his illness. Oland died in Stockholm on August 6, 1938 at the age of fifty seven.

It has been reported that *CHARLIE CHAN AT THE RINGSIDE* was transformed into *MR. MOTO'S GAMBLE* after Oland's death, but this is entirely false, since the Moto film was in circulation five months before Oland passed away. The picture was previewed on March 11 and received general release on March 25, 1938. The retooling of the property into a Moto picture happened very quickly after the film was suspended. Lorre was both under contract and available. The main plot of the film was left unaltered, except for having the character of Moto pinch hit for Chan. Some of Moto's lines were changed to be more in line with his personality, but the film can still be regarded as a Chan film since Charlie's "Number one" son Lee Chan plays a major role. Moto still has several Chan-like quotes that he inherited in the script. Other Chan factors include a number of traditional Chan film veterans in the cast, regular Chan scriptwriters and James Tinling, the director of one of the greatest Chan films, *CHARLIE CHAN IN SHANGHAI*. This was the first Chan film not directed by Norman Foster, the regular Moto director, who in the Forties later directed a number of the finest Chan films of Sidney Toler.

One must also remember that almost a third of the scenes for this film was shot during the week it was a Chan film. Mr. Moto behaves in an atypical manner for most of the film. He dons no disguises, and has only two quick judo scenes, one as a classroom demonstration. It is the only film where Moto acts like a detective rather than a secret agent. The picture is successful because it is a good film, and the premise is plausible. One could easily imagine Moto taking a sabbatical in order to teach a specialized crime course at an American university. Still, Charlie Chan would have better suited to the scenario, and the picture would have been an admirable recovery from the weak *CHARLIE CHAN AT MONTE CARLO*, both for Warner Oland and Harold Huber.

The picture opens with Moto lecture to a class about aspects of criminology. After the class, Lee Chan and Mr. Moto are taken to the fights by Lt. Riggs., who is also an old associate of Charlie Chan. The colorful pageantry of the boxing arena fascinates Moto. He and Lee Chan fully enjoy the spectacle, and Riggs introduces them to many major figures involved in the sport. During the main bout, however, a homicide occurs right under his nose.

One of the main event fighters, Frankie Stanton, is murdered when a deadly poison enters a cut above his eye. This occurs during the middle of the fight. The poison was presumedly squirted onto the glove of Bill Steele, his opponent.

Steele is later charged with manslaughter by a grand jury, and Riggs asks Moto's help in uncovering the real solution. The plot is filled with many colorful characters, possible suspects who were at the ringside. These include: Tom McGuire, Steele's manager; Jerry Connors, Stanton's manager; Biff Moran, the heavyweight champ; Philip Benton, head of the boxing corporation; his daughter Linda, a friend of Steele; Penny Kendall, a reporter also in love with Steele; sports newsman Gabby Marden and Clipper McCoy, a high stakes gambler. Lee's friend Horace "Knockout" Wellington, a punch-drunk former boxer, also attended the fights. He is a kleptomaniac with memory lapses, and he is taking Moto's criminology seminar to try to correct his aberrant behavior.

At the *Daily Chronicle*, Penny Kendall suggests to her editor that the newspaper put up bail for Steele. At the same time, Linda Benton persuades her father to post bail, outmaneuvering her romantic rival Penny.

After concluding another classroom lecture, Moto discovers a coat stolen by Wellington is stained with the same poison that killed Stanton. A label with the name "John Howard" is sewn inside to the coat.

Benton visits Biff Moran's training camp. The champion is taking it easy, since his upcoming fight with Bill Steele may not ever occur. Benton urges the boxer to train hard, since Steele may be cleared at any time. Gabby Marden is preparing a campaign to publicize and hype up the fight. Gambler Clipper McCoy taunts Moran, claiming that Steele could defeat him. McCoy lost a fortune on the Stanton fight, and warns that it will never happen again. An investigation of the wagers on the fight reveal that John Howard placed the largest bets with bookies across the country.

Lee Chan and Wellington are arrested after the ex-boxer drives off with someone else's car. When Moto learns of this, he decides to leave them in jail for their own safety. Riggs is frustrated in his search for John Howard, who finally turns up in the morgue. His real identity is discovered to be Whitey Goodman, a former convict. He died by the same poison as Stanton. Moto convinces the district attorney, in typical Chan fashion, to stage the Moran-Steele fight as a trap. He promises to name the killer after the fight.

That evening, Moto is assaulted in his hotel room, but he uses judo to easily overcome his opponent. During the middle of the night, someone tampers with the official time clock at the ringside in the arena.

Still in jail the next morning, Lee Chan tells Wellington that his father, like Moto, sometimes left him in prison for protection. Suddenly, Wellington discovers he has a gun in the pocket of his topcoat. He fires it at the wall, and is startled to see that the weapon sprays poison. Lee asks the boxer where he got the gun, but he cannot remember. He asks Lee to hit him, since that sometimes stimulates his memory. This fails, but the sheriff enters their cell, and they escape after tricking him. They rush to the arena to bring the new evidence to

Moto.

The championship fight is brutal, and both the champion and the challenger find themselves victims of knockdowns. As the battle drags on, Moran appears to be gaining the upper hand, until Steele launches a spectacular comeback and knocks Moran out in the ninth round.

Moto asks all suspects to remain at the ringside after the fight, but he deliberately changes his seat. He subtly maneuvers another individual to sit in his original location. This is his "gamble" alluded to in the title. The killer is then forced to reveals himself, since the clock at ringside is wired to a gun that was originally intended to kill Moto. The bullets had been removed by Moto, who had earlier discovered the deadly device.

The murderer escapes, but is shot by Clipper McCoy as revenge for trying to ruin him. Lee appears with the murder weapon, but Moto informs him that the killer has already been executed. In class the next day, Moto praises both Wellington and Lee Chan for their fine detective work and assistance in the difficult case.

PERFORMANCES

Peter Lorre does a good job filling in for Warner Oland. He fits neatly into the fast-placed story. At one point, he humbly comments that he is a "floundering amateur" compared to his friend Charlie Chan, at least as a detective. Charlie's presence is also reflected by the presence of Keye Luke as Lee Chan, and this film bridges both the Chan and Moto film series. In fact, the Moto series later paid a special tribute to Oland. *MR. MOTO'S LAST WARNING* was in production in August, 1938, the same month as Oland's death. In one scene of this film, there is a close-up of poster. A Charlie Chan film is featured at the theater "Starring Warner Oland." Obscuring the name of the film is a strip reading "Last Day" crossing over Oland's name. It is a subtle but genuine and moving eulogy to the great performer.

The overall cast of this fast-paced film is outstanding. Harold Huber is particularly good as Lt. Riggs. Dick Baldwin (Steele), Cliff Clark (McGuire), John Hamilton (Benton) and Bernard Nedell (McCoy) play their roles to the hilt. Lynn Bari (Penny) and Jayne Regan (Linda) are especially delightful as the rival girlfriends of Bill Steele. They bring an excellent edge to the plot as well.

The major drawback to the story is Maxie Rosenbloom (Wellington) as the comic sidekick to Lee Chan. His portrayal of the forgetful kleptomaniac is so outlandish that it quickly becomes annoying. The ex-prizefighter (who was nicknamed "Slapsie" in the ring because of his tendency to slap at his opponents) is a natural talent who is quite good in smaller doses. Ward Bond (Moran) is ideal as the heavyweight champ. Lon Chaney, Jr. has a very minor part as a thug named Joey who can be seen lurking around whenever Douglas Fowley (Nick Crowder) is present.

This picture is a genuine hybrid, but it was a smart move by Fox to "save" the footage shot for *CHARLIE CHAN AT THE RINGSIDE* and still produce an entertaining picture. It should also be noted that there were also alternate titles for the original Chan film. First there was simply *CHARLIE CHAN AT RINGSIDE,* then the expressive *CHARLIE CHAN'S KNOCKOUT* and *CHARLIE CHAN'S GAMBLE.* Of course, the final variant was what was eventually selected for the Moto film.

MOTO'S OBSERVATIONS, ORIGINALLY INTENDED FOR CHAN

- ◇ Much information can be obtained from tongues loosened by anger.

- ◇ I have often noticed that the dog and the human are very much alike. Each will go to any length to obtain something he desires or to destroy something he believes dangerous.

- ◇ The usual way to avoid trouble is to lock it out. In this case, we lock it in.

- ◇ To reveal a snake, one must overturn a rock.

- ◇ Some people save strings. I pull them.

- ◇ In poker, the man with the poorer cards very often wins on a bluff.

MURDER OVER NEW YORK
(1940)
Rating: **

TWENTIETH CENTURY FOX. Written by Lester Ziffren; Photographed by Virgil Miller; Edited by Louis Loefler; Musical direction by Emil Newman; Produced by Sol M. Wurtzel; Directed by Harry Lachman. 65 minutes.

ANNOTATED CAST LIST

Sidney Toler...................Charlie Chan
Victor Sen Yung..............Jimmy Chan (Number two son)
Marjorie Weaver..............Patricia Shaw (Wife of saboteur)
Robert Lowery................David Elliot (Chemical researcher)
Frederick Warlock............Hugh Drake (British intelligence agent)
Ricardo Cortez................George Kirby (Aircraft manufacturer)
Donald MacBride.............Inspector Vance (New York detective)
Melville Cooper..............Herbert Fenton (Drake's college friend)
Joan Valerie...................June Preston (Actress)
Kane Richmond..............Ralph Percy (Airplane designer)
John Sutton...................Keith Jeffrey (Stockbroker)
Leyland Hodgson.............Robert Boggs (Kirby butler)
Clarence Muse................Servant (Temporary helper for dinner party)
Lal Chand Mehra.............Ramullah (Hindu servant of saboteur)
Frank Coghlan, Jr...........Gilroy (Clerk at British Imperial club)
Shemp Howard...............Shorty McCoy (Phony Hindu suspect)

SYNOPSIS AND APPRAISAL

This routine effort is a reprise of the plot of *BEHIND THAT CURTAIN* and *CHARLIE CHAN'S CHANCE*. There are a few good scenes, but the story never really gels. The scene where Inspector Vance orders all Hindus in New York rounded up is surreal, and the entire production becomes completely contrived when this ridiculous notion appears to succeed. The most suspenseful moment is the short scene where two shadowy figures are observed trailing Chan. This bit is well photographed and very atmospheric. The climax in the plane is also well done, if somewhat artificial.

The credits roll looking down upon the lower Manhattan skyline. In atypical fashion, Sidney Toler is billed last. Chan is flying to New York to attend a police convention, and he finds himself seated next to an old friend, Hugh Drake, formerly of Scotland Yard, now working for British military intelligence. Drake is trying to track down a notorious saboteur, Paul Narvo, who may be active in the United States. His only lead is Narvo's wife, a former actress, now in hiding in Manhattan. Drake is alarmed by the recent crash of a new bomber on a test flight, which he thinks could have been sabotaged by Narvo. Chan promises to help and makes plans to meet his friend later.

At the airport, Charlie is greeted by Inspector Vance of the New York City police. Jimmy also shows up, having driven to New York with his college roommate to see the World's Fair. That evening, Chan and his son call at George Kirby's apartment where Hugh Drake is staying. The agent left Kirby's dinner party early to work in the library, which his host turned over to him.

They find Drake slumped over his desk. Upon seeing a dead canary in a cage, Chan deduces that poison gas was used. Jimmy detects the scent of tetrogene emanating from a broken vial on the floor. This deadly gas quickly evaporates, leaving behind a distinct odor. Since the windows are latched, the murderer had to be one of Kirby's guests. Drake's briefcase with Narvo's photo and fingerprints are missing.

Chan and the police question the suspects: Herbert Fenton, Drake's college friend and his wife; June Preston, an actress; Keith Jeffrey, a stockbroker; Ralph Percy, an airplane designer who works for Kirby; and Boggs, Kirby's butler. Another servant, hired only for the evening diner party, had finished his duties and left. Chan notices that a pearl is missing from June Preston's elaborate necklace.

Jimmy catches Boggs steaming open a cablegram that was sent in reply to Drake's inquiry about him. The butler admitted he was once the primary suspect in a crime, and that Drake must have recognized the man when he worked for Scotland Yard. After the suspects are sent home, the temporary servant is brought in, and he reports that Drake had a visitor that evening in the library named David Elliot.

While preparing a cablegram to his wife, Chan discovers June Preston's pearl on the desk where Drake died. Charlie goes to June's apartment to return the pearl from her lavaliere. She admits that Drake questioned her in the library. He wanted some information about an actress with whom she had worked several years earlier, but June denied knowing the woman's whereabouts. Now, however, she gives Chan the woman's current name and address.

Chan is followed as he visits Patricia Shaw, who reluctantly confides in the detective about her troubled marriage to Paul Narvo. They were wedded in London, and later moved to India where she learned that he was responsible for the murder of an air ministry official with the assistance of his Hindu servant named Ramullah. Narvo imprisoned her, but she escaped, and he has been pursuing her around the world. A commotion is heard outside her window, where Jimmy is trying to catch a Hindu who was spying on Chan. Patricia is positive it was Ramullah, which means that Paul Narvo is in Manhattan.

At police headquarters the next day, Inspector Vance brings in David Elliot, thinking he might be Paul Narvo, but Patricia identifies him as her friend who met with Drake. He tried to convince Drake that Patricia was not working with Narvo.

In an absurd move, Vance launches a manhunt for "every Hindu in New York" to be gathered for a massive police line-up. Hundreds of Hindu suspects are paraded before Jimmy. The most ridiculous of these detainees turns out to be Shorty McCoy, a phony swami. Jimmy narrows his identification to a final choice, a curio shop owner, who is shot dead when Patricia Shaw recognizes him as Ramullah. The shots came from a warehouse across the street from the police station.

That night, Charlie and Jimmy investigate the curio shop and discover a man smashing up a chemical laboratory in a back room, where the deadly gas had been manufactured. The vandal flees after firing a shot at Jimmy. Charlie locates the plans for a new bomber, identical to the plane that recently crashed.

Meanwhile, the night clerk at the British Imperial Club informs Inspector Vance that Drake had checked his briefcase with him, and the police stake out the club. Boggs, Kirby's butler, arrives to claim it. When the police question him, he shows them a note from Kirby instructing him to retrieve it, but Chan believes the note is a forgery. Jimmy, entrusted with bringing the briefcase to headquarters, is attacked in the elevator as he leaves Kirby's apartment. Chan finds Kirby's body behind the same desk where Drake was murdered. The remnants of his glass of brandy show he was poisoned, while the liquor in a second glass is uncontaminated. Chan and Vance decide to keep the news of Kirby's death a secret.

The suspects gather the following morning at the airfield where another bomber is being tested. Before the flight, two unobserved workers plant a vial with poison gas on the plane, positioning it to fall when the aircraft descends.

Percy signals the plane to take off while the passengers are still in the cargo hold. Jimmy panics, but Chan merely observes everyone's reaction. As the plane starts a steep dive, the killer catches the vial as it falls. When the plane lands, Charlie reveals that the vial is a harmless substitute.

The killer's two henchmen were responsible for the attack on Jimmy, the shooting of Ramullah, and the sabotage on the earlier plane that crashed. At police headquarters, Chan reveals that the killer is not Paul Narvo, but only his confederate. Narvo, his face altered by plastic surgery, gives himself away while trying to poison the killer. Vance is amazed by Charlie's strategy in solving the case, but Jimmy boasts that this adventure was merely routine.

PERFORMANCES

Sidney Toler's best moments in the film are during his interviews with June Preston and Patricia Shaw. He is gentle, yet direct and quite comforting, putting these troubled women at ease while obtaining vital information. He also reacts with lightly disguised mirth at the cavalcade in the line-up where every Hindu in New York is forced to appear. Finally, Toler's poker-faced reactions the bomb dives is another great moment.

Victor Sen Yung lets a whiff of haughtiness slip into his characterization of

Jimmy in the film, which is unfortunate. His part is better written than usual, and his knowledge of chemistry proves of value in the case. He also saves his father when he notices a Hindu following him. But he is distracting when he overacts in the dive bomber sequence, almost ruining the climax of the film.

The picture contains a number of sound performances by Chan series regulars like Marjorie Weaver (Patricia Shaw), Kane Richmond (Ralph Percy) and Ricardo Cortez (George Kirby). Donald MacBride is a bit too camp as Inspector Vance to be effective, but his genuine liking for Jimmy Chan is a nice touch.

The other players likewise do fine work, with three standouts. The first is Clarence Muse, a major black actor who is sometimes underappreciated. Muse combines charm and dignity in his numerous film appearances, such as the low budget Bela Lugosi thriller *THE INVISIBLE GHOST* (1941). He wrote and starred in some films for black audiences. Muse also composed songs, and was active in films until 1979. Frank Coghlan, Jr. is excellent as the sharp-eyed clerk who works with the police. Often known as "Junior," the feisty serial hero is often remembered for *THE ADVENTURES OF CAPTAIN MARVEL* (1941) where he would yell "Shazam!" to transform himself into the superhero played by Tom Tyler. Coghlan previously played a race horse jockey in *CHARLIE CHAN AT THE RACE TRACK*. Finally, Shemp Howard from The Three Stooges has a hilarious cameo as a phony Hindu swami whose ineffective make-up fails him in the police line-up.

CHARLIE CHAN'S SAYINGS

⋄ Needle can be found when correct thread located.

⋄ British tenacity with Chinese patience like royal flush in poker game, unbeatable.

⋄ Canary, unlike faithful dog, do not die for sympathy.

⋄ Coincidence like ancient egg, leave unpleasant odor.

⋄ Thought at present like dog chasing own tail, getting no place.

⋄ Nut easy to crack often empty.

⋄ Will inform honorable mother that aid from Number two son like interest on mortgage, impossible to escape.

⋄ Fresh weed better than wilted rose.

⋄ Person who asks riddle should know answer.

⋄ Happy solution never see light if truth kept in dark.

⋄ One man with gun have more authority than whole army with no ammunition. Door of opportunity swings both ways.

⋄ Wishful thinking sometimes lead to blind alley.

⋄ Faces may alter, but fingerprint never lie.

⋄ Important events, like insistent alarm clock, demand attention.

⋄ Eye easily deceived.

⋄ Same leopard can hide beneath different spots.

⋄ Kitchen stove most excellent weapon, good for cooking goose.

⋄ Desire to live still strongest instinct in man.

⋄ Confidence of favorite son like courage of small boy at dentist, most evident after tooth extracted.

THE RED DRAGON   (1945)
Rating: **

MONOGRAM. Written by George Callahan; Photographed by Vincent Farrar; Edited by Ace Herman; Musical Direction by Edward J. Kay; Produced by James S. Burkett; Directed by Phil Rosen. 64 minutes.

ANNOTATED CAST LIST

Sidney Toler...................Charlie Chan
Benson Fong..................Tommy Chan (Number three son)
Willie Best.....................Chattanooga Brown (Chan chauffeur)
Fortunio Bonanova..........Luis Carvero (Mexican police inspector)
Robert E. Keane..............Alfred Wyans (Nuclear scientist)
Carol Hughes.................Marguerite Fontan (American tourist)
Marjorie Hoshelle............Countess Irena (Nightclub singer)
Barton Yarborough..........Joseph Bradish (Oil salesman)
George Meeker................Edmund Slade (Farm machinery salesman)
Don Costello..................Charles Masack (Importer)
Charles Trowbridge..........Prentice (U.S. Embassy attache)
Mildred Boyd..................Josephine (Fontan's maid)
Jean Wong.....................Iris Ling (Chinese artist)
Donald D. Taylor............Walter Dorn (Undercover detective)

SYNOPSIS AND APPRAISAL

It is rare for Monogram to portray a foreign setting, but they do a credible job. The film has a strong supporting cast and a quick pace. Unfortunately, the plot is basically a retread of the same story from *CHARLIE CHAN IN THE SECRET SERVICE*. The film bogs down with too many long, rambling sequences in the hotel storage basement. The plot is constructed around a trick gimmick which had become routine for the Monogram Chan series.

The picture opens with Walter Dorn visiting the U.S. Embassy in Mexico City to request the assistance of Charlie Chan. He warns of an espionage plot to steal the papers of his employer, the nuclear scientist Alfred Wyans. Inspector Carvero of the Mexico City police also wishes that the American Embassy would send for Chan at once.

Inspector Carvero attends a luncheon given by Wyans at which Walter Dorn is shot. He manages to type out a message on a typewriter before he dies. This puzzling message is "TH E$M OST."

Chan arrives at the airport with Tommy, who speaks fluent Spanish, and Chattanooga Brown, Birmingham's cousin. Inspector Carvero tells them about the murder of Dorn. No gun was found at the scene or in the possession of any of the suspects, guests at Wyans' luncheon: Marguerite Fontan, an American tourist; Countess Irena, a singer; Joseph Bradish, an oilman and suspected smuggler; Edmond Slade, a salesman and gun runner; Charles Masack, an importer who was previously suspected of distributing Nazi propaganda; and Alfred Wyans himself. All these people reside at the same hotel.

There are odd aspects to the Dorn case. Two bullets were uncovered at the scene, but only one shot was fired. A rare bottle of Chinese ink called *Red Dragon* is spotted by Tommy near the typewriter. Charlie cannot decipher Dorn's dying message. The police laboratory reports a bizarre conclusion. The bullet used to kill Dorn lacked any gun barrel markings whatsoever. It had not been fired from any firearm. There also are strange metal fragments found in Dorn's pocket.

Wyans reports his typewriter has been stolen, and Chan discovers that Countess Irene is married, and that her husband may be an enemy agent. Each suspect is observed searching the baggage room of the hotel by Tommy and Chattanooga. Chan conducts his own search and locates the missing typewriter in Wyans' own luggage. Tommy saves his father's life when some heavy crates come crashing down towards him.

Alfred Wyans makes his own discovery and tries to notify Chan. When he attempts to telephone the detective, the professor is shot and killed. Masack, who was standing near Wyans at the time, is interrogated. The death of Wyans is similar to Dorn's murder, in that two bullets are found, but only one shot was heard. Chan believes the strange fragments in Wyans' pocket is the key to the mystery.

The inspector and Chan go to the Capitol Club to question Countess Irene, who admits to being married to Masack. She is about to name the killer when she is shot by a device hidden in her purse. All the suspects are present at the nightclub, and they are searched, but no evidence is found.

Charlie returns to the hotel to talk over the case with Tommy and the inspector. While searching for his notes, he discovers a strange device in his own pocket, and he determines the bullets came from this object. He hands the device to Tommy, and it explodes while his son is holding it, sending two bullets off in opposite directions. Chan is unable to determine how this deadly device is triggered.

Inspector Carvero discloses that the bottle of *Red Dragon* ink might have come from Iris Ling, an artist visiting Mexico. She frequents nightclubs, and Charlie and Tommy track her down in a popular night spot. Iris dances the rumba with Charlie, and tells him that she sold Wyans the ink. The scientist told Ling it was for his "banderillas," which is the word for the ornamental bullfighting pikes with streamers that adorn the walls of Wyans' apartment. This statement intrigues Charlie. All of Wyans' banderillas are examined, but nothing is found on them. Charlie ascertains that the literal meaning of "banderilla" is "small flag," but he thinks these ornamental streamers look more like ribbons than anything else. On a hunch, Charlie checks an old ribbon from Wyans' typewriter, which is found to actually contain his secret nuclear formula written in indelible red ink.

Chan reveals that this formula was actually the property of Marguerite Fontan, since the discovery was actually conceived and stolen from her late uncle. Chan solves the mystery of the message **"TH E\$M OST"** by substituting **"R"** for the dollar sign. Dorn was trying to indicate that the firing mechanism for the death apparatus was hidden in a phony thermostat. The murderer placed this mechanism on the wall, and used it to detonate the bullets. Later, he would simply remove the thermostat. Chan quickly uses the lethal thermostat to locate which suspect has a supply of the deadly bullet devices. He uses the thermostat to trigger them, and unveils the identity of the killer, who is trapped after a shootout with the authorities in the basement of the hotel.

The film concludes with Charlie threatening to tell Tommy's girlfriend in Honolulu about his flirtation with Iris Ling. Tommy in turn kids Charlie about his hot rumba with the same young artist, and they make a deal not to mention Miss Ling to anyone.

PERFORMANCES

Toler shows Chan's suave side in this film, although he seems rather slow on the uptake figuring out the gimmick of the murder weapon. His most memorable scene without doubt is his rumba with Jean Wong as Iris Ling. Tommy is more important to this plot of the film than usual, and it gives Benson Fong an opportunity to shine. He is the one who first notices the clue of the *Red Dragon* ink, he saves his father's life and his fluent Spanish is a definite asset. He unsuccessfully pursues Iris Ling, who slaps him in the face near the end of the film, also putting an end to his flirtation. For the only time in the series, Tommy appears to get the better of his father in the final fadeout.

Willie Best takes over for Mantan Moreland as his cousin, Chattanooga Brown. His material isn't very strong, but he has one very funny scene involving a remote control gun in the police lab. He tries to woo Josephine, Miss Fontan's beautiful black maid, which makes a charming subplot, particularly when he wins a kiss from her while Tommy gets slapped by Iris. On the whole, Best lacks Moreland's sense of timing, but he gives an adequate performance.

Fortunio Bonanova is very strong as Inspector Carvero. His personal romance with a prime suspect, Miss Fontan, is a fresh element, unique in the series. In fact, all of the supporting players are first rate in this endeavor, making this one of the most interesting grouping of suspects in the entire Monogram series. George Meeker, who plays Slade to sneaky perfection, is well remembered for many roles, including Maximilien Robespierre in Fox's epic, *MARIE ANTOINETTE* (1938). Barton Yarborough, another screen veteran, is appropriately slimy as Bradish, and Don Costello even wins audience sympathy as Masack, especially upon the death of his wife.

The actresses are also superb, and provide textbook performances on how to act in a low budget mystery. Carol Hughes (Fontan) is a very winning heroine, and Marjorie Hoshelle (Irene) also gets to sing quite nicely in a nightclub scene.

Even the minor characters, Jean Wong (Iris Ling) and Mildred Boyd (Josephine), are memorable and well played, providing added sparkle to the film. It is a shame that the script didn't give them more opportunity to perform in the film instead of having them wander about aimlessly for long stretches in the hotel basement.

CHARLIE CHAN'S SAYINGS

◇ Confucius could give answer to that...unfortunately Confucius not here at moment.

◇ Puppy cannot fool old dog.

◇ Good detective always look for something unusual.

◇ Hens sit often, but they lay eggs.

◇ Like Chinese army, Chinese ink cannot be wiped out.

◇ Number three son is like rooster, who thinks sun come up just to hear him crow.

◇ There is an old saying, "Mother know best," but perhaps in this case, it best Mother know nothing whatsoever.

THE RETURN OF CHARLIE CHAN (1970) Alternate title: *HAPPINESS IS A WARM CLUE*

Rating: **

UNIVERSAL. Written by Gene Kearney after a story by Simon Last and Gene Kearney; Photographed by Richard C. Glouner; Edited by Frank Morris; Music by Robert Prince; Produced by Jack Laird; Directed by Darryl Duke. 91 minutes.

ANNOTATED CAST LIST

Ross Martin....................Charlie Chan
Rocky Gunn...................Peter Chan (Number eight son)
Virginia Ann Lee............Doreen Chan (Number three daughter)
Leslie Nielsen.................Alex Hadrachi (Greek billionaire)
Richard Haydn................ Andrew Kidder (Novelist friend of Chan)
Louise Sorel...................Ariane Hadrachi (Alex's second wife)
Joseph Hindy..................Paul Hadrachi (Alex's son)
Kathleen Widdoes............Irene Hadrachi (Alex's daughter)
Don Gordon................... Lambert (Head of Hadrachi security)
Peter Donat....................Noel Adamson (Ariane's illicit lover)
Soon-Teck Oh................ Stephen Chan (Number six son)
Ernest Harada..................Oliver Chan (Number seven son)
Pearl Hong....................Jan Chan (Stephen's wife)
Adele Yoshioka...............Mai-Ling Chan (Oliver's wife)
Otto Lowy..................... Anton Grombach (German scientist)
Pat Gage........................Sylvia Grombach (Anton's wife)
William Nunn................. Fielding (Member of security team)
Ted Greenhalgh...............Dr. Howard Jamison (Alex's doctor)
Graeme Campbell............McKenzie (Vancouver police inspector)
Neil Dainard...................Richard Lovell (Andrew's secretary)
John Juliani................... Gian Carlo Tui (Italian playboy)

SYNOPSIS AND APPRAISAL

This interesting but unconvincing film had an unusual history. It was produced in Vancouver in 1970 by Jack Laird as a pilot for Universal television. The original title on the script was *THE CRADLE OF HERCULES*, but that was dropped after the film was shot. The show was not picked up, and the picture then had a brief theatrical run in Australia in 1972. BBC broadcast it in England in 1973 as *HAPPINESS IS A WARM CLUE*. It was finally shown on NBC television network in the United States on July 17, 1979.

The story involves the ultra-rich Hadrachi family, referred to by Chan as the modern equivalent of the Borgias. The head of the clan, the fifth richest man in the world, is shipping magnate Alex Hadrachi. Someone shoots at him on his luxury boat one evening while he is talking with Richard Lovell, one of his guests. Hadrachi refuses to call in the police from the nearest city, Vancouver. Another guest, writer Andrew Kidder, suggests calling in Charlie Chan.

Chan is now retired to a large Hawaiian pineapple farm run by his grown children. Charlie is busy teaching his grandchildren how to observe and make deductions when Andrew Kidder arrives. He convinces Chan to take the case. The family decides to assign Peter, his "Number eight" son to accompany him as bodyguard, along with his daughter, Doreen. When Chan arrives at the Vancouver airport, an assassin tries to shoot him. Lambert, Hadrachi's head of security, intervenes and kills the attacker.

Chan interviews all of the passengers on Alex's ship. They include Alex's children from his first marriage, Paul and Irene. Their mother is dead, and Alex has remarried a vivacious younger woman named Ariane. Alex suffers from heart trouble, and is always attended by Dr. Jamison, his personal physician. Other guests include Noel Adamson, a former actor now active in real estate, Gian Carlo Tui, an Italian playboy, an eccentric wine grower, Anton Grombach and his wife Sylvia. Kidder and his secretary, Richard Lovell, are the remaining guests. Alex's son, Paul, is hostile to Chan's presence. Chan suspects Grombach is a fraud, and tells Alex. Alex reveals that Grombach is actually a German scientist named Henniger, who is working for him.

After a lively party on board, Alex's wife runs off in a speedboat with Noel Adamson. Alex orders Lambert to follow, and he brings them back. Meanwhile, Richard Lovell is found dead. Chan starts an investigation with Inspector McKenzie from the mainland. Chan concludes that Lovell was first struck on the head by the nozzle of the firehose, and later killed by a paperweight. He determines that Lovell was typing something incriminating at the time of the attack, and that this page was then replaced by a harmless one in his typewriter. He now believes Lovell, not Alex, was the target of the initial shooting.

Police suspicion falls on Adamson, who ran off with Alex's wife. Adamson was trying to pull a fast land deal on Alex. A letter found by the police suggests Lovell was blackmailing Adamson. Chan notices that Adamson had changed his shirt because of a small wine spill before he left the ship. He doesn't believe a murderer in flight would interrupt his escape to do this. Instead, he thinks the actual murderer knew of Adamson's plans, and used them as camouflage for his crime.

Kidder plans to leave the yacht, but is stopped by Ariane. Chan continues to investigate, and learns that the assassin at the airport was Gunnar Johanson, Alex's former head of security. He believes that Dr. Jamison had known Johanson. There is another attempt on Alex's life when a man in a raincoat breaks into his bedroom and fires a shot. Alex shoots back, and the attempt fails. Chan then finds Dr. Jamison dead in his cabin an apparent suicide. Charlie quickly rules this out, and discovers some curious evidence in the doctor's files relating to both Alex and Johanson. He also finds Kidder's packet of eye glass cleaners next to the body. Soon, Chan is stalked and fired upon by Kidder, who tells Charlie he does not want to hurt him, but that he has no choice. He is risking all because of Ariane, whom he adores. Chan overcomes Kidder, and the police take him into custody.

Chan then gathers all the suspects at police headquarters. It is learned that Ariane had begged Kidder to kill Alex. Kidder killed the doctor, who had discovered his plans, and shot in vain at Alex and Chan. Charlie reveals, however, that another individual had killed Lovell. He explains that Lovell was actually John Sebastian, a scandalmonger who was completing a nasty expose about the Hadrachi family. Chan's suspects are Lambert, the Grombachs, Tui, Adamson, and the members of the Hadrachi family.

Lambert confesses, and Chan accepts the confession, but after the other suspects leave, he shows that Lambert couldn't be guilty. He unmasks the real killer and his motive, the hidden "secret" of the Hadrachi family. Dr. Jamison had discovered that Alex had a rare, incurable illness that leads to complete physical deterioration. This disease would also recur in his children. This explanation is very long and involved. Nevertheless, the film comes to a powerful, if sentimental conclusion.

It is not a bad picture, but it is loaded with so many misdirections and complications, that it is rather difficult for the casual viewer to follow. The main confusion is due to Kidder's crimes. They provide the film's climax, but they are basically irrelevant to the main plot. Kidder never knew the Hadrachi family secret, nor did he know his secretary was actually an impostor. He was merely acting out of love for Ariane.

The picture ends with Chan being summoned to another case. Apparently, his retirement is over, and he plans to continue as a consulting detective.

PERFORMANCES

Ross Martin was an interesting choice to play Chan. The well-known character actor was actually born in Poland, and his real name was Martin Rosenblatt. He was brought to America while still a baby, and he grew up in New York City. He obtained a law degree, but found greater rewards in acting. One of his first motion pictures was as the tragic hero of the science fiction thriller *THE COLOSSUS OF NEW YORK* (1958). His greatest success in films was his phenomenal performance as a psychopath who tormented Lee Remick in Blake Edwards' highly-charged thriller *EXPERIMENT IN TERROR* (1962). Martin wasn't billed in the opening credits of this picture, and received a special billing headlining the end credits. Martin was highly regarded for his versatility, showcased in the television series *THE WILD, WILD WEST* where his character, Artemus Gordon, assumed a variety of disguises and accents each week. Ross Martin performs the role of Charlie Chan in this film with dignity and affection. He wears little make-up, except for his mustache and goatee which look rather artificial in some scenes. As successful and competent as Martin is in the part, the production missed a golden opportunity to cast Keye Luke in the role. Luke would not only have made a superb Chan, but he would have provided a vital link to the original film series. If Luke had been cast, perhaps the production might have sold as a series.

Leslie Nielsen, the son of a Canadian Mountie, has had two different careers as an actor. His earlier films presented him in serious or light romantic roles. His later career, inspired by his appearance in the television series *POLICE SQUAD* in the early Eighties, was as a satirical comedian. He has perfected a brilliant, deadpan style, and became so effective in these roles that it is difficult to watch some of his earlier, straight parts without chuckling. Nielsen's performance as Alex Hadrachi is such a case. He uses the same thick accent he later employs in the Mel Brooks farce, *DRACULA: DEAD AND LOVING IT* (1995). His portrayal of Alex is so broad, especially in his exaggerated "Greek dance" sequence, that it is hard to take this character seriously. One interesting point is that Alex endlessly quotes homilies from Homer. Alex spends so much time doing this, that it leaves little chance for Charlie to deliver any of his own observations when Alex is present.

Richard Haydn is difficult to believe as Andrew Kidder. It would be hard for any actor to be successful in this part as it is written, but Haydn has a fussy, prim manner that makes his performance seem artificial. He was acceptable as Charlie's old friend, but when he starts a killing spree because of Ariane, his characterization falls apart. While shooting at Chan, he apologize to him in such a casual manner as though he accidentally stepped on his toe instead. It is most ineffective.

Louise Sorel is quite good as Ariane, but her motivations seem inconsistent. It was actually Don Gordon as Lambert and Ted Greenhalgh who are most effective in their performances. Soon-Teck Oh and Ernest Harada are quite likable and irreproachable in their brief appearances as two of Chan's sons. Rocky Gunn, as Peter Chan, is given the most screen time however, but he is rather bland and unmemorable. Virginia Ann Lee, however, is particularly engaging as Doreen Chan.

CHARLIE CHAN'S SAYINGS

⋄ Unexpected appearance of long absent friend is like finding five dollars in pocket of old suit...pleasant and most rewarding surprise.

⋄ Grandchildren are a joy like summer rain...disconcerting but very necessary.

⋄ (Appealing to Hadrachi for cooperation) The fruit of the litchi nut cannot be preserved without first removing the shell. There can be no secrets kept from me.

◇ Indeed, the ultimate in privacy is the tomb.

◇ Indeed, happiness is a warm clue.

◇ It is wisely written, even a strand of hair casts a shadow.

◇ Infidelity is one of the most common motives for murder.

◇ Wisdom like molasses, although sweet, is very slow to pour.

◇ The truth does not go away because one is absent for a little while.

◇ Bad news travels fastest.

THE SCARLET CLUE   (1945)

Rating: **

MONOGRAM.   Written by George Callahan; Photographed by William
Sickner; Edited by Richard Currier; Musical direction by Edward J. Kay; Produced by James S. Burkett; Directed by Phil Rosen.   65 minutes.

ANNOTATED CAST LIST

Sidney Toler...................Charlie Chan
Benson Fong..................Tommy Chan (Number three son)
Mantan Moreland............ Birmingham Brown (Chan chauffeur)
Ben Carter......................Ben Carter (Birmingham's friend)
Virginia Brissac.............. Mrs. Marsh (Radio show sponsor)
Robert E. Homans...........Flynn (Police Captain)
Jack Norton...................Willie Rand (Radio actor)
Janet Shaw.....................Gloria Bayne (Radio actress)
Helen Devereaux............. Diane Hall (Radio actress)
Victoria Faust.................Hulda Swenson (Cleaning woman)
I. Stanford Jolley..............Ralph Brett (Radio station manager)
Reid Kilpatrick............... Wilbur Chester (Radio announcer)
Charles Sherlock............. McGraw (Police Sergeant)
Milt Kibbee................... Herbert Sinclair (Marsh's assistant)
Charles Jordan................ Nelson (Police doctor)
Leonard Mudie................ Horace Carlos (Shakespearean actor)
Emmett Vogan............... Professor Hamilton (Radar specialist)
Kernan Kripps................ Police detective

SYNOPSIS AND APPRAISAL

This picture is a mixed bag, but quite enjoyable even though some parts are
much better than the whole. The central story is cluttered with too many complicated murder devices. The biggest plot loophole is that Chan and the police
let a modified elevator remain in service after learning it is a death trap. Chan
then foolishly enters the same elevator at the film's climax. He would never do
anything so preposterous. Incidentally, the harrowing shot of a man plunging to
his death down an elevator shaft may be the most effective single insert in any
Chan film.

The screenplay has many redeeming features, especially by letting the audience know the identity of the killer quite early in the story. The picture then
becomes an inverted mystery, in which the audience watches the killer and Chan
match wits against each other. This is the format favored in the *COLUMBO*
television series, as well as in authentic Chinese detective literature from the
17th century. Eventually, this malefactor is slain by his superior in the spy

ring, an individual whose name remains a secret until the end of the picture.

The picture opens at night with the police following a foreign agent named Roche on behalf of Chan and the Secret Service. Captain Flynn greets Charlie when he arrives at the waterfront scene, and they discover that Roche has been killed while hiding on a boat. Chan notes the license of a car parked on the dock. This car speeds off while Chan and Flynn are still on the boat. Charlie notices a bloody shoe print near the body. The police trace the car and discover that the automobile was reported stolen by Diane Hall, an actress at the Cosmo Radio and Television Center, which is in the same building as the Hamilton Research Lab. Chan believes that foreign spies have targeted Hamilton, a genius in the field of radar who is developing an advanced radar system.

Chan, Tommy and Birmingham go to the broadcast studio to question Diane Hall, who says that her car has now been returned to the building's parking lot. Chan takes note of a bloody heel print in the corridor, proving that the murderer is an individual at the studio.

After Chan leaves, the audience learns that Ralph Brett, the station manager, is the culprit. He telephones the leader of his espionage cabal to report that he eliminated Roche, who was planning to confess to Chan. Brett himself is unaware of the identity of his superior, who replies to all his queries by teletype.

At a radio show rehearsal the next day, Chan explains that he is working on a murder case, and needs to question the studio personnel: Ralph Brett; Diane Hall; Mrs. Marsh, the abrasive sponsor of the most popular show; Herbert Sinclair, her assistant; Gloria Bayne, an actress; Willie Rand, an actor who specializes in playing old ladies; and Wilbur Chester, the radio announcer.

Meanwhile, Tommy and Birmingham have a humorous encounter with the eccentric Horace Carlos, a Shakespearean actor who is now reduced to playing the role of a masked phantom on television. Chan then goes to visit the scientist Hamilton, who has found evidence of an attempted break-in at his laboratory. He believes thieves or spies are trying to steal his patents. Hamilton shows Tommy and Birmingham some of his his audacious discoveries, including a climatic tunnel that can simulate extreme weather conditions.

Gloria Bayne tries to blackmail Brett, knowing he stole Diane's car. Brett calls his boss, whose typed reply tells him not to be concerned about Gloria. Charlie watches the next rehearsal, where Gloria appears unsteady. She feels better after smoking a cigarette, but then collapses in the corridor. Tommy notices the cleaning woman has pocketed the cigarette dropped by Gloria, and he steals it back from her. This puzzled Birmingham, who knows Tommy doesn't smoke.

A coroner's report shows that Gloria died from an exotic poison. Tommy and Birmingham follow Brett, and Chan gathers evidence against the station manager. Brett begins to panic after he overhears Chan and Jimmy talking. After calling the spy master, Brett is lured into riding on a particular elevator, and falls to his death in the shaft when the elevator floor gives way.

As the police search for Brett, Tommy and Birmingham suspect the cleaning woman. They notice that the door to Hamilton's lab has been forced open, and they discover that his safe has been robbed. They search the premises, but get trapped in the climatic tunnel which is accidentally activated by Birmingham. Captain Flynn and Charlie rescue them and uncover the body of Brett, buried in snow in the climatic tunnel.

Chan ferrets out the office from which Brett's phone calls are relayed. After using a mimic to impersonate Brett on the telephone, Charlie gets a typed message leading him to the trick elevator. Birmingham takes the elevator, but grasps a side rail when the trap door opens. Chan and Tommy rescue him, and conclude Brett was killed by the trick elevator.

Willie Rand tells Chan that Gloria Bayne made an unusual remark that he is trying to remember. He collapses, however, after doing an experimental television broadcast, and Chan analyzes the cigarette Rand was smoking. He locates the hidden switch which triggers the elevator's trap door in Wilbur Chester's office. Since Chester's office is never locked, anyone could use the switch.

Chan finds out that the poison which killed both Gloria and Rand was delivered by cigarettes interacting with gas pellets hidden in flowers. These pellets were shattered by a short-wave signal.

Captain Flynn and Chan begin a detailed search to locate the mastermind's teletype machine and short-wave radio. Tommy and Birmingham locate them in an office, but are fired upon by a masked phantom. Chan and Tommy almost enter the booby-trapped elevator, but exit when they hear shots being fired. Flynn is pursuing the phantom on the stairway. The killer discards the phantom disguise, but then falls victim to his own deadly elevator trap.

The identity of the killer is revealed when the authorities examine the body at the bottom of the shaft. Chan thanks the cleaning lady, who is really a government agent installed by him to monitor the activities at the Hamilton laboratory. Birmingham, upset by these events, flees the building while wearing the phantom's disguise.

PERFORMANCES

Sidney Toler's acting becomes inexplicably weak in the second half of this film, especially when his character almost commits the fatal blunder of using the sabotaged elevator. At this point, he seems to be following events rather than using his logic to control them. This poor characterization is both the result of the screenplay and Toler's lazy reading of the part. There are also very few bona fide Chan sayings in this picture. There is one curious moment in the lab scene in which Toler appears to get a genuine electrical shock from the equipment. Toler does a quick ad lib, and completes the scene like a real trouper.

The usually reliable Benson Fong delivers his poorest rendition of Tommy Chan. He seems juvenile and silly, rather than the well-meaning innocent he performs so well in the other films. On the other hand, this is one of the best performances by Mantan Moreland, whose clever quips and asides are very effective. His reactions are hilarious when he spots his own photo in the police mug book. (For the record, Birmingham is 5'5" tall, weighs 158 pounds and is 38 years old.) His fright by the electric equipment seems genuine, and his reaction when the elevator floor gives way is priceless.

The highlight of the film is Moreland's two routines with Ben Carter, his old vaudeville partner. Carter is dapperly dressed, and delivers his lines with an infectious zest. Moreland and Carter are simply wonderful together. Their timing when each man completes the other one's thoughts is phenomenal. Monogram should have considered a Moreland/Carter series, a black comedy team that could have rivaled Abbott and Costello in many ways.

I. Stanford Jolley (Brett) , a classic serial and Western villain, portrays the radio manager with style and sinister grace. Leonard Mudie (Carlos) is a riot as the Shakespearean actor reduced to playing a masked phantom. His lavish accent reminds one of the relish John Carradine brought to similar roles. Jack Norton (Willie Rand) is also outstanding playing a grandmother on the radio. He also gets a chance to do his well-known drunk routine, which is excellently woven into the plot. On the other hand, Victoria Faust overacts in her guise as a Swedish cleaning lady, and Robert E. Homans' dithering Captain Flynn is simply annoying and a complete distraction.

CHARLIE CHAN'S SAYINGS

⋄ What detective needs is great patience.

⋄ (To Tommy) Number three son have excellent head. Question have always been...what it contain.

⋄ So many fish in fish market, even flower smell same.

SHADOWS OVER CHINATOWN
(1946)
Rating: *

MONOGRAM. Written by Raymond Schrock; Photographed by William Sickner; Edited by Ralph Dixon; Musical direction by Edward J. Kay; Produced by James S. Burkett; Directed by Terry Morse. 64 minutes.

ANNOTATED CAST LIST

Sidney Toler....................Charlie Chan
Victor Sen Yung..............Jimmy Chan (Number two son)
Mantan Moreland............ Birmingham Brown (Chan chauffeur)
Tanis Chandler.................Mary McCoy (Alias of Mary Conover)
John Gallaudet.................Jeff Hay (Private detective)
Paul Bryar......................Mike Rogan (Fake bus driver)
Bruce Kellogg.................Jack Tilford (Alias of Joe Thompson)
Alan Bridge....................Captain Allen (Police inspector)
Mary Gordon..................Mrs. Conover (Mary's grandmother)
Dorothy Granger............. Joan Mercer (Escort service hostess)
Jack Norton....................Cosgrove (Bus pickpocket)
Charlie Gordon............... Jenkins (Police detective)
George Eldredge.............. Flannagan (Police Chief)
Tyra Vaughn.................. Miss Johnson (Mrs. Conover's friend)
Lyle Latell.....................Desk clerk
Harry Depp.................... Veterinarian on the bus trip
John Hamilton................Lawyer on the bus trip

SYNOPSIS AND APPRAISAL

SHADOWS OVER CHINATOWN is a rambling and confusing entry, distinguished only by somewhat greater production values than usual for a Monogram film.   On the plus side, the film includes a fine variety of decent sets and a larger than usual cast. Most of the players are unnamed extras who appear only briefly. Raymond Schrock's screenplay is the main weakness, providing little mystery since the identity of the killer is almost unmistakable. There are gruesome aspects to the script which do make this entry stand out. Schrock had written a number of good scripts for *THE WHISTLER* series and others, but the Chan formula seems to have eluded him. The humor is stilted and forced, and the writer had no concept about how to incorporate Birmingham and Jimmy into his story. Their scenes, except for one or two moments, is simply extraneous filler. Schrock overplays the references to Confucius, whom Birmingham refers to as Confusion. It is amusing, however, when at one point,

Chan says, "What Confucius say to this, too terrible for even Charlie Chan to repeat."

The film opens with a sequence lifted from an earlier documentary, where a narrator explains the function of the Bureau of Missing Persons in cities across the nation. After this prologue, the scene shifts to a bus traveling on a blustery night to San Francisco. Charlie, Jimmy and Birmingham are among the passengers. Charlie is reading about a recent torso killing, a gruesome crime where the victim was dismembered.

The bus stops for repair, and the passengers wait at a rural depot. After one of them discovers his wallet is missing, a gunshot is fired at Chan from outside the station. He is unharmed since the bullet was stopped by his pocket watch. A stranger enters the station an instant later, and the passengers cross-examine him about his identity. The stranger has a gun, but it hasn't been fired. As the travelers return to the bus, Chan detains one of them, a man named Cosgrove, and advises him to return the wallets he has just pickpocketed. Chan says he will not press charges if the thief returns the stolen items the same way he lifted them, and Cosgrove is grateful that Chan gave him a break.

Charlie converses on the bus with Miss Johnson and Mrs. Conover, an elderly lady whose granddaughter Mary Conover is missing. She fears that Mary may be the victim in the torso murder case, and Chan offers to ascertain if this is possible.

The bus driver is mysteriously driven away in a car as soon as the vehicle arrives at the San Francisco bus depot. This disappearance confuses the personnel at the depot.

Chan visits the police to offer his aid on the torso case, which he believes is related to a similar crime in New Orleans where a widow vanished after she collected a large insurance policy. Chan believes the torso murder may be another missing widow, Mrs. Pendelton. He notices a police flyer about an AWOL soldier, Joe Thompson, whom Chan identifies as the stranger who showed up at the rural bus depot. Chan closely examines the unidentified torso, then visits Mrs. Conover at her hotel and tells her that Mary is not the torso victim. Unlike Mary, the dead woman once had an appendectomy.

Jeff Hay, a private detective who was also on the bus, sees Charlie and tells him he had learned the driver on their trip was an impostor. The real driver was knocked out and replaced. Jeff was assigned the case by the bus company.

Jimmy and Charlie have lunch at a restaurant, where Charlie identifies the waitress as Mary Conover. After Charlie leaves to telephone Mrs. Conover, Mike Rogan, the counterfeit bus driver arrives at the restaurant and also notices her. Rogan tries to blackmail the young woman. Mary flees, but Jimmy follows her back to her apartment.

Jimmy recruits Birmingham to fetch his father, but they find Jimmy unconscious in Mary's apartment. Jeff Hay is also hiding in another room, having trailed the bus driver. They discover the body of Miss Johnson, the traveling companion of Mrs. Conover. Chan assumes she was knifed to death by mistake in the dark, and that Mary was the intended victim.

Searching through the police files, Chan finds that Mrs. Pendelton was once involved with an unscrupulous theatrical manager named Craig Winfield. The police pick up serviceman Joe Thompson, who tells Chan he was just trying to locate his missing girlfriend, Mary Conover. He said that Mary was frightened by the owners of the Bay Escort Service where she worked. Chan deduces these people were Mike Rogan and a man named Kearney.

Jeff gets a tip that Rogan is hiding out in Chinatown. They rush off and find Rogan dead from a gunshot wound. On his body they also find the knife that killed Miss Johnson. Meanwhile, Birmingham and Jimmy get involved in a series of misadventures in a Chinese curio shop.

Mary Conover is finally located by Jenkins, a police detective. She explains that she went into hiding because Mike Rogan, whom she knew as Mike Roberts, had discovered that her boyfriend Joe Thompson was rich. He had an insurance scheme to make her a wealthy widow. Mary never met the mysterious Mr. Kearney and could not describe him. Chan reunites Mary with both Joe and her grandmother.

Mary agrees to act as bait in Chan's gambit to capture Kearney. But Chan's scheme almost backfires when the criminal learns of the set-up and manages to kidnap Mary. Charlie believes the kidnapper is using an apartment as a hideout in Chinatown. With the unexpected assistance of Cosgrove the pickpocket, Chan confronts and captures the wrongdoer, who had assumed various aliases while committing his crimes, such as Kearney, Winfield, as well as his current identity. The killer had arranged to substitute Rogan as the bus driver in order to shoot Chan. He also admits killing Mrs. Pendelton (the torso victim), Miss Johnson and Mike Rogan. Mary Conover is now free to marry Joe Thompson. The film ends as Birmingham, Jimmy and Charlie discuss whether Abraham Lincoln was a disciple of the works of Confucius.

PERFORMANCES

Sidney Toler provides the few good moments in this film, particularly in his dealings with Mrs. Conover, Cosgrove the pickpocket and Joe Thompson. In each case, his personal warmth and caring attitude enrich both the characters and the plot. At other moments, Toler seems completely disengaged in the role and merely going through the motions. More commitment on Toler's part would have made this picture a more successful entry. The writer also has Toler engage the criminal in a tussle at the end of the picture, which appears very unconvincing.

Victor Sen Yung, now billed as Victor Sen Young, returns to the role of Jimmy Chan after four years, since the last Fox Chan film *CASTLE IN THE DESERT*. Unfortunately, his role as written is rather shallow and poorly conceived, except for the sequence when his father finds him unconscious in the closet. There is no evidence of any further growth or development in the part either. Jimmy had been maturing as a character in the last few Fox films. It could have just as easily been Tommy in the picture. Still, the actor's charm and good nature make his return a welcome one.

The script provides little opportunity for Mantan Moreland to display his comic talents. His best vignette is when he thinks he is conversing with Chan on the telephone when he actually is standing right behind him. There is little humor in his inability to get the car started. His endless confusion about Confucius becomes tiring. Moreland's longest sequence, totally unrelated to the plot, is spent wandering through a Chinese curio shop where he converses with life-sized Chinese figures and is inexplicably frightened by some convex and concave funhouse mirrors.

There are a number of solid performances from some of the supporting players. Mary Gordon, Mrs. Hudson from the Basil Rathbone Sherlock Holmes series at Universal, is quite convincing and appealing as the fretful Mrs. Conover. This was her first appearance in a Chan film since *THE BLACK CAMEL* in 1931. Alan Bridge (Captain Allen) is excellent as usual. Veteran performer John Hamilton appears all too briefly as a lawyer in the rural bus depot, and he always manages to add interest in any scene in which he appears. Viewers may best remember the busy actor as Perry White in the *SUPERMAN* television program. John Gallaudet (Jeff Hay), usually overlooked in the Chan series, does a fine job with a somewhat meatier role in this outing. Jack Norton (Cosgrove) is charming as the inept pickpocket who later assists Charlie. His line, "I must be slipping," when Chan easily notices his criminal activity, is one of the best in the film.

Bruce Kellogg and Tanis Chandler are both first rate as the young couple whose fate becomes entwined with murder. The villains of the piece, especially Paul Bryar (Mike Rogan) are cardboard performances that provide little interest for viewers.

CHARLIE CHAN'S SAYINGS

⋄ Numbers cannot control destiny.

⋄ Hot stove make all the world kin on a night like this.

⋄ Momentarily I think United States lose one Chinese detective, but now I discover I am living on borrowed time.

⋄ As nurse say to father of newborn twins, pleasure is double.

⋄ Goods returned, crime prevented.

⋄ Sometimes surgeon's scar speak louder than fingerprints.

⋄ Confucius say, "Sleep only escape from yesterday."

⋄ Business conversation at table very bad for digestion.

⋄ Deception is bad game for amateurs.

◇ Ancient proverb say, "Never bait trap with wolf to catch wolf."

◇ I recall story of farm hand who find cow by trying to figure out where he would go if he were cow.

◇ Cornered rat usually full of fight.

◇ What Confucius say to this too terrible for even Charlie Chan to repeat.

SHANGHAI CHEST   (1948)
Rating: *

MONOGRAM. Written by W. Scott Darling and Sam Newman with additional dialogue written by Tim Ryan; Photographed by William Sickner; Edited by Ace Herman; Musical direction by Edward J. Kay; Produced by James S. Burkett; Directed by William Beaudine. 56 minutes.

ANNOTATED CAST LIST

Roland Winters...............Charlie Chan
Victor Sen Yung.............Tommy (Jimmy) Chan (Number two son)
Mantan Moreland............Birmingham Brown (Chan chauffeur)
Tim Ryan......................Mike Ruark (Police Lieutenant)
Pierre Watkin.................Armstrong (Murdered Judge)
Deannie Best..................Phyllis Powers (Judge's secretary)
Tristram Coffin...............Edward Seward (Judge's attorney)
John Alvin.....................Vic Armstrong (Nephew of Judge)
Russell Hicks.................Frank Bronson (District Attorney)
Phillip Van Zandt...........Joseph Pindello (Dead convict's brother)
Milton Parsons...............Grail (Funeral director)
Olaf Hytten....................Bates (Armstrong butler)
Erville Alderson..............Walter Sommerville (Former court clerk)
Edward Coke..................Cartwright (Juror in Pindello case)
George Eldridge...............Pat Finley (Police detective)
Louis Maso....................Custodian
William Ruhl.................Police jailer
Chabing........................Insurance company receptionist
Willie Best....................Convict (Birmingham's friend)

SYNOPSIS AND APPRAISAL

This is a rather feeble entry, and it likely is the picture that many reviewers consider when they express a harsh judgment on the entire Winters/Monogram series. It is no doubt the low point of Winters' films, but there are still a few good points, such as the addition of the character of Lt. Ruark and the use of a number of original Biggers' Chan precepts. The plot is very contrived and artificial, borrowing elements from *DARK ALIBI* as well as Agatha Christie's novel *THE A. B. C. MURDERS.* Even the pointless title refers partly to a more successful effort, *THE SHANGHAI COBRA.* The best part of the film is the opening sequence, with its creepy depiction of the murder of Judge Armstrong. His nephew Vic Armstrong is knocked unconscious while answering a phone call from the judge's secretary, who then calls the police. When he regains consciousness, he finds the judge murdered and foolishly removes the knife from the dead man's back exactly at the moment when the police arrive. His sweetheart, Phyllis Powers, has to admit that Vic had an argument with his uncle.

Tommy and Birmingham, returning from the movies, follow a man they see crawling into the window of a house. They think they are going to catch a burglar, but instead they are arrested for breaking and entering, since the man is the district attorney who merely lost his keys. They get placed in jail, and Charlie gets involved in the Armstrong case while arranging their release. Lt. Ruark is baffled when the murder weapon is found to contain the fingerprints of Tony Pindello, a murderer executed six months earlier. Meanwhile, Birmingham has a very funny comic exchange with another convict played by Willie Best.

Lt. Ruark visits Chan the next day with the latest development, the murder of the district attorney and the discovery of Pindello's fingerprints again at the crime scene. Chan questions Edward Seward, Armstrong's attorney who was also the defense council in the Pindello case. Ruark asks Vic Armstrong about his whereabouts during the time of the district attorney's murder. The private safe of the judge is opened, and a letter is discovered by the judge to his nephew states that he had uncovered evidence that Tony Pindello was an innocent man. Charlie suggests that all individuals connected with the Pindello case be given police protection.

Pindello's grave, exhumed by Tommy and Birmingham under Ruark's supervision, is found to be empty. Chan carefully studies the details of the Pindello case, and suspects that the case has some connection to an insurance swindle the judge was also researching. This leads him to an intensive investigation of all the insurance agencies in town. The Winter Island Insurance Company in Chinatown is particularly evasive to his inquiry, and the receptionist makes an urgent call as soon as Chan leaves the office.

Thomas Cartwright, one of the Pindello jurors, is killed by a masked figure in his hotel room. Pindello's fingerprints are uncovered at the crime scene, and Chan notes all the victims, Armstrong, Bronson and Cartwright, are being slaughtered in alphabetical order.

Birmingham aids Charlie in producing forged fingerprints, a process that was previously revealed in *DARK ALIBI*. Chan, Ruark, Vic and Phyllis visit Judge Armstrong's den and find that his papers have been searched. A masked man locks them in a closet, and Ruark believes the voice of the assailant sounds just like Pindello. After they break free, Chan suggests that the police investigate if any recently released prisoners were involved with Pindello.

Chan visits all the undertakers in San Francisco to see if anyone had reburied Pindello. This action is covered in a long, tedious montage. The only character who arouses Charlie's suspicious is Mr. Grail of the AAA Funeral Parlor.

After dark, he breaks into the establishment with Tommy and Birmingham, and finds important information in the office files. Grail is awakened by the intruders, and he threatens them at gunpoint. Chan defiantly tells him to shoot, as he and the others calmly leave the premises. His next stop is a rooming house, where Chan confronts Joseph Pindello, the dead man's brother, and asks him to co-operate with his investigation.

Ruark gathers all the suspects at Chan's house, and Charlie discloses the story of Joseph Pindello, who recently escaped from prison. Joseph then makes a dramatic entrance brandishing a gun, but he is tackled from behind by Tommy. Pindello, who was responsible for stealing his brother's body, is actually working with Chan to trap the murderer. When Chan reveals the man's identity, the killer grabs Joseph's gun to make his escape. The gun is unloaded, however, and the perpetrator runs into Birmingham who tussles him to the ground.

Chan describes the insurance scam that was the authentic motive for the murders. He also gives ample credit to Tommy and Birmingham as the film winds down, and jokes about the fact that his chauffeur is still handcuffed to the killer.

PERFORMANCES

Roland Winters comes across very poorly as Chan, primarily due to the way that his role was written. His stilted speech is agonizing at times to the viewer, even if some of the quotes are unadulterated Earl Derr Biggers. This is the only film where Chan seems to speak broken English, with incorrect syntax, such as "What are your good news?" Some critics incorrectly claim Chan spoke pidgin English in the films, but in *SHANGHAI CHEST* that claim seems to have merit.

A number of interesting moments also misfire in the story. When Ruark jokes about a Chinese puzzle, Chan's deadpan remark, "Very funny," falls flat. His forbidding reaction to Birmingham's amusement when Tommy is caught eavesdropping is also a dud. On the other hand, the fingerprint sequence with Mantan Moreland simply sparkles, as does the humorous bit at the fade out of the picture.

Victor Sen Yung becomes somewhat irritating in this film, again largely due to the way his role is constructed. Tommy's plans to continually sneak in through windows is overdone and not amusing. His best moment is at the end of the long montage sequence, when he suggests to his father that at least one of the undertakers must have aroused his suspicions.

Mantan Moreland comes across quite well overall. At one point he says to his employer, "Mr. Chan, there ain't no limit to the cleverness of us detectives, is there?" He tosses off the remark with such style that the viewer can't help but smile. His short sequence in jail with Willie Best is also marvelous. Willie Best, who plays Birmingham's cousin in two other films, matches Moreland with perfect timing, and their division helps to lighten this dreary film.

Tim Ryan, who also wrote some of the dialogue, is quite successful as Lt. Mike Ruark, whom Charlie refers to affectionately as "Lieutenant Mike." His Irish cop may be earthy, but he also unexpectedly quotes Shakespeare when it suits his mood. His quirky character is a welcome addition, and recurs in two later films.

Tristram Coffin (Seward), Milton Parsons (Grail) and Phillip Van Zandt (Pindello) are all praiseworthy, but they are not given much of a chance in the screenplay. Deannie Best (Phyllis) and John Alvin (Vic Armstrong), the young lovers, are simply unmemorable cardboard characters.

CHARLIE CHAN'S SAYINGS

⋄ Night in Bastille not exactly bed of roses.

⋄ Happiest walk in life of mailman are on holiday.

⋄ Sometimes better to lull suspected person with false sense of security.

⋄ Surprised detective might just as well clutch iron ball and jump in lake.

⋄ Patience are virtue one must hug to bosom.

⋄ Sometimes muddy waters, when stirred sufficiently, bring strange things to surface.

⋄ Certain facts begin to gleam clear like snow on distant mountain top.

⋄ So seldom brains and beauty dance in street together.

⋄ Man who have gun either afraid or have guilty conscience.

THE SHANGHAI COBRA (1945)
Rating: **

MONOGRAM Written by George Callahan and George Wallace Sayre, based on a story by George Callahan; Photographed by Vincent Farrar; Edited by Ace Herman; Musical direction by Edward J. Kay; Produced by James S. Burkett; Directed by Phil Karlson. 64 minutes.

ANNOTATED CAST LIST

Sidney Toler....................Charlie Chan
Benson Fong...................Tommy Chan (Number three son)
Mantan Moreland............ Birmingham Brown (Chan's chauffeur)
James Cardwell...............Ned Stewart (Private detective)
Joan Barclay....................Paula Webb (Bank secretary)
Addison Richards.............John Adams (Bank guard)
Arthur Loft.................... Bradford Harris (Bank Vice-President)
Roy Gordon................... Walter Fletcher (Bank President)
Janet Warren...................Lorraine (Juke Box girl)
Gene Roth..................... Morgan (Ex-con staking out the bank)
Joe Devlin..................... Taylor (Ex-con staking out the bank)
James Flavin..................H. R. Jarvis (Chemical engineer)
Walter Fenner.................Harry Davis (Police Inspector)
George Chandler.............Joe (Coffee shop owner)

SYNOPSIS AND APPRAISAL

This is a solid, atmospheric film, well-photographed with a very sinister opening sequence. The last half of the picture is somewhat of a letdown, with too many wanderings back and forth in the sewer system underneath the bank. The plot is built around a clever gimmick: a poison needle concealed in a juke box is used to kill individuals the gang wishes to eliminate. There is also a clever flashback sequence, establishing Chan's presence in Shanghai at the time of the Japanese bombing in 1937.

The picture opens using elements of the "film noir" style portraying a rain-storm at night in a large city. Two men and a woman enter a coffee shop, all behaving in a mysterious fashion. One man plays a juke box that is run by a live attendant in a studio using remote control. The woman pretends to know the second man, in order to avoid the attentions of the first one, a bank guard named Mr. Black. The woman leaves, but she is followed by Black who claims he has something vital to tell her. Black then collapses. The second man shows up, and asks the woman to call a doctor. She heads back to the coffee shop, but slips out the back door of the shop. A crowd starts to gather, and the second man heads off to try and locate the elusive woman. He, in turn, is chased by a policeman.

It is discovered that Black was killed by cobra venom, the third recent victim of this bizarre method. The only similar case was solved in Shanghai eight years earlier by Charlie Chan. Harry Davis, the police inspector, is an old friend of Charlie, so he cables him at the federal building in Washington to ask for his help.

When Chan arrives, he tells Davis the details of the Shanghai case when he arrested Jan Van Horn on circumstantial evidence. Van Horn was seriously burned during the Japanese raid, and his entire face was wrapped in bandages. He proclaimed his innocence, and managed to escape while being transported on a police boat. Chan believes that Van Horn may be behind these new crimes, but he may be difficult to identify because his face would be totally changed after his injuries.

The three victims of the cobra killer were all employees of the same bank, two guards and a woman from the posting department. This large bank is the government depository of radium, which Chan thinks may be the ultimate target of any criminal scheme. He visits the bank with Tommy and Birmingham to check on the radium in the vault, and question bank officials, including Vice President Bradford Harris, President Walter Fletcher, his secretary Paula Webb and John Adams, a bank guard.

He visits the coffee shop with Tommy and Birmingham. Joe, the owner, is not very helpful. Chan is startled by a voice coming from the juke box. He learns the device is operated by remote control and video screen. The woman who operates the juke box tells Chan that she overheard the name of the second man, Ned Stewart. Charlie thanks her, and is surprised when the juke girl tells him that he is cute!

Using the phone book, Chan tracks down Ned Stewart, the owner of the Apex detective agency. Stewart was hired by mail to secretly protect a girl named Pauline Webster, and he was following her when Black was slain. Chan pretends to arrest Stewart to see if the woman will respond, which she does by phone on the following day. She is actually Paula Webb from the bank, and when Chan detects a possible romance between the two, so he leaves them together at a restaurant.

Inspector Davis, meantime, gets an urgent late night telephone call to come to the bank from Larkin, a police detective working undercover as a custodian. When Chan and Davis arrive, the guard tells them that Larkin has vanished.

The next day, Charlie finds Tommy and Birmingham arguing over a U-turn ticket. Davis tells them that he suspects two ex-convicts, Morgan and Taylor, who were seen at the bank. Chan wants to investigate the sewer and service tunnels underneath the bank.

Tommy and Birmingham bump into Morgan and Taylor in the street, and they follow them to a Chinese laundry. Sneaking into the back room, they locate a secret passage into the sewer, where they find Larkin's body. Morgan and Taylor shoot at them, but Chan and the police arrive and recover the body.

The coroner informs them that Larkin was also killed by cobra venom.

The police investigate the Chinese laundry but no trap door can be found. Chan learns from the postman that the laundry had just moved next door. After finding the concealed entrance to the sewer, Chan, Davis and Stewart uncover a secret passage leading directly into the bank, where they startle the bank officials with their unconventional entrance. Chan asks Paula to accompany them to the coffee shop. Chan has deduced that the shop is the location where the "cobra" infected his victims. The owner explains that the juke box was placed in the shop by a man named Jan Van Horn. Paula seems startled after hearing the name.

Chan and Davis leave to track down the juke box studio, which is hidden in the office of Jarvis, a chemical engineer. They question the juke girl. Chan broadcasts to the coffee shop, telling Stewart to push the juke box coin return button, but not using his fingers. This procedure reveals a poison needle that pricks the victim's finger when he presses the return button when a lever is activated from the studio. The method of the cobra killings has been found.

Chan releases a false story that the radium deposits will be removed from the bank the next day. He plans to set a trap. Meanwhile, Tommy and Birmingham track the criminals into the sewer where Morgan tries to kill them with a bomb. Charlie hears the explosion, and investigates. He finds Tommy and Birmingham, but a cave-in traps them. Chan locates a telephone line, and sends out a message in Morse code. One of the telephone operators detects the message. The police rescue them, and round up the gang in the act of robbing the vault.

Chan then gathers the bank officials to unveil the mastermind of the murders and attempted robbery. He first discloses that the guard, John Adams, is really Van Horn, and Paula is his daughter. They were in disguise to find the planner of the Shanghai robbery for which Van Horn was framed. They suspected Black, whom Paula was following. Van Horn hired Stewart to protect Paula. Chan clears Van Horn and his daughter by exposing the real criminal. With the case finished, Charlie learns that he too has received a traffic ticket in the mail for making an illegal U-turn.

PERFORMANCES

Sidney Toler appears to have a good deal of fun while doing this entry. His performance is filled with numerous winks and nods, and far more explosions of laughter than usual. This is balanced by his abrasiveness and even rudeness when dealing with the bank officials. He often seems exasperated by Tommy and Birmingham, but his expression changes to a grin when they are not watching him. Two moments are particularly infectious. The first is when the juke girl tells him he is cute. Chan is taken aback, and then he, Tommy and Birmingham roar with laughter. The second is at the picture's end. Charlie gets a ticket because Captain Davis told him "No U-turn here!" and Charlie thought he said "No, you turn here!" Chan's dour expression melts into a chuckle as the end credits roll.

Benson Fong and Mantan Moreland work very well together in this picture too. Their earlier version of the "U-turn" routine was very sharp. Moreland's comic asides are hilarious and his delivery is impeccable and very well-timed.

James Cardwell and Joan Barclay are very believable and likable as Stewart and Paula, whose romance is largely brewed by Charlie himself. Joe Devlin and Gene Roth are entertaining as the hoods, Taylor and Morgan. Joe Devlin is well known for his comic portrayal of Mussolini in several Hal Roach shorts with Bobby Watson playing Hitler. Burly Gene Roth, originally billed as Gene Stutenroth, changed his name during the mid-Forties. He became one of the most popular serial and Western villains in the late Forties and early Fifties. His most broad performance was in the serial *CAPTAIN VIDEO* as the dictator Ventura of Atoma, where his odd costume combined medieval armor with tights, which stressed his rather rotund figure.

Most of the other players make very little impression, except for Addison Richards (John Adams/Jan Van Horn). Janet Warren is particularly bland as the juke box girl, except for her one line telling Charlie he is cute. Her character doesn't make sense as written. She is part of the criminal gang, yet she deliberately draws Chan's attention to the juke box, and provides him with a useful tip. If she remained quiet, Chan might have wasted valuable time, searching for other clues.

CHARLIE CHAN'S SAYINGS

◇ In my business, always expect to find something wrong.

◇ Ancient ancestor once say, "Even wise man cannot fathom depth of woman's smile."

◇ Cannot sell bearskin before shooting bear.

◇ Police do not read Emily Post.

◇ Mice will never play so long as cat is in house.

◇ Too many hands sometimes spoil pudding.

THE SKY DRAGON (1949)

Rating: **

MONOGRAM. Written by Oliver Drake and Clint Johnson after a story by Clint Johnson; Photographed by William Sickner; Edited by Roy Livingston; Musical direction by Edward J. Kay; Produced by James S. Burkett; Directed by Lesley Selander. 64 minutes.

ANNOTATED CAST LIST

Roland Winters...............Charlie Chan
Keye Luke......................Lee Chan (Number one son)
Mantan Moreland............Birmingham Brown (Chan chauffeur)
Tim Ryan......................Mike Ruark (Police Lieutenant)
Noel Neil.......................Jane Marshall (Head stewardess)
Elena Verdugo................Marie Burke (Stewardess-in-training)
Milburn Stone.................Tim Norton (Pilot)
Iris Adrian......................Wanda La Fern (Popular showgirl)
Lyle Talbot....................Andy Barrett (Wanda's companion)
Paul Maxey....................John Anderson (Private Detective)
Joel Marston..................Don Blake (Co-pilot)
John Eldredge.................W. E. French (Head of insurance company)
George Eldredge..............Stacey (Ruark's assistant)
Eddie Parks....................Jonathan Tibbets (Justice of peace)
Louise Franklin..............Lena Franklin (Wanda's maid)
Lyle Latell.....................Ed Davidson (Murdered detective)
Bob Curtis.....................Watkins (Stage manager)

SYNOPSIS AND APPRAISAL

This is the last of the seventeen Monogram films featuring Charlie Chan. Three additional films were planned to be filmed in England, but they were scrubbed when the British devalued their currency. So this picture unintentionally beacame the swan song of the series. It chould have been a better film, given the strong cast of excellent supporting actors and the presence of Keye Luke. The focus in the last half of the film drifted however, and the picture became routine and somewhat stale, with the identity of the murderer being painfully obvious to almost any viewer familiar with the series. The audience only stick around because they enjoy the characters of Chan and his son Lee, not because of interest in the plot.

The film has a promising start with Charlie and Lee on a late night airplane flight to San Francisco. Lee is a close friend of the plane's captain who has been helping him with his flying lessons. Stewardess Marie Burke, on her first flight is startled when two passengers, Wanda La Fern and Andy Barrett, call her

"Connie." She begs them to keep quiet. Coffee is served in mid-flight, after which all the crew and passengers fall into a trance-like sleep.

Lee, who spilt most of his father's coffee, awakens first, but cannot rouse anyone else. He checks that the plane is on automatic pilot, and discovers a man stabbed to death in the cockpit. Lee douses his father with water, explaining the situation to his groggy father. Charlie determines that the coffee was drugged. He observes the condition of the cockpit crew, and Lee assumes control of the plane.

The passengers are eventually revived by Chan, who learns that a quarter of a million dollar shipment was stolen while everyone was blacked out. John Anderson, a plainclothes detective guarding the money, tells Chan that the murdered man, Edwards Davidson, was in charge of the money satchel and rode in the cockpit. Chan radios Lt. Ruark of the San Francisco Police to meet the plane when it lands. Anderson adds that everyone on the plane, himself included, has to be regarded as a suspect.

Upon landing, he confers with his employer, W. E. French, the head of the bonding company that insured the cash shipment. At the airport, Birmingham flirts with Lena, Wanda La Fern's maid. Ruark interrogates the crew and passengers. The main suspects of the crime are: Tim Norton, the pilot; Don Blake, the co-pilot; Stewardesses Jane Marshall and Marie Burke; and the remaining passengers including Wanda La Fern and Andy Barrett. The police suspect the money bag was parachuted out of the plane after being stolen. W. E. French decided to hire Chan to solve the murder of Davidson and recover the stolen shipment of money.

Don Blake and Tim Norton go backstage to see Wanda La Fern at her lively burlesque show the next evening, while Ruark and Chan follow them. Marie is already in Wanda's dressing room, being pressured by the showgirl to repay sixty thousand dollars belonging to Andy Barrett. Marie says she has no money and was not involved in the airline theft, but Wanda doesn't believe her. Blake overhears them arguing, and confronts Marie after Wanda leaves to do her number. Lee and Birmingham show up at the theater, conducting their own investigation, and climb through the window of La Fern's dressing room. They find Blake on the floor and pursue a suspect, while alerting Ruark and Chan. The fleeing man turns out to be Captain Norton, who is arrested by the police. Blake is not dead, but seriously injured and rushed to the hospital.

Chan surprises Marie Burke and Andy Barrett in Andy's apartment, sitting in the dark as they enter. Andy admits that he was living under an alias and that he has a police record. Charlie points out that Anderson and Davidson arrested him for a sixty thousand dollar fraud scheme five years ago. Barrett claims his presence on the plane was a coincidence, and he refuses to co-operate. Chan leaves, after revealing that Lee was hidden in the closet with a drawn gun in case of emergency.

Jane Marshall is waiting at Chan's house, insisting that Tim Norton is completely innocent. She relates that her roommate, Marie Burke, has become very evasive and nervous, and that she was present in the burlesque theater when Blake was attacked.

Charlie confers with Ruark on the phone, after which Barrett sneaks into Chan's house and holds him at gunpoint. He offers to give the detective some valuable information about his wife when Lee and Birmingham tackle him. Andy regains his gun, but he is shot by John Anderson who enters by the French windows.

Lee and Charlie search through the county records to learn about Andy's wife. The trail leads them to a talkative justice of the peace, who believes he owns a photo of Barrett's wedding ceremony. The man is knocked out while searching for it, and his files are set ablaze by a hidden assailant. Waiting in the car, Birmingham notices the :attacker escaping, and alerts the Chans. Lee rescues the justice of the peace, who then finds an address book. He had previously mailed photos of the ceremony to the La Fern sisters, and the name of the bride was Connie.

At the theater, Wanda gives very elusive answers when questioned by Chan. Lee does further research and uncovers a newspaper photo that reveals that Marie Burke is Connie La Fern, Wanda's sister and Bartlett's wife. Chan calls Ruark, and plans a special conference on the plane including all the suspects. Everyone is positioned in the same seats they had on the night of the robbery, and Chan stages a reconstruction of the event.

Four people were near the coffee dispenser: Tim Norton, Joan Marshall, Wanda La Fern and Marie Burke. Don Blake, his face covered in bandages, emerges from the cockpit, and Chan asks him to identify the person who drugged the coffee. He vaguely points at the suspects, and Marie/Connie pulls a gun. She is shot by Anderson, much to the consternation of Chan. When Blake removes his bandages, we learn that Lee is masquerading as Blake, who died that morning. Chan had no proof, so he tricked the guilty woman into revealing herself. His next conclusion is that the money never left the plane, but was hidden in a trick coat that was exchanged with a collaborator at the airport. The killer whips out a gun and takes the plane up. He locks the cockpit, planing to parachute to safety. Double-crossed, the guilty woman turns on the killer, who is then easily overpowered. Chan produces a key to the cockpit, and Lee lands the plane as the picture concludes.

PERFORMANCES

This is the last of Roland Winters' six film portrayals of Charlie Chan. He delivers an admirable presentation, and works especially well with Keye Luke. Their scene together with Tibbets shows their performances to be both rich and subtle.

This is the last of Keye Luke's eleven screen performances as Lee Chan, Number one son. As in *THE FEATHERED SERPENT*, Lee is more actively helpful to his father than his other offspring and much less of a bungler. At one point, Charlie pays him a wonderful compliment, saying, "Increasing wisdom of Number one son give much pleasure to humble father." Luke's rescue of Tibbets and his disguise as the murdered co-pilot are excellent scenes.

Mantan Moreland played the part of Birmingham Brown in fifteen Chan films. His role is less prominent in this film, and his best scenes are with Louise Franklin as Lena, the maid. Their banter and byplay make for a very amusing subplot.

Tim Ryan as Lt. Ruark is a bit more cantankerous than usual in this film, but he gets in a number of smart comments. For example, when the stage manager implores him, "Please, quiet, the show, the show!" Ryan mumbles, "Yeah, I've seen it," and continues to fire his gun.

The very capable supporting cast are all fine, but the static script didn't provide them with any good material. Almost all of them won later fame on television...Noel Neil as Lois Lane in *SUPERMAN*, Lyle Talbot as neighbor Joe Randolph in *THE ADVENTURES OF OZZIE AND HARRIET*, Elena Verdugo as Nurse Consuelo Lopez in *MARCUS WELBY, MD,* and Milburn Stone as Doc Adams on *GUNSMOKE.* Iris Adrian started her career as a Ziegfeld showgirl, and played numerous roles as a wisecracking blonde similar to Wanda La Fern. The most memorable character role in the film belongs to Eddie Parks who is outstanding as Jonathan Tibbets, justice of the peace. His comic sales pitch and later sincere assistance to Chan are among the best bits in the film.

Two other cast members of interest are George Eldredge (Stacey) and John Eldredge (W. E. French). Both are character actors who are often confused with each other, and this picture and *DARK ALIBI* may be the only films in which they appeared together. In some earlier films, George's last name was spelled Eldridge. George appeared, usually as a villain, in over thirty westerns, but may be best remembered as the scheming Dr. Tobor in the serial *CAPTAIN VIDEO* (1951) and as "the Baron" in *ROAR OF THE IRON HORSE* (1951), both directed by Spencer G. Bennet who directed the very first Chan effort. John appeared in a greater variety of roles, doing about a dozen westerns and a variety of "B" films such as *CHAMPAGNE FOR CAESAR* (1951) and *THE FIRST TRAVELING SALESLADY* (1956). Both of them appeared in many Chan films, with John starting as far back as 1937 in *CHARLIE CHAN AT THE OLYMPICS*. John also has a unique distinction among Chan guest stars that is revealed in Appendix A.

CHARLIE CHAN'S SAYINGS

⋄ Would much prefer to wait a few minutes more to soar with eagle than rush to fly with fledgling sparrow.

⋄ Small flower receive blessing of rain with thanks.

⋄ Tired man's idea sometimes very much like child's nightmare, easily dispelled by bright light of day.

- ◇ Innocent act without thinking. Guilty always make plans.

- ◇ Revenge and profit two of oldest motives for murder and robbery.

- ◇ Justice must be blind to friendship.

- ◇ Ideas planted too soon often like seeds on winter ground, quickly die.

- ◇ The case very much like photographic negative...proper development sometimes bring very interesting things to light.

- ◇ To think is one thing. To have proof is another.

- ◇ Death, even to deserving, never pleasant.

THE TRAP (1947) Alternate title: *MURDER IN MALIBU BEACH*

Rating: *

MONOGRAM. Written by Miriam Kissinger; Photographed by James Brown; Edited by Ace Herman; Musical direction by Edward J. Kay; Produced by James S. Burkett; Directed by Howard Bretherton. 62 minutes.

ANNOTATED CAST LIST

Sidney Toler...................Charlie Chan
Victor Sen Yung.............Jimmy Chan (Number two son)
Mantan Moreland............ Birmingham Brown (Chan chauffeur)
Larry Blake.................... Rick Daniels (Publicity agent)
Kirk Alyn......................Reynolds (State Police officer)
Howard Negley............... Cole King (Theatrical impresario)
Lois Austin...................Irene Thorn (Wardrobe mistress)
Minerva Urecal............... Mrs. Weebles (Housekeeper)
Walden Boyle................. George Brandt (Physiotherapist)
Tanis Chandler................Adelaide (French showgirl)
Rita Quigley.................. Clementine (Showgirl)
Anne Nagel....................Marcia (Lead showgirl)
Helen Gerald..................Ruby (Showgirl)
Bettie Best.................... Winifred (Showgirl)
Jan Bryant.....................Lois (Murdered showgirl)
Barbara Jean Wong.......... San Toy (Chinese showgirl)
Margaret Brayton.............Madge (Show assistant)

SYNOPSIS AND APPRAISAL

The final Toler/Monogram picture is a rambling production loaded with red herrings, long dreary scenes of pointless searches, and too many subplots. The suspects are largely a gaggle of silly showgirls, who seem upset that murders are occurring that interferes with their frolicking on the beach. The missing metal box, which is the central clue, becomes a pointless diversion by the end of the story. In Great Britain, this film was released under the more marketable title of *MURDER IN MALIBU BEACH*.

The establishing scene of the picture introduces the Cole King variety show troupe as they arrive at the Rutherford mansion in Malibu Beach for a month's holiday. Marcia, the lead showgirl, is disliked by the entire company, and the arrogant star is supposed to be having an affair with Cole King. She is also blackmailing Adelaide, who is secretly married to the show's physical therapist, and Lois, who lied about her age to get the job. Marcia asks Lois to steal letters from a metal box stored in Adelaide's trunk. All the girls store their valuable papers in this box.

While everyone takes an ocean swim, Lois rummages through Adelaide's room. She is strangled with a knotted silken cord, and Marcia disappears. The metal box is also missing. When someone mentions that the technique of strangling with a silken cord is a Chinese custom, San Toy calls her newest acquaintance, Jimmy Chan.

A sleepy Birmingham answers the telephone, and mistakenly believes that Jimmy is the victim. He drives Chan to the Malibu address, where the great detective is relieved to learn that Jimmy is not involved in the crime. He agrees to help Reynolds, the state policeman handling the case.

Meanwhile, Jimmy comes home late, and after catching sight of the note with the Malibu address, hurries off. Chan interviews everyone connected with the case, including showman Cole King; publicity agent Rick Daniels; George Brandt, the show's physical therapist; Irene Thorn, the wardrobe mistress who oversees the showgirls; Mrs. Weebles, the housekeeper; Madge, the showgirls' attendant; and the remaining performers, Adelaide, Clementine, Winifred, Ruby and San Toy. Jimmy shows up, frightening the girls as he enters by a porch window.

Chan posts Jimmy and Birmingham at the back entrance of the house, to make sure no one leaves. They notice a man sneaking into the cellar, trying to burn a mysterious bundle. They investigate, and Birmingham is clubbed as the man escapes. San Toy is attacked (smothered with ether), but is unharmed.

The next day, Jimmy is asked by his father to follow Rick Daniels. Marcia's body washes up on the beach, with a cord from King's robe still tied around her neck. Jimmy alerts his father that Rick Daniels is burying a parcel further down the beach, which is found to contain Marcia's robe. Daniels says the robe was deliberately planted in Cole King's closet, and he was trying to destroy this evidence to save his employer embarrassment. He was the man Jimmy and Birmingham saw in the basement.

A theory is proposed that Marcia was killed on the beach, then the killer donned her robe and went into the house to kill Lois. All the suspects start hurling accusations at each other, as Chan listens closely and finally declares, "I am convinced the murderer is in this room."

Ruby later sneaks away by car, attempting to post a letter. Jimmy notices her, and Reynolds tracks her down. Adelaide admits giving her the letter, which contains George Brandt's application to the State Medical Board for reinstatement. Chan allows the letter to be mailed, as Brandt and Adelaide explain they are secretly married. Brandt had been a doctor whose career was ruined when he was accused but then cleared of murdering his first wife six years earlier. He also admits that he found Lois' body and removed the metal box that contained his wife's letters. As Brandt tries to retrieve the box, he finds that it was stolen from his suitcase.

That night, Jimmy searches Cole King's quarters for evidence, and Mrs.

Weebles, the housekeeper, is caught spying and taking notes about the show-girls. Cole King has a breakdown, and admits to Brandt and Daniels that he took the metal box, fearing it contains papers that could ruin him.

Jimmy finds the box hidden in the ventilation system, and searches for his father who is in San Toy's bedroom, baiting a trap. Jimmy accidentally blunders into the scene, interrupting the killer, a woman, who then flees outside and races away in a car. Birmingham drives in pursuit, until the killer's car cracks up. Badly injured, she explains her motivation, which was to incriminate and ruin Cole King, who is actually her ex-husband. She was trying to kill San Toy, thinking she had the box that included her papers that implicated her. She dies, saying about King, "I hope he suffers!"

Chan explains the loose ends to the remaining suspects back at the house. Cole King explains that his former wife had deserted him years earlier, and when she returned he gave her a job, but kept their former marriage secret. The film ends as Birmingham arrives with a mouse he caught, which upsets the entire household.

PERFORMANCES

This is the last of Sidney Toler's twenty-two performances as Charlie Chan. Toler died mere weeks after completing the film, on February 12, 1947 at his home in Beverly Hills. This is a difficult film to enjoy because Toler appears quite tired. Chan's onscreen time is much briefer than usual, and perhaps this was an accommodation for Toler.

Victor Sen Yung seems more helpful and mature in the story, and is a genu-ine asset to his father in the story. His main interest is San Toy, and their rela-tionship provides a nice underpinning to the adventure. Mantan Moreland has a mixed bag of material, but his activities are all relevant to the plot.

There is, however, one outstanding scene in *THE TRAP* where Toler, Sen Yung and Moreland all shine. It really is Toler's last momentous scene as Chan. Birmingham enters a room, and sees Jimmy lying on the floor, with Charlie standing over him with a strangler's cord. Mantan exclaims, "Good gracious alive, Mr. Chan, I knew it was going to happen some day!" This line, delivered in mock seriousness, is delivered perfectly by Moreland, and it is one of his most hilarious reactions in the entire series. Chan is actually making a point about the attack, with Jimmy playing the victim. He then asks Birmingham to play the victim, as Charlie dramatically acts out the killer's movements. Bir-mingham reacts, proving Chan's point that the killer couldn't have caught Lois unawares, so Lois must have considered her murderer a friend. He then leads Jimmy through a series of clever deductions, ending with a preposterous theory by Birmingham. This short scene is a gem, providing the best moment in the film and typifies the best of Monogram Chan.

Most of the other performers deliver silly, giggling presentations. Lois Austin as Irene and Tanis Chandler as Adelaide acquit themselves particularly well. Minerva Urecal is disappointing as Mrs. Weebles, even though the part seems a natural for her. Among the men, Howard Negley is quite hammy as Cole King, but he is lively. His pronunciation of Marcia's name is quite amusing. Larry Blake is brash and annoying as the publicity agent, but Walden Boyle is convincing as Doc Brandt. Kirk Alyn (Reynolds), who later played Superman in two serials, is pleasant as the young officer who works with and learns from Chan. Finally, Barbara Jean Wong is wonderful as San Toy, Jimmy's girlfriend. Barbara should not be confused with Jean Wong, who appeared in *THE RED DRAGON* and *THE CHINESE RING*. In fact, both these actresses later appeared together in the William Holden and Jennifer Jones romance, *LOVE IS A MANY SPLENDORED THING* (1956).

CHARLIE CHAN'S SAYINGS

⋄ Mistake sometimes bring most fortunate relief.

⋄ Obstructing justice is a very serious crime.

⋄ Best laid plans of mice and men sometimes go a little bit haywire.

⋄ Puzzle always deepest near the center.

⋄ Leisurely hunter have time to stalk prey, but hunter in haste must set trap.

APPENDICES

APPENDIX A

Rogue's Gallery of Chan Film Criminals

This appendix reveals the guilty parties in each of the films, usually revealed in the climax by Chan himself in a soft voice saying, "You are murderer." The characters are identified in this appendix both by their names in the film as well as by the actors who portrayed them. The only actor who appears in the Rogue's Gallery twice is John Eldredge. Further explanations are also provided for complicated solutions. In the films, the killer is sometimes in disguise, and sometimes a vital clue requires elucidation.

◇ *BEHIND THAT CURTAIN*
Eric Durand (Philip Strange).

◇ *THE BLACK CAMEL*
Mrs. Denny Mayo, posing as Anna the maid (Violet Dunn), killed Shelah Fane. Jessop (Dwight Frye) murdered Archie Smith.

◇ *BLACK MAGIC*
Paul Hamlin (Frank Jaquet).

◇ *CASTLE IN THE DESERT*
Wayne King (Henry Daniell) is Lucy's stepbrother.

◇ *CHARLIE CHAN AND THE CURSE OF THE DRAGON QUEEN*
Sylvia Lupowitz (Lee Grant).

◇ *CHARLIE CHAN AT MONTE CARLO*
Gordon Chase (Robert Kent).

◇ *CHARLIE CHAN AT THE CIRCUS*
Tom Holt (J. Carrol Naish).

◇ *CHARLIE CHAN AT THE OLYMPICS*
Cartwright (John Eldredge) stole his own device and killed
Miller, in order to defraud his partner.

◇ *CHARLIE CHAN AT THE OPERA*
Anita Barelli (Nedda Harrigan).

◇ *CHARLIE CHAN AT THE RACE TRACK*
George Chester (Alan Dinehart).

◇ *CHARLIE CHAN AT THE WAX MUSEUM*
Tom Agnew (Ted Osborn) is Butcher Degan.

◇ *CHARLIE CHAN AT TREASURE ISLAND*
Rhadini (Cesar Romero).

◇ *CHARLIE CHAN IN CITY IN DARKNESS*
The butler did it ...Antoine (Pedro de Cordoba).

◇ *CHARLIE CHAN IN EGYPT*
John Thurston (Frank Conroy).

◇ *CHARLIE CHAN IN HONOLULU*
Captain Johnson (Robert Barrat).

◇ *CHARLIE CHAN IN LONDON*
Geoffrey Richmond (Alan Mowbray).

◇ *CHARLIE CHAN IN PANAMA*
Reiner is Jennie Finch (Mary Nash).

◇ *CHARLIE CHAN IN PARIS*
Henri Latouche (Murray Kinnell) is Max Corday's partner.

◇ *CHARLIE CHAN IN RENO*
Vivian Wells (Phyllis Brooks).

◇ *CHARLIE CHAN IN RIO*
Helen Ashby (Kay Linaker) is really Mrs. Manuel Cardosa and
the murderess. Chan trapped her by showing her cigarette was
not drugged. Marana (Victor Jory) was only trying to protect
his sister-in-law, but was not guilty of the crime.

◇ *CHARLIE CHAN IN SHANGHAI*
James Andrews (Russell Hicks) The real Agent Andrews was
killed and this man was an impostor. Chan tells him, "You
pretend to be 'G' man, now turn out to be 'NG' man."

◇ *CHARLIE CHAN IN THE SECRET SERVICE*
Mrs. Winters (Lelah Tyler) is the master spy Manleck.

◇ *CHARLIE CHAN ON BROADWAY*
Speed Patten (Donald Woods).

◇ *CHARLIE CHAN'S MURDER CRUISE*
Professor Gordon (Leo G. Carroll) is Jim Eberhart.

◇ *CHARLIE CHAN'S SECRET*
Fred Gage (Edward Trevor).

◇ *THE CHINESE CAT*
The Bishop chess piece left by the dying man was a clue to the killer's identity...like a bishop, a deacon is a church official. Webster Deacon (Cy Kendall) killed Manning and Kurt Karzos. Deacon was then killed himself by Catlen (Anthony Warde).

◇ *THE CHINESE RING*
Armstrong (Byron Foulger).

◇ *DANGEROUS MONEY*
Joe Murdock, posing as Mrs. Whipple (Alan Douglas) and Theodore Kane, posing as Dr. Whipple (Leslie Dennison) are the culprits. Their accomplices include Mr. & Mrs. Erickson (Rick Vallin and Amira Moustafa) and Harold Mayfair (Bruce Edwards).

◇ *DARK ALIBI*
Hugh Kenzie (George Holmes).

◇ *DEAD MEN TELL*
Jed Thomasson (Don Douglas).

◇ *DOCKS OF NEW ORLEANS*
Oscar Swenstrom (Harry Hayden) is the killer, assisted by his wife Mrs. Swenstrom (Dian Fauntelle), who planted the poison gas radio tubes and detonated them during her radio broadcasts.

◇ *ERAN TRECE*
John Ross (Martin Garralaga) is Jim Maynard.

◇ *THE FEATHERED SERPENT*
John Stanley (Robert Livingston), assisted by Sonya Cabot (Carol Forman) who actually stabbed Professor Scott. Stanley later murdered Cabot.

◇ *THE GOLDEN EYE*
Talbot Bartlett (Bruce Kellogg).

◇ *THE JADE MASK*
Lloyd Archer (Jack Ingram) killed and disguised himself as
Walter Meeker (Hardie Albright). His partner was Stella
Graham (Dorothy Granger).

◇ *MR. MOTO'S GAMBLE*
Philip Benton (John Hamilton).

◇ *MURDER OVER NEW YORK*
Herbert Fenton (Melville Cooper) is the killer. Keith Jeffrey
(John Sutton) is Paul Narvo.

◇ *THE RED DRAGON*
Joseph Bradish (Barton Yarborough).

◇ *THE RETURN OF CHARLIE CHAN*
Paul Hadrachi (Joseph Hindy).

◇ *THE SCARLET CLUE*
Mrs. Marsh (Virginia Brissac).

◇ *SHANGHAI CHEST*
Edward Seward (Tristram Coffin).

◇ *THE SHANGHAI COBRA*
Bradford Harris (Arthur Loft).

◇ *SHADOWS OVER CHINATOWN*
Jeff Hay (John Gallaudet).

◇ *THE SKY DRAGON*
John Anderson (Paul Maxey), assisted by W. E. French (John
Eldredge).

◇ *THE TRAP*
Irene Thorn (Lois Austin).

APPENDIX B

Chan Offspring on Film

This is a guide to appearances by Chan's children in each film. There are naturally several inconsistencies. Charlie Chan, Jr. was described as Number two son in *CHARLIE CHAN AT THE OLYMPICS*. His character was then discontinued after only one film and replaced by Jimmy Chan starting with *CHARLIE CHAN IN HONOLULU*. Jimmy later had a confusing name change near the end of the Monogram series to Tommy Chan, starting with *THE CHINESE RING*. At this point, the original Tommy Chan, Number three son, disappeared from the series, leading to fan speculation that the character of Tommy died in World War Two, and his brother assumed his name in tribute. These are also conflicting numerations in different films. For example, Tommy accidentally gets called Number five son instead of Number three son, again in *CHARLIE CHAN IN HONOLULU*.

LEE CHAN, Number one son
(Played by Keye Luke)

◊ *CHARLIE CHAN AT MONTE CARLO*
◊ *CHARLIE CHAN AT THE CIRCUS*
◊ *CHARLIE CHAN AT THE OLYMPICS*
◊ *CHARLIE CHAN AT THE OPERA*
◊ *CHARLIE CHAN AT THE RACE TRACK*
◊ *CHARLIE CHAN IN PARIS*
◊ *CHARLIE CHAN IN SHANGHAI*
◊ *CHARLIE CHAN ON BROADWAY*
◊ *THE FEATHERED SERPENT*
◊ *MR. MOTO'S GAMBLE*
◊ *THE SKY DRAGON*

(Played by David Hironane)

> ◇ *CHARLIE CHAN AND THE CURSE OF THE DRAGON QUEEN*

CHARLIE CHAN, JR, Presumably Number two son
(Played by Layne Tom, Jr.)

> ◇ *CHARLIE CHAN AT THE OLYMPICS*

JIMMY CHAN, Number two son. See also name change below.
(Played by Victor Sen Yung)

> ◇ *CASTLE IN THE DESERT*
> ◇ *CHARLIE CHAN AT THE WAX MUSEUM*
> ◇ *CHARLIE CHAN AT TREASURE ISLAND*
> ◇ *CHARLIE CHAN IN HONOLULU*
> ◇ *CHARLIE CHAN IN PANAMA*
> ◇ *CHARLIE CHAN IN RENO*
> ◇ *CHARLIE CHAN IN RIO*
> ◇ *CHARLIE CHAN'S MURDER CRUISE*
> ◇ *DANGEROUS MONEY*
> ◇ *DEAD MEN TELL*
> ◇ *MURDER OVER NEW YORK*
> ◇ *SHADOWS OVER CHINATOWN*
> ◇ *THE TRAP*

TOMMY (JIMMY) CHAN, Number two son after name change.
(Played by Victor Sen Yung)

> ◇ *THE CHINESE RING*
> ◇ *DOCKS OF NEW ORLEANS*
> ◇ *THE FEATHERED SERPENT*
> ◇ *THE GOLDEN EYE*
> ◇ *SHANGHAI CHEST*

TOMMY CHAN, Number three son
(Played by Benson Fong)

> ◇ *CHARLIE CHAN IN THE SECRET SERVICE*
> ◇ *CHINESE CAT*
> ◇ *DARK ALIBI*
> ◇ *THE RED DRAGON*
> ◇ *THE SCARLET CLUE*
> ◇ *THE SHANGHAI COBRA*

(Played by Layne Tom, Jr.)

   ◊ *CHARLIE CHAN IN HONOLULU*

EDWARD CHAN, Number four son
(Played by Edwin Luke)

   ◊ *THE JADE MASK*

STEPHEN CHAN, Number six son
(Played by Soon-Teck Oh)

   ◊ *THE RETURN OF CHARLIE CHAN*

WILLIE CHAN, Number seven son
(Played by Layne Tom, Jr.)

   ◊ *CHARLIE CHAN'S MURDER CRUISE*

OLIVER CHAN, Number seven son
(Played by Ernest Harada)

   ◊ *THE RETURN OF CHARLIE CHAN*

PETER CHAN, Number eight son
(Played by Rocky Gunn)

   ◊ *THE RETURN OF CHARLIE CHAN*

FRANCES CHAN, Presumably Number one daughter
(Played by Frances Chan)

   ◊ *BLACK MAGIC*

IRIS CHAN, Number two daughter
(Played by Marianne Quon)

   ◊ *CHARLIE CHAN IN THE SECRET SERVICE*

DOREEN CHAN, Number three daughter
(Played by Virginia Ann Lee)

   ◊ *THE RETURN OF CHARLIE CHAN*

COMPLETE FAMILY APPEARANCES
(Individual actors unspecified)

   ◊ *THE BLACK CAMEL*
   ◊ *CHARLIE CHAN AT THE CIRCUS*
   ◊ *CHARLIE CHAN IN HONOLULU*

APPENDIX C

Lost Films of Charlie Chan

There are six missing Charlie Chan films, including one serial. According to film producer Alex Gordon, who served as Twentieth Century Fox's one man film preservationist (1968-78), one of his principal efforts was to try and locate the missing Chan films. He was successful in the case of *BEHIND THAT CURTAIN*, the first sound Chan picture and *THE BLACK CAMEL*.

CHARLIE CHAN IN PARIS. was also discovered in a European film collection. The other films have remained elusive, and the last known prints of the four missing Warner Oland films were lost in a laboratory fire in 1962. Of course, time is running out due to nitrate deterioration for any prints that might exist in some remote location. For the devoted Chan fan, the dim hope remains that one or more of them might be found.

1. *HOUSE WITHOUT A KEY* (1926)

PATHE. Silent serial in ten chapters. Written by Frank Leon Smith; Directed by Spencer G. Bennet. Cast: George Kuwa as Chan; With Walter Miller, Allene Rey, Frank Lackteen, Charles West, John Webb Dillon, Natalie Warfield and William N. Bailey.

Earl Derr Biggers' first Charlie Chan novel, *THE HOUSE WITHOUT A KEY* was published in 1925, and this ten chapter Pathe serial was released relatively quickly in November, 1926. The basic plot was considerably altered, and concentrated on a chest that contained evidence of a twenty year old crime committed by one of a pair of rival brothers. The struggle for possession of this enigmatic chest made up the main action of the plot throughout the serial. The lead performer was screen veteran Walter Miller, former leading man for D. W. Griffith.

The very first screen Chan was played by a Japanese actor named George

Kuwa, who had appeared in bit parts in many productions such as the Rudolph Valentino film *MORAN OF THE LADY LETTY* (1922). His participation in the story was reduced to a minor, background character. Kuwa played Charlie as clean-shaven, wearing a dark business suit and an occasional white hat. Chan received eleventh billing in the original cast list. The individual chapter titles are as follows:

- Chapter One....... The Spite Fence.
- Chapter Two...... The Mystery Box.
- Chapter Three..... The Missing Numeral.
- Chapter Four...... Suspicion.
- Chapter Five...... The Death Buoy.
- Chapter Six........Sinister Shadows.
- Chapter Seven.... The Mystery Man.
- Chapter Eight..... The Spotted Menace.
- Chapter Nine...... The Wrist Watch.
- Chapter Ten....... The Culprit.

2. *THE CHINESE PARROT* (1927)

UNIVERSAL. Silent film. Written by I. Grubb Alexander; Directed by Paul Leni. Cast: Kamiyama Sojin as Chan; With Hobart Bosworth, Edmund C. Burns, Marian Nixon, Albert Conti, Anna May Wong and George Kuwa.

This was the first Chan feature film. Based on Biggers' novel written in 1926, the picture was directed by the brilliant German director Paul Leni. Leni actually started as an avant garde painter who became a set designed for the theatrical virtuoso, Max Reinhardt. He entered films as an art director in 1914 and by 1916, he began to direct films such as *THE DIARY OF DR. HART*. He became a central figure for works specialized in works in the Expressionist style, such as *WAXWORKS* (1924), which featured historical vignettes about figures in a wax museum such as Ivan the Terrible and Jack the Ripper. In 1927, he emigrated to America to direct *THE CAT AND THE CANARY*, a trend setting comic thriller starring Laura LaPlante and Tully Marshall. *THE CHINESE PARROT* was his second American production. The *New York Times* praised the film for its "Ingenious use of lights, shadows and photographic angles" that created and sustained an eerie atmosphere. The forty-four year old Leni died quite suddenly from blood poisoning two years after completing this motion picture.

Another Japanese actor, the stage magician Kamiyama Sojin, was featured as Charlie Chan. Sojin is best remembered as one of the villains from *THE THIEF OF BAGHDAD* (1924) starring Douglas Fairbanks. The Japanese actor was tall, quite thin, and wore a moustache for the part. He reportedly played the role in a humorous vein. Sojin return to Japan shortly after 1930, influenced in part by the advent of sound films. Curiously, the first screen Charlie Chan, George Kuwa, also appears in *THE CHINESE PARROT* in a different role. There is much speculation about the quality of this picture. The reviews at the time of release were mixed, notwithstanding the enthusiastic praise from the *New York Times*.

3. *CHARLIE CHAN CARRIES ON* (1931)

FOX. Written by Philip Klein and Barry Conners; Directed by Hamilton Mac-Fadden. Cast: Warner Oland as Chan; With John Garrick, Marguerite Churchill, Warren Hymer, Marjorie White, C. Henry Gordon, William Holden, George Brent, Peter Gawthorne, John T. Murray, John Swor, Goode Montgomery, Jason Robards, Zeffie Tillsbury and Betty Francisco. 76 minutes.

This was the first actual Chan film. It closely followed Earl Derr Biggers' novel, so Chan doesn't appear until the second half of the film. The detailed analysis of *ERAN TRECE*, the Spanish version of this film, gives a reliable insight into this lost picture. It is most regrettable to miss Oland's introduction to the role while wearing the garb of a Chinese mandarin in his home laboratory. The killer in the film was depicted by C. Henry Gordon, one of the most sensational of all Chan supporting players. The reaction to Warner Oland as Chan was fully enthusiastic with both critics and the public, and the Charlie Chan series became officially launched. Incidentally, the William Holden listed in the cast was an actor from the silent film era who died in 1932, unrelated to the famous star who used the same name.

4. *CHARLIE CHAN'S CHANCE* (1932)

FOX. Written by Barry Connors and Philip Klein; Directed by John Blystone. Cast: Warner Oland as Chan; With Ralph Morgan, H.B. Warner, Marian Nixon, Linda Watkins, Alexander Kirkland, James Kirkwood, James Todd, Charles McNaughton, Herbert Bunston and Edward Peil, Jr. 73 minutes.

For their follow-up to the successful *THE BLACK CAMEL*, Fox chose to remake its 1929 film *BEHIND THAT CURTAIN*, restoring the Chan role to prominence as in the original novel. Other changes included shifting the setting from San Francisco to New York and altering the role of an Oriental servant who tries to assassinate Chan in the film. Another Chan staple, the use of poison gas as a weapon, also makes its debut in another plot modification. A romance between Marian Nixon and Alexander Kirkland was also introduced. Many of the characters names were changed for the plot, so it is unclear identifying any additional changes in the plot. Critics generally praise the film, but complained that the plot was a very complicated one for casual observers to follow. The picture was also highly praised for the technical detail in the scene of the East River at night. Earl Derr Biggers was credited with providing of few lines of dialogue specifically for Chan in the final script. Ralph Morgan, older brother of Frank Morgan (who played The Wizard of Oz) was singled out for his fine performance as Barry Kirk. H. B. Warner, the distinguished British actor who portrayed Inspector Fife from Scotland Yard in the film, is best remembered for playing Jesus Christ in the silent *KING OF KINGS* (1927). Fife became the second Scotland Yard official murdered in the plot. One Chan saying made a marked impression and was quoted by several critics: "Some heads, like hard nuts, much better if well-cracked." Various elements of this film were later recycled in *MURDER OVER NEW YORK*.

5. *CHARLIE CHAN'S GREATEST CASE* (1933)

FOX. Written by Lester Cole and Marion Orth; Directed by Hamilton MacFadden. Cast: Warner Oland as Chan; With Heather Angel, Roger Imhof, John Warburton, Walter Byron, Ivan Simpson, Virginia Cherrill, Francis Ford, Robert Warwick, Gloria Roy, Claude King, Clara Blandick, Frank McGlynn and William Stack. 70 minutes.

This title was a remake of the serial *HOUSE WITHOUT A KEY* as an authentic Chan film, setting it in Honolulu and restoring the original plot. One interesting feature of this version was the casting of Virginia Cherrill in the role of Barbara Winterslip. Cherrill starred in Charlie Chaplin's *CITY LIGHTS* as the blind girl, and in real life she was just about to marry screen idol Cary Grant. Francis Ford, older brother of John Ford, makes the first of many Chan appearances in this film as Captain Hallett. Another screen veteran, Robert Warwick, also appears in a key role as Dan Winterslip. If the film kept the novel's original ending, Walter Byron played the murderer, Harry Jennison. Reviews of the film were vague and not very revealing except to suggest that stock footage from *THE BLACK CAMEL* was used to suggest the Hawaiian setting.

6. *CHARLIE CHAN'S COURAGE* (1934)

FOX. Written by Seton I. Miller; Directed by George Hadden and Eugene Forde. Cast: Warner Oland as Chan; With Donald Woods, Drue Leyton, Murray Kinnell, Paul Harvey, Jerry Jerome, Harvey Clark, Si Jenks, Jack Carter, James Wang, Reginald Mason, Virginia Hammond, DeWitt C. Jennings, Francis Ford, Lucille Miller, Sam McDaniels, Wade Boteler, Carl Stockdale, James P. Burtis and Teru Shimada. 70 minutes.

The last of the lost films, this is a remake of *THE CHINESE PARROT* as a traditional Chan picture based more closely on Biggers' novel. Virginia Hammond plays Sally Jordan, daughter of the notable Phillimore family, where Chan served as a houseboy in his youth. Charlie is now a dear friend of Sally, and he is deeply devoted to her. She entrusts him with a special mission to deliver an important family heirloom, a valuable pearl necklace, to J. P. Madden (P. J. Madden in the novel). Madden later requests that Chan bring the item to his remote desert ranch. Things seem amiss when Chan arrives there, and he assumes an undercover identity. The film featured many actors who became regulars in the series, such as Murray Kinnell and Drue Leyton. Francis Ford makes his second Chan film appearance as Hewitt. The romantic lead was played by the capable Donald Woods later starred in *CHARLIE CHAN ON BROADWAY*. The film drew mixed reviews at the time, in part because of disapproval that Oland spent much of the film posing as a servant named Ah Kim. Since this is atypical of the usual Chan formula, this picture could possibly be the most interesting of the missing films. At one point, Chan says of his pose, "Silly talk hard business for me. Chinese without accustomed dignity is like man without clothes, naked and ashamed." The words of a dead parrot provide Charlie with a vital clue in solving the case. An additional subplot in the picture introduces a film company who wish to shoot some scenes at Madden's ranch. Following the original denouement, Paul Harvey plays a dual role as the criminal Jerry Delaney, an impostor who kidnaps the genuine J. P. Madden in an effort to steal the pearl necklace, assisted by Martin Thorne, Madden's secretary (Murray Kinnell). Various elements from this film were later recycled in such films as *CHARLIE CHAN IN RENO*, *DEAD MEN TELL* and even *THE GOLDEN EYE*.

APPENDIX D

1935
Pennsylvania Referendum

There are many examples of short films made by the studios promoting their films, including interviews and other vignettes usually regarded as "fluff" pieces. More unusual is this short film by Warner Oland, an endorsement delivered in the persona of Charlie Chan of a referendum in the state of Pennsylvania. Wearing a dark suit, Chan speaks directly to the camera, with several jump shots alternating between mid-frame poses and moderate close-ups. The short opens with a title card introducing Warner Oland as Charlie Chan. Charlie bows, and begins to speak.

Biggest mysteries are not always crimes. Most mysterious is what mankind does to itself for reasons difficult to understand. For instance, Eskimo will not eat meat of seal in certain seasons even if starving. Men in India will go barefoot on hot coals to prove devoutness. South Sea Islanders may not smoke before grandfather. African tribeman put painful sticks through nose to be beautiful, and his lady love stretch neck like ostrich to be more beautiful. And in honorable state of Pennsylvania, populous will not permit itself to enjoy motion pictures on Sunday. Old proverb say, strange laws make even more strange bedfellows! Humble self very much puzzled why one man may play golf game on Sunday and other man cannot see Charlie Chan bring criminal to justice on same day. Respectfully suggest, you use mighty power of ballot on fifth day of November to remove unnecessary obstacle to innocent pursuit of pleasure. Thank you so much!

APPENDIX E

Chan in Mexico

Like Sherlock Holmes, the character of Charlie Chan has been parodied in numerous films and television skits over the years, the most famous being Peter Sellers' performance as Sidney Wang in *MURDER BY DEATH* (1976). The first name is a tribute to Sidney Toler. Unlike Holmes, Chan has not had the same international fascination, except for Latin American audiences. There Chan has proved very popular. The Mexican film *EL MONSTRUO EN LA SOMBRA* (1955) or *THE MONSTER IN THE SHADOW* is not really a parody so much as a literal replication of Chan. In fact, the star of the film, Eduardo Noreiga, told me that they called him Charlie Chan in the original script.

Actually, the film was based on a Cuban production from 1937 called *LA SERPIENTE ROJA*, which was directly inspired by the Warner Oland series. The role of the Oriental detective was somewhat downplayed in that picture. This elusive film is difficult to locate, but the 1955 picture is has been in release and is occasionally shown on television in Spanish-speaking countries.

Eduardo Noreiga plays a man accused of murder who is finally cleared through the efforts of Chan. An element of drug-smuggling is also in the plot, similar to *CHARLIE CHAN IN SHANGHAI*. Chan is portrayed by the Cuban actor Orlando Rodríguez, and although the film was shot in Mexico, Producciones Cub-Mex financed the film as a joint venture with considerable Cuban financing.

According to Noreiga, Rodríguez based his performance largely on Warner Oland. His approach was soft-spoken, and his dialogue contained bits of folksy wisdom. Rodríguez wore an elaborate mustache, but omitted the goatee. He also enjoyed staying in character between scenes. In the final film, Chan is called Chan Li Po, which is interesting because some of Chan's sayings are based on Li Po (701-762), a renowned Tang Dynasty poet. The female lead in this film is Martha Roth, who is still quite busy as an actress. Among her films are *THE BLACK PIRATES* (1954) with Lon Chaney, Jr., Robert Clarke and Anthony Dexter and *MASSACRE* (1956) with James Craig and Jaime Fernández. One of the highlights of this Chan film is a stunning dance number she performs that is featured on some posters of the film. Other actors in the picture include Carmen Ignarra, Luis Beristaín, Rudolpho Landa, Prudencia Grifell and Jaime Fernández. The director was Zacarías Gómez Urquiza, and the screenplay was by Félix B. Caignet, a Cuban writer. The production was photographed by Gabriel Figueroa. and the producers were Roberto Martínez Rubio and Agustín R. Delgado. Eduardo Noriega reports the picture started production on October 25, 1954, and was filmed rather quickly. He recalls the atmosphere on the set as quite enjoyable.

Noriega himself had a very distinguished film career, both in the United States and Mexico. He is featured in a number of films with John Wayne. In *THE FAR HORIZONS* (1955), the story of the Lewis and Clark expedition with Charlton Heston and Fred MacMurray, Eduardo played Donna Reed's brother. One of his last American films was *ZORRO, THE GAY BLADE* (1981) with George Hamilton. Noriega remains quite proud of having starred in this Chan feature.

EL MONSTRUO EN LA SOMBRA remains a curious hybrid, a serious but not quite authentic facsimile of the beloved detective.

APPENDIX F

Charlie Chan on Television

Charlie Chan did not enjoy anywhere near the esteem on television as he did in the movies. The character was employed in only two rather marginal series, discussed in this appendix. A later attempt by Quinn Martin to produce a weekly series in the Seventies failed.

Chan's major success on television was in the many packagings of *Charlie Chan Theater*, when many local networks ran a Charlie Chan film each week in the same time slot. WSBK, Channel 38 in Boston for years ran their series on Saturdays with a classy piano introduction as a gothic house appeared through the fog. Other stations created other special introductions, some eerie and effective, and a few embarrassing and silly. Nevertheless, these programs for years satisfied many veteran fans and created generations of new fans. More recently cable networks like *American Movie Classics* have had their own Chan festivals, sometimes running Chan films non-stop for twenty-four hours, and other times having a weekly series in the same time slot.

Chan's two series, one animated and one live-action, did have some curiosity value, and do round off a full portrait of Chan in the media.

1. *THE NEW ADVENTURES OF CHARLIE CHAN* (1956-1957)
39 half hour episodes. Independent syndication.

This series, produced principally in Europe, features a London-based Chan, usually accompanied by Barry, his son. J. Carrol Naish specialized in playing roles with foreign accents, and some assumed he would make an acceptable Charlie Chan. Naish might have been entertaining as an Italian in *LIFE WITH LUIGI* or an Indian in *GUESTWARD HO*, but he was completely miscast as Charlie Chan. His rendition is without doubt the poorest of all the filmed Chans. The make-up devised for him is ludicrous, and the delivery of his lines is stilted, artificial and irritating. Even the bow ties he wears seem entirely wrong for Chan. The talented James Hong played Barry Chan, Charlie's Number one son. His character's name was derived from Biggers' novel *BEHIND THAT CURTAIN*, where Barry Chan was the name of Chan's newborn baby, his last-born son named after Charlie's friend Barry Kirk. Hong is consistently good and credible in the series, but cannot offset the poor job done by Naish.

The general production values were weak, but not quite bottom level. The saving factor was that a number of the episodes were earnestly well written, and might have been excellent if Roland Winters, for example, had been cast as Charlie. Some of these plots include *The Man in the Wall*, where Charlie is asked to solve the mystery of a skeleton found in the wall of a building that is torn down; *Secret of the Sea*, where Chan investigates the death of a ship's steward who is killed while trying to warn his shipmates of some unknown danger; *The Noble Art of Murder*, where Barry is the prime suspect in a murder in a gymnasium; and *Without Fear*, in which Chan helps an amnesiac who just recalls she is an escaped convict accused of murder. Even other traditional plots like *Exhibit in Wax* are fun when Charlie investigates some mysterious occurrences at *Madame Tussaud's Waxworks*. Unfortunately, an equal number of plots are trite, boring and poorly contrived.

The settings of the various episodes included Paris, Venice, Rome and Amsterdam. The supporting players were also a mixed bag. Some outstanding guests were Philip Ahn (who was outstanding in two Chan films), Hans Conreid, Strother Martin and Honor Blackman (who later played "Pussy" Galore in the James Bond film *GOLDFINGER*). The three principal directors were also known for their past and future work on feature films. These individuals were Alvin Rakoff (*CITY ON FIRE*), Leslie Arliss (*THE NIGHT HAS EYES*) and Don Chaffey (*JASON AND THE ARGONAUTS*).

The program was syndicated starting in June 1957. Critical reaction and ratings were largely negative, and the series was quickly canceled and forgotten. Several of the episodes have been resurrected and released on home video, a tribute to the popularity of Chan even in this format. The titles of the thirty nine individual episodes, in alphabetical order, are as follows:

- *The Airport Murder case*
- *Backfire*
- *Blind Man's Bluff*
- *A Bowl by Cellini*
- *Charlie's Highland Fling*
- *The Chippendale Racket*
- *Circle of Fear*
- *The Counterfeiters*

- *Dateline-Execution*
- *Death at High Tide*
- *Death of a Don*
- *Exhibit in Wax*
- *The Expatriate*
- *The Final Curtain*
- *The Great Salvos*
- *Hamlet in Flames*
- *The Hand of Hera Dass*
- *The Invalid*
- *Kidnap*
- *The Lost Face*
- *The Man in the Wall*
- *The Man with a Hundred Faces*
- *No Future for Frederick*
- *No Holiday for Murder*
- *The Noble Art of Murder*
- *Patient in Room 21*
- *Patron of the Arts*
- *Point of No Return*
- *The Rajput Ruby*
- *Rhyme or Treason*
- *Safe Deposit*
- *Secret of the Sea*
- *Something Old, Something New*
- *The Sweater*
- *Three for One*
- *Three Men on a Raft*
- *Voodoo Death*
- *Without Fear*
- *Your Money or Your Wife*

2. *THE AMAZING CHAN AND THE CHAN CLAN* (1972-1973)

Animated.   16 half hour episodes.   CBS   Saturday mornings.

Charlie Chan was resurrected in cartoon form by William Hanna and Joseph Barbera, the production team who created *THE FLINTSTONES, THE JETSONS* and many other projects.   CBS ran the program in its Saturday morning lineup starting in the fall of 1972.   The most memorable thing about the project was the fact that the role of Charlie Chan was voiced by Keye Luke.

The main focus of the series was Charlie's kids, who formed a band called "The Chan Clan."   The children portrayed in the series were not counterparts to those seen in the film series, and their names were Henry, Stanley, Suzie, Alan, Anne, Tom, Flip, Nancy, Mimi and Scooter.   They were mostly played by Asian-American performers, including Virginia Ann Lee, who played Doreen Chan in *THE RETURN OF CHARLIE CHAN*.   The most exceptional member of the cast was child actress and future star Jodie Foster, who alternated with Leslie Kumamota in the role of Anne.   Although aimed at juveniles, the cartoons offered an occasional tip of the hat to established Chan fans, particularly in the episode *The Crown Jewels*, where Mr. Moto, Mr. Wong and Philip Marlowe made an appearance.   Appropriately, the actors performing these parts impersonated Peter Lorre, Boris Karloff and Humphrey Bogart.   In one episode, *Will the Real Charlie Chan Stand Up?*, found Charlie being accused of being a jewel thief.   In another, *The Mardi Gras Caper*, Chan is asked to trace a stolen ring that once belonged to Marie Antoinette.   Charlie usually opened and closed each episode, often providing answers to the mystery presented in the story.   The kids also had a big, lovable dog named Chu-Chu.   The setting ranged around the world, and included episodes set in Trinidad, India, England, Egypt and Bavaria.   The main emphasis remained the kids and their misadventures, and usually one pop song was performed by "The Chan Clan" each episode.   The names of some of their songs were *Number One Son*, *I Got the Goods on You* and *Who done it?*

The artwork in the series, of marginal quality, was done by the Eric Porter Animation Studio in Sydney, Australia.   A team of about ten different writers contributed to the series, including Jamie Farr of *M*A*S*H* fame.   Charles A. Nichols was director of animation, Don Kirshner was musical director, and six different individuals provided story direction.   The titles of the 16 individual episodes, in alphabetical order, are as follows:

- *The Bronze Idol*
- *Captain Kidd's Doubloons*
- *The Crown Jewel Affair*
- *Double Trouble*

- *Eye of the Idol*
- *The Fat Lady Caper*
- *The Great Illusionist Caper*
- *The Greek Caper*
- *The Gypsy Caper*
- *The Mardi Gras Caper*
- *The Mummy's Tomb*
- *The Phantom Sea Thief*
- *Scotland Yard*
- *To Catch a Pitcher*
- *White Elephant*
- *Will the Real Charlie Chan Stand Up?*

APPENDIX G

Actors Who Played Charlie Chan

ARBO, Manuel.
Mexican actor active in Hollywood in the early Thirties. He played Chan in *ERAN TRECE* (1931), the Spanish language version of *CHARLIE CHAN CARRIES ON.* He remained active in films thropugh the mid-Sixties.

BEGLEY, Ed. (1901-1970)
Famous American character actor who played Chan on radio in a half hour NBC show from July, 1944 through April, 1945. The program switched to ABC in a fifteen minute format from June through November, 1945. His film career began in 1947, and he later won an Academy Award for his performance in *SWEET BIRD OF YOUTH* (1962).

CONNOLLY, Walter. (1887-1940)
Burly character actor who launched the role of Charlie Chan on radio starting on December 2, 1932. The Blue network series was a half hour in length and ran through May, 1933. He was featured later in a fifteen minute series on Mutual from September, 1936 through April, 1938. Connolly also played Nero Wolfe on screen in *THE LEAGUE OF FRIGHTENED MEN* (1937) and G. K. Chesterton's *FATHER BROWN, DETECTIVE* (1935). He was best remembered for his role as Claudette Colbert's millionaire father in *IT HAPPENED ONE NIGHT* (1934).

HARRIGAN, William. (1894-1966)
Character actor who played Chan on stage in *INSPECTOR CHARLIE CHAN* in 1933. The play by Valentine Davies (author of *MIRACLE ON 34TH STREET*) was based on the final Biggers' novel *KEEPER OF THE KEYS,* which became the play's alternate title.

KUWA, George. (1887- ?)

Japanese actor who was the first screen Chan in the silent serial *THE HOUSE WITHOUT A KEY*. He later appeared in the second Chan film *THE CHINESE PARROT* in a different role.

LUKE, Keye. (1904-1991)

Beloved actor who was most famous for playing Number one son, Lee Chan, in eleven films. He himself finally had the opportunity to play Charlie in the animated series *THE AMAZING CHAN AND THE CHAN CLAN*.

MARTIN, Ross. (1920-1981)

Versatile character actor best remembered as Artemas Gordon in *THE WILD, WILD WEST*. Martin starred in the pilot film for a projected television series called *THE RETURN OF CHARLIE CHAN*.

NAISH, J. Carrol. (1900-1973)

New York-born actor descended from the Irish nobility. He specialized in playing character roles with foreign dialects or Indians such as the title role in *SITTING BULL* (1954). Oddly enough, he seldom played an Irishman. He starred as Chan on television for thirty-nine episodes of *THE NEW ADVENTURES OF CHARLIE CHAN* in 1956 and 1957.

OLAND, Warner. (1880-1938)

Called "the complete Chan" by Keye Luke, the Swedish-born completed sixteen films as Chan from 1931 to 1937. He is generally regarded as the definitive Chan.

ORTEGA, Santos. (1900-1976)

Actor who was the third and final Chan on radio from 1947 until the final broadcast on June 21, 1948.

PARK, E. L.

Korean part-time actor who appeared briefly as Chan in *BEHIND THAT CURTAIN*.

RODRIGUEZ, Orlando.

Cuban born actor who played Chan (called Chan Li Po) in the Mexican film *EL MONSTRUO EN LA SOMBRA* (1955). He also performed under the name Rafael Hernandez. Rodríguez later appeared in *MONDAY'S CHILD* (1967) with Arthur Kennedy and Geraldine Page.

SOJIN, Kamiyama. (1884-1954)

Japanese stage magician and actor who played Chan in *THE CHINESE PARROT* in 1927. He retired to Japan in 1930.

TOLER, Sidney. (1874-1947)

Born in Warrensburg, Missouri, Toler assumed the role of Chan at the age of sixty four, and he became the most prolific of all Chan performers, playing the role in twenty-two films from 1938 through 1947.

USTINOV, Peter. (1921-)

Multi-talented celebrity, he was born in London with a Russian and French background. Acclaimed as a writer, director, producer and cultural ambassador, he is one of the few undisputable geniuses of the theater. He starred as Chan in the spoof *CHARLIE CHAN AND THE CURSE OF THE DRAGON QUEEN* (1981) with a performance that was not one of the highlights of his career.

WINTERS, Roland. (1904-1989)

Boston-born Roland Winternitz became interested in stock theater in his youth, and even appeared in bit parts in a handful of silent films. He eventually switched to radio, and broadcast games for the Boston Braves and Boston Red Sox. Winters tested and was assigned to replace the late Sidney Toler in the Monogram series starting in 1947. Despite his incongruous casting as Chan, he brought much style and enthusiasm to the role. He played Chan in the last six series films (1947-1949).

Index

About the Author

CHARLES P. MITCHELL has served as director of a number of Maine libraries and has been Chairman of the Southern Maine Library District. He has lectured on theater, film, and books at various sites throughout Maine and on radio.

ISBN 0-313-30985-X

HARDCOVER BAR CODE